CU00695621

Bridget was born in a thatched cottage to a beekeeper father and nature-loving mother. She grew up in the Welsh border town of Hay in the frugal post-World War ll years. While campaigning against nuclear power stations in rural Northumberland, UK, she and her American husband raised four children. In recent years, she has written local history books, been a teacher of English language to new citizens, promoted green energy schemes and studied ancient woodlands.

She is a septuagenarian who can't be stopped.

By the same author

Bridget Gubbins' Morpeth Local History series:
de Merlay Dynasty, 2018
The Conquest of Morpeth, 2017
Juliana and Ranulph of Morpeth Castle, 2016
Newminster: Monks, Shepherds and Charters, 2014
The Mysteries of Morpeth's Workhouse, 2013
The Drovers are Coming to Morpeth Town, 2012
The Curious Yards and Alleyways of Morpeth, 2011

Power at Bay, 1997
Generating Pressure, 1991

Cover design by Stephen Ashton, Llansor Mill Press
Rear cover painting with permission of Sue Jenkins

To Helen, Rosie, Richard and Stephen
my sisters and brothers who all lived in Hay.

My childhood in Hay has remained in my mind for more than six decades, and we all know that childhood recollections are unreliable. My siblings, friends and acquaintances may remember things differently, which I acknowledge. But I have been as true as I am able to those times, and to those upstanding people.

Bridget Ashton

HAY BEFORE THE BOOKSHOPS OR THE BEEMAN'S FAMILY

Steam trains, a cinema and
free cod liver oil – a child's-eye
view of post-war Hay

AUSTIN MACAULEY PUBLISHERS™

LONDON * CAMBRIDGE * NEW YORK * SHARJAH

A CIP catalogue record for this title is available from the British Library.

ISBN 9781398452060 (Paperback)
ISBN 9781398452244 (ePub e-book)

www.austinmacauley.com

First Published 2022
Austin Macauley Publishers Ltd ®
1 Canada Square
Canary Wharf
London
E14 5AA

Acknowledgement

Helen and Rosie, my sisters, who willingly described their earliest memories.

Richard, my brother, who prompted me at suitable points along the way.

Stephen, my brother, who brought the work to fruition.

Roddy Williams, who clarified areas of fuzziness, gave technical support and offered his own stories.

Pauline Manfield, my mother's cousin, a nonagenarian, who offered wartime stories; Alison Hutchison and Bob Hutchison, who carefully read the text;

Brenda Barker, who carefully read the text and helped with graphics.

And finally, Lyndsay Robinson, who contributed to the cover author photograph, and Sue Jenkins, who gave us permission to use the rear cover painting.

Table of Contents

When the Beeman needs some shorts, to be economical he simply
cuts the bottom off his trousers…

"I went for a walk, just baby and me. It was a glorious sunny
day – blue sky, warm sun. Went up the Clyro road, then turned round and
looked at little Hay, shut in by its mountains.
When one goes outside the house, everything seems to fall into its true
proportions."
From my mother's diary, 7 February 1953

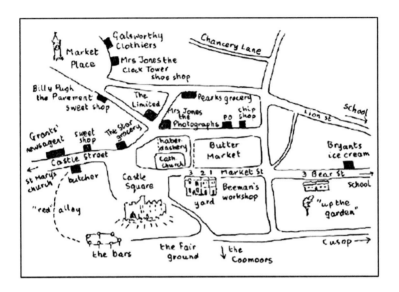

Bridget's 1950s Hay

my childhood world of streets, shops and places to play

Bridget, aged 9

Introduction

"Nana, tell me one of your naughty stories. When you put the extra sugar in the cake."

My nine-year-old grandson loves to hear about all the bad things I'd done as a child, how I was reprimanded, and sometimes avoided trouble. Hasn't every one of us stories like this, when we got away with our naughty tricks, or when we were confused by the unexplainable things adults did or said? We hold the stories in our minds for years, for decades.

Later, we realise that our childhood friendships, our toys, even the food we found so delicious, have become history. Whether we grow up in blackened city streets, green leafy suburbs, remote farms or seaside villages, every child has stories to tell. My sisters and brothers and I were born into the frugality of the post-war decade, with ration books, the new National Health Service, and strict teachers at school. Our father was a beekeeper, and at the dinner table, the bees that buzzed out of our father's clothes left us unperturbed. Our mother, like most women in those days, scrubbed dirty clothes, shopped, cooked and cleaned. Safe streets to play in, a half-abandoned castle, steam trains and a sandy beach beside the River Wye: this was my childhood world. In Hay, before the bookshops.

1 At the Door

I am standing at the door of my house, looking out over my childhood world, thinking about games I shall play in the day which lies ahead. Mine is a world of street and stone, of solidity and permanence. This is 1950s Hay.

The narrow streets lie in front, a grey pattern with a few dots of colour here and there. This town is my playground. Out there, I may be the queen who leads my tribe to victory against the invading Romans. Or I may run down to the sweetshop because I have managed to obtain a big round penny. One day, I know I will have my own sweetshop, and then I can eat as many sweets as I want. Or maybe I will take the narrow alley behind the butcher's shop where watery red stuff sometimes leaks across the path. At the end of that are the bars around a little green, where I can be a trapeze artist, tucking up my dress and swinging upside down by my knees.

Behind me, in the house, my mother is cleaning up after breakfast, washing my baby brother, dressing my little sister, scrubbing nappies in the cold water of the scullery sink.

To my right is a house with a workshop where my father is working with his honey. Opposite me is the door leading up big stairs to the Catholic church.

Around the corner is a big square where I play ball games with my sister. Further down the alley opposite, there is a wall where I can practise balancing.

I decide to try to jump across the street in two leaps, as far as the pillars of the butter market. But however hard I try, I cannot do it in less than two long ones and a bit. Then I go in to ask my mother if I may go to play with my friend. This time, we will definitely defeat the Romans.

My mother agrees because this world holds no dangers, or almost none. The streets are not noisy with traffic. When a car comes, it can be heard from a distance so children can stay out of the way. I run off past the castle on its hillock which overlooks the square. It has a grey stone gatehouse, tumbledown and sprouting with weeds and next to it is a turreted building. I am going to play with my friend at the castle.

....

Hay has everything

Whatever you need to buy in Hay, you can find it. This is a town of shops. My mother's priority is to feed the family.

"It is order day today," she says on a Tuesday, the day she gets her family allowances at the post office. She has prepared her shopping list. Putting my little sister in the pushchair, she heads to The Star.

This is one of three grocery shops just yards away from our front door. The other two are Burtons and Pearks. Burtons is right next door to the Star, but more expensive.

"Would you like to sit down, madam?" says Mr Price. He is standing in his clean white apron behind the counter which separates the stock from the customers. She takes a seat on the round wooden chair. It is nice to relax and be served politely. She reads out the order, cheese, butter, sugar, flour, and he makes a list. It will all be delivered later.

Another customer comes in. "Half a pound of cheddar cheese, please." Mr Price's assistant cuts it off from a big block. "A little more, madam?" Or perhaps it is too big, and a piece must be cut off.

Butter, sugar, currants and flour all come in big containers from which the selected produce is taken, weighed and then wrapped. Boxed packages are beginning to appear, Kellogg's Corn Flakes, Quaker Puffed Wheat and Shredded Wheat.

Washing powders are being advertised. *Persil Washes Whiter* informs hardworking housewives that they will have the cleanest white cottons. If the budget stretches to it, lavatory paper may be purchased.

Once a week, on Saturday, my mother gets her housekeeping money from my father. It is never enough, but it has to do.

"A nice piece of roast beef, Madam?" enquires Mr Keylock, the butcher in Castle Street, indicating a juicy sirloin. How she wishes she could afford it.

"Not today, thank you. I'll take a piece of shoulder of lamb, with plenty of fat, please," she says, and watches while he cuts if off. With luck, there will be enough meat left over for Monday's meal. "And a pound of pork sausages."

Later in the week, if she can set the money aside, she'll get a pound of mince, which can be made into two meals with a shepherd's pie.

"Eight pounds of potatoes please," she says at the greengrocer. This is enough for most meals of the week, and she will cook some of them every day. She fills up her basket with the cheap everyday vegetables, cabbage, carrots and turnip. Only in summer are there fresh peas and runner beans, and in the autumn tasty Brussels sprouts. She buys some apples and oranges, but they must be cut up sparingly and shared. A lettuce and some tomatoes vary the diet in the summer months.

"I swear I would never complain again if I just had enough money to feed the family," my mother says to herself as she counts her coins.

We are not allowed to eat meat on Friday, and so it is always a fish day. The fishmonger's window is cool and tempting, and the fish are all laid out neatly. Their eyes are open and look sideways at us as we peer through the window. The insides of their mouths are pink, and their backs scaly grey.

"Perhaps a small piece of smoked haddock," my mother tells herself. "Daddy could have most, and leave a piece to be shared between the girls and me."

She finds that the size of fish she can afford is very small, so she changes her mind. "I'll take five fishcakes, please," she says. Mainly potato with fish scraps mixed in, and coated with golden breadcrumbs, they will make a tasty substitute. Anyway, she knows the children like them better. On other weeks when she manages to keep a little more aside, she might choose a piece of cod, or a plaice or two. Sometimes we have a few herrings, and then we must be careful not to get their tiny bones stuck in our throats.

Once a month, my mother has need for feminine sanitary items. This is another expense to be skimped out of the weekly housekeeping. It isn't just the money though. It's the embarrassment.

"Good morning, madam," says Mr Gwilliam at the haberdashery down the steps from 3 Market Street. "How can I help you?"

"Good morning to you, Mr Gwilliam," she replies. She doesn't want to tell him directly. "Is Mrs Gwilliam around at the moment?"

"Certainly, madam," he says, and disappears discreetly. Mrs Gwilliam appears, and she quickly realises what is required, handing over the packet of sanitary napkins wrapped in anonymous brown paper.

The shop contains other items of a delicate nature. Most women wear stockings which ascend to just above the knee. They are held up with suspenders which dangle from a belt around the waist, or in the case of those who can afford it, a 'corsnip'. My sister and I giggle if we get a glimpse of the large pink corsets which pull in the roundness of our mummy's abdomen. The garment is held together by an arrangement of elastic and hooks-and-eyes. Gwilliams' shop sells them, and ladies' knickers, capacious bloomers, keeping them well out of general display. More easily accessible are the little items for babies.

My mother has budgeted to buy some tiny vests for her new baby. Mrs Gwilliam pulls open one of the wooden drawers in her cabinet, where all the clean pieces of clothing are neatly folded. The sets of sliding shelves and drawers in the shop are a masterpiece of joinery. There are no plastic or cellophane wrappings, and items are sold wrapped in tissue paper.

Three sleeveless vests are chosen, small but with a little growing room, smelling deliciously fresh and clean. They are made of knitted cotton It is a treat to have something new. The old ones are thin and worn after being used for her three girls.

As winter approaches, she takes us to be measured for liberty bodices. Made of padded soft cotton, these are vests to keep us warm and they fit comfortingly around our chests and tummies. They also have hanging suspenders if we have long stockings.

"Mummy, please can I have my pocket money?" I ask on a Saturday, for me the most important shopping day of the week. Clutching my threepenny bit, I decide which sweetshop I'll go to. There is one across the square, on Castle Street, where two very thin ladies hold guard over rows of glass jars filled with delicious sweets of every imaginable variety.

There are coloured hard boiled fruit sweets to suck and make last for ages; chewy jelly babies which don't last so long; butterscotch and fudge which is expensive and so you don't get many for your pennies, but which is so creamy and delicious.

When someone chooses a quarter of a pound, the sisters pour the sweets out, tinkling onto the scales, and then into a paper cone. With my thruppence, I can't afford a whole quarter.

Some shopkeepers let you have half the quantity a little reluctantly, but the packet is small.

There is another sweetshop. Billy Pugh the Pavement really loves children. I know this because he will sell you a ha'penny sweet if that is all you have. I decide I'll go to him. He has Sherbet Dips for tuppence and flavoured chews two for a penny. There is bubble gum, pink and stretchy which is forbidden to me as a nasty, messy American habit. The same rule applies to chewing gum. Four little pieces are wrapped into inch-long packets. There are two varieties, the white-coated mint flavoured Beech Nut or the four coloured fruity ones, each sold in packets costing a penny. A tube of fruity acidic Refreshers in many colours is tempting. I could choose Rowntree's fruit pastels, which are sugar-coated jellies, or fruit gums, which last longer. Both cost thruppence for a paper tube. There is Cadbury's chocolate, but those bars of eight pieces cost more than thruppence. How about pink snakes, lurid coloured babies' dummies, black liquorice sticks with green sprinkles?

The Saturday drama between me and the patient shopkeeper is finally resolved, and I skip away chewing my purchase. After the sweetshop, for me, the best shop in town is Grant's the stationers. Once a week, my mother goes to pay the bill for the papers. While she chats with Mr Grant, my sister and I look longingly into the back of the shop where toys are displayed, but they are not for us. There is a box containing out of date children's comics, and as I get older I am allowed to rummage through it if I have some pennies, and buy old editions of *School Friend* for my collection.

For anyone who might need their wireless repaired, there is the Bon Marché in Castle Square. A little international wartime flavour has crept in. Sid Williams, the owner, saw the name in a shop in Gloucester, and decided it would be a good name for his repair business in Hay. My parents use the French pronunciation, but most people aren't having any of that, and they call it the Bon Marsh. An ironmonger's shop, known by everyone as The Limited, is just a few steps from our house. It has pans and tools hanging outside.

Maddy's is the baker across Castle Square. My sister and I are often sent with four pennies for a large white or brown loaf, warm in our hands as we run home.

It is always hard to find money for non-everyday items such as shoes. Many a jar is hidden away by thrifty mothers who put a few coins out of the housekeeping allowance for those big expenses.

When I grow out of my winter lace-up shoes, they are put aside ready for my younger sister. I am taken to the shoe-shop of Mrs Jones the Clocktower where I am bought some t-shaped summer sandals. On rare occasions, my sister is lucky and not stuck with hand-me-downs.

"Let's go and choose your shoes for your special day," our mummy says to her when her First Holy Communion approaches. She must be dressed beautifully, so they go together down The Pavement.

The darkish interior smells of shoe-shop leather. Cardboard boxes are opened and the contents displayed. Among them is a pair of white shoes with blue and pink flowers printed on to the canvas. A size that fits is found, and the purchase is agreed. This is a luxury, something frivolous, not the usual sensible, long-lasting shoes with room to be grown into. A little girl glowing with happiness is holding her mother's hand as they leave with the cardboard box.

When a man needs a haircut, he can go the barber on The Pavement. For an engagement ring, he can go to Billy Mayall the jeweller. Watches and clocks can be repaired at Pyrzakowski's shop next to the post office. Mr Hawkins on Castle Street is the cobbler who will make everyone's shoes last longer.

Indeed, a mother or a farmer or a labourer can find almost anything they need among the shops of this busy market town. If you want to inform yourself of current affairs, or entertain yourself in an idle hour, you can buy a newspaper or a magazine. If you want something more substantial to read, there is always the local library. But should you want to browse among dusty shelves, or purchase a current best-seller, there is one kind of shop you won't find in Hay at this time…

....

The beekeeper's family

Our parents are English, with outsiders' ways, newly embedding themselves in this Welsh border town. My father is a beekeeper and a former conscientious objector. My mother with her gentle friendly smile has had a liberal education. In these days, so soon after the end of World War II, Hay is a little-known town with no special status. It is a place where my father could practise his trade, and together with our romantic, poetic mother bring up the children. Here, she will struggle to feed, wash and clothe the family, and he will make his living selling honey.

In future years, my mother was wont to say, "Everyone has a story." No matter how humble, how ordinary a person is, or at the other end of the scale, how privileged, how extraordinary, there is a story to tell. A person could be a miner or a domestic servant, a teacher or a politician, a farmer or a nurse. Each

20

individual's hopes and disappointments, sorrows and joys, are their own. What is true of a person is equally true of a family. We may feel that destiny is set out for us, and we have no choice but to follow its path, or contrarily that our lives are the consequence of our own decisions. Either way, my father and mother's particular path brought us to Hay in the years after the war when everyday life was still a struggle. Their lives together had started a few years previously while the war was going through its final agonies. A few hundred miles from Hay in a cottage in Norfolk, among the beehives and under a thatched roof, I am about to take my first breath.

2 Under the Thatched Roof

The bees are humming busily among the flowers in the garden of the thatched cottage, and some newly fledged sparrows are cheeping.

The beekeeper is pacing along the paths between the vegetables, ignoring his hives. His attention is focussed on the cottage's upstairs window where the drama is taking place.

The Beeman with four-week old Bridget

Eventually, there is a sense of bustle, and he hears a squawking cry. Behind the window glass, the midwife and the relieved exhausted woman are focussed on the new creature, who is wiped and washed, and handed into her mother's arms. That is me, a pink and wriggling body, demanding to be held, to be nourished, to feel secure in the world into which I have been thrust. I am nuzzling, pounding the source of food and snuggling close to the body of the one who means everything, my mother. My father arrives and looks at his miracle daughter, the bees forgotten, the war a million miles from his consciousness.

It is August 1944. The soldiers are burning, bombing, battling in Normandy. The Jews of Europe are still being transported to the gas chambers. The baby's uncle is suffering in a Japanese prisoner-of-war camp in Thailand. But for the moment, the beekeeper's world is focussed on this bedroom in the cottage in Norfolk. The people of the market town on the Welsh borders, to which destiny will lead this family, are busy with their everyday lives, managing without the many brothers and husbands who are away at war. The future pathway of our family between Watton Green in Norfolk and Hay is not even a dream.

....

Wartime marriage

A year or so before the birth, the man who would become my father was seeing Eileen onto a train. To her surprise, he said, "Do you think you would marry me one day?"

She was on the way to visit her mother, and she brooded over the question. She couldn't marry another man with whom she was in love because he was about to become the father of another woman's baby.

So she agreed to marry John. "A good-looking, young man who was a conscientious objector and worked in the garden and with the bees."

Money was tight for this wartime marriage, as her notebook records:

I was engaged – and one day, when we were walking about in Norwich, John bought me a ring from a little junk-shop. I think it cost five shillings. It had four 'jewels'. Before long, one fell out, but I did not mind. I liked it, and when the other three fell out, I still liked it.

She wrote a poem:

My Ring
I like my ring.
It is a nice and comfortable
Kind of thing.
And mine –
Although it has a stone too few,
I like because it makes me
Always think of you.

And oh! It's nice to think
I'm not too far away
From Watton (Norfolk) and my J.R.A.

They married in October 1943, at the Catholic church of Our Lady of Walsingham in Ampthill, Bedfordshire. This was a 'mixed marriage', defined by the church's Catechism as 'between a Catholic and one who, though baptized, does not profess the Catholic faith'. The Catholic church has always considered mixed marriages 'unlawful and pernicious'. Strong words indeed! However, it 'sometimes permits mixed marriages, by granting a dispensation, for very grave reasons, and under special conditions'[1].

The most significant condition was that my father must agree to any future children being brought up Catholic.

Their wartime wedding photographs are a few tiny black and white survivors, two inches by one-and-a-half, taken with a simple camera, probably my father's Box Brownie. My mother is wearing a knee-length dress in a pale colour, gathered at the waist, short sleeved, with a small bouquet of roses pinned to the bodice. My father is wearing a smart suit and tie.

There is one photo only of the thirteen guests of the wedding group. My father's parents, Grandfather and Grandmother Ashton, are on the left, and next to them my Grandmother Cumberbatch.

I would grow up to know my Ashton grandparents as Granny Annie and Granfer. There were tensions. Their only son was marrying a Catholic, and Grannie Annie was a dedicated Protestant from Ireland. Grandmother Cumberbatch was my Granny Izzie, who had been brought up as a Catholic during her childhood in Chile.

In the wedding photos, the bride is radiant, and the bridegroom looks modestly proud. Simplicity was the order of the day. The newly married couple, changed into ordinary clothes, are off for a honeymoon picnic. My father is holding a flask for tea, and over his shoulder is a strap probably for the camera he held in his other hand. Being economical was a wartime necessity and also in the case of my parents an undoubted virtue.

Cottage life

They move to their first home together, Thatched Cottage, Watton Green, Norfolk. John is employed as a beekeeping assistant. He goes off to his work at the honey farm every day, being paid the lowly wartime rates. He is surely wondering about his future. The war is beginning to change direction, and it may end soon. What can the future hold for a beekeeper who is also a conscientious objector? The newly married mother-to-be is meanwhile learning how to manage her household. My mother is a writer, and she describes her daily life before I am born in a long ditty of rhyming couplets:

The Cottage Wife
Down with blackouts, windows ope
Fetch in coal and wash (with soap)
Then I must the porridge cook
Take down the cups from off the hook.
Then at last, the breakfast eat
A crusty loaf and porridge sweet.
With husband gone, I wash the plates
Dust the parlour, sweep the grates.
Then there is the bed to make,
The milkman comes – a pint I take.
Soon it's time to think of dinner
Chocolate pudding is a winner
So I scrape and cut and peel
All to make the midday meal.

(After midday dinner)
I'll get up and stretch and frown
Take my basket to the town.
It's nice to look around the shops
At wool and fruit and books and mops.

(After going home)
I must go and get the coal
Fetch in water for the bowl

Think about the evening meal –
And now away the light does steal
So before the light gets dim
The lamps I get, the wicks I trim.
When they're alight, the curtains draw
Poke up the fire a little more.

(John comes home)
We will sit around the table
Talk and eat as we are able
The kettle on the hob does sing
The pussy purrs like anything.
I must my little candle light
Go bedwards by its beam so bright.
At last the day is ended, so
All peacefully to sleep I go.

This is a picture of wartime cottage life: windows blacked out, lighting of fires and carrying coal, no mains water and outside earth closet, shopping, cooking, washing up and going to bed by candlelight. Bedroom intimacy is not mentioned but it must take place because before long a baby is on the way. Another poem of rhyming couplets is dated 1 May 1944, when her five months' pregnancy would be beginning to show:

In the Garden
We have a garden shared by both
Full of every kind of growth.
Over there you like to grow
Peas and beans all in a row.
But here, all planted at the edge
Are wallflowers and a rosemary hedge.
So all beside the things to eat
Are primroses and violets sweet,
In fact, it is easy to see,
What belongs to you, and what to me.
We like the unofficial things
The shrew that squeaks, the bird that sings.
The hasty rabbit in the bank

The frog among the nettles dank.
Oh, it is nice when skies are blue,
To walk around it all with you.
In fact, you cannot take the measure
Of the different kinds of pleasure
There is in gardens made by two,
Especially when they're Me and You.

He likes the practical vegetables and she the romantic cottage flowers. They enjoy their garden together, both appreciating natural things, but the priorities are different.

....

The beekeeper's baby

At birth, I weighed seven and a quarter pounds. My wartime birthday presents are listed in *My Baby's Progress Book*. Money was short and it was helpful when friends and relations gave presents. I was given pram suits, a cardigan, knitted frock, jackets, socks, matinee coat, knitted rompers, silk dress socks, vests, smock, petticoat, mittens, bootees. They are all useful.

There were also pillows, an eiderdown, blankets, bath thermometer and feeders. To keep me on the right track, I was given a prayer book, and for my pleasure a beautiful book of nursery songs by H Willebeek de Mair.

I was given money too. Granny Izzie, Granny Annie and Great Aunt Lily each gave £10. Great Aunt Katie gave 10 shillings and a cardigan. There were two gifts of National Savings stamps.

I am an important and wanted baby girl, the first grandchild on both sides of the family.

....

My father

Who was this beekeeper who would bring his trade to Hay? It is an unusual trajectory, being a beekeeper rather than a miner, a builder, a teacher, a tradesman, or a civil servant. He was born in 1915, the oldest child of four, his younger sisters being Grace, Margaret and Catherine. My grandfather Percy Ashton was a middle-class civil servant who worked in customs and excise. At least some of the time he was posted in Ireland which is where he met my grandmother, Annie Smith, daughter of a shopkeeper and farmer in the town of Adare.

John was sent to John Wycliffe school in Stonehouse, Gloucestershire, as a weekly boarder. In those days, it was a day and boarding school for boys. The school's magazine in 1933 reports the boys debating the rise of Hitler's Germany. Their views ranged from sympathising with Hitler's action against the 'vermin' Communists, objecting to the German internment camps, questioning if Jews should be controlling politics, banks and professions and pointing out that the obligation for all Germans to use the Nazi salute was contrary to English ideas. John, aged 18, is reported saying that he "did not believe that Germany wanted war to restore her prestige. England ought to support Germany in her endeavour to regain equality of status." The arguments go back and forth. The boys are young, and there is time for their views to evolve, to harden, to change.

My grandparents had paid so much money for my father's private school education that when he left school he was told he must earn his own living. Their resources now had to be spent on his sisters. He took a job at a printing firm, which had Quaker connections, and was training as a chartered accountant. He was in contact with Whiteway Colony, a utopian settlement with Tolstoyan ideals of going back to the land, whose residents included anarchists, conscientious objectors and refugees from the Spanish Civil war. During this period, he and some friends made a cycling expedition into Germany where they came across one of the Nuremberg rallies, attended by around half a million participants. He was certainly not sympathetic to militarism, and the influence of this event on his thinking is uncertain.

After receiving conscription papers, he convinced the wartime tribunal that he would not take up arms. His parents accepted his position, even if they didn't agree with him. He opted to work producing food for the war effort instead of going to prison.

He became a registered conscientious objector, and worked as gardener and beekeeper at the Rudolf Steiner home for disabled children at Clent Grove in Worcestershire, which is where he met my mother. From there, he moved to Norfolk as a beekeeping assistant in Madoc and Moore's honey farm. He had been interested in honey and bees since at least Christmas 1937, as we know from a surviving book of his of that date. It is not a beginner's book but a technical study on swarm control.

....

My mother

Who would marry a pacifist beekeeper in wartime conditions? Born in 1921, Eileen Meriel Cumberbatch came from a well-to-do doctor's family in London. She was used to comforts and pretty things. As a child, life downstairs in the kitchen attracted her much more than being dressed in silk and having her hair tied up in ringlets. She agonised through years of early schooling, until her mother arranged for her to have a private education after the age of sixteen. She studied poetry and literature, languages ancient and modern, and learned to play the piano.

Her doctor father, a heavy smoker, died of a heart attack in 1939, and her only brother Richard went off to war around the same time. She then spent two years' teacher training at the Charlotte Mason College at Ambleside in the English Lake District.

While there, she converted to Roman Catholicism, taking the name of Francesca Mary Cumberbatch. She wrote:

I felt very unhappy there, what with my becoming an R. C. convert in a Protestant stronghold, and my solitary habits of reading and thinking and wandering about.

At this college, she was obliged to study botany. The students collected floral specimens, drew and painted them, and studied botanical families with their Latin names. She came to love botany and the beauty of the lakes and mountains.

Refusing to take the final vows with their religious element, with which she no longer agreed, she left without her teaching qualification. From there, she moved to a Rudolf Steiner school:

Here I was at home from the first day and it was such pleasure and happiness to be truly myself, instead of twisting myself up in vain efforts to be someone else.

Here I met James and John. John I married – James with whom I had a perfect friendship for thirty years.

John was the beekeeper, and James, who had been invalided out of the army, worked in the nurseries with the children. In an early letter from 1941, she had written about James to her mother: "He said he loved me ever since one night when we went out on the hills when the snow was on the ground, and the moon was in my hair." And "he wrote poems which I thought most beautiful."

At the Rudolf Steiner school, she absorbed ideas of bringing up children close to nature which had an innate appeal. From there, she moved to Downham Market in Norfolk, where she took a post 'nursing backward children'. In January 1943, she started a nature notebook which survives, with lovely illustrations, and this record moves with us all the way to Hay.

Her developing love of the natural world and experience of the Steiner movement were positive influences which she would take to Hay, and the bringing up of her children. The presence of James in the background was a touch incongruous.

Soon after my birth, on 17 September 1944, I am christened a Catholic baby at Our Lady and St Thomas church in Wymondham. My name is to be Bridget Mary, the first being a nod to my Irish side and to my mother's admiration of Saint Bridget of Kildare. Eighteen guests were at the christening including my mother's aunt on her father's side, Aunt Alice, who lived not too far away. They are all Protestant, but it is clear that I am to be nurtured in my mother's Catholicism. This is accepted by my father.

I am a first baby, a first grandchild and a source of wonderment. Everything is new and experienced as though never realised before, my gurgles, my first smiles, my looks of recognition, my grunts of contentment and even my complaints at babyish discomforts. It is all recorded in My Baby's Progress Book.

The district nurse instructs my mother. I am put on a strict routine as is the habit of the day. I must be fed every four hours, and after that 'winded' over my mother's shoulder.

Next, she is to change my nappy, wash me and put me in my cot to sleep until the next feed time. She must ignore me if I cry for food before four hours is up. If she doesn't follow the routine I will be spoiled and she will be making a rod for her back.

When I am four weeks old, I am taken to the clinic for my check-up, and weighed.

"Mrs Ashton, this is not satisfactory. Bridget is underweight," she was told. "You have not enough milk to feed her properly, and you must put her straight onto a bottle."

My mother has been breast-feeding me, but despite my poundings and greedy suckling at the source of life, and my regular four-hour feeds, I am not growing properly. The fashion for feeding on demand, which stimulates the milk supply, had not reached Watton Green in 1944.

My distraught mother complies. She supplements her breastfeeding with cow's milk from a bottle, and I begin to thrive. Her milk supply slowly lessens and that for her is a deep sorrow.

....

Wartime village

Our cottage is near an American base. This entry appears in one of my mother's notebooks:

An American army aerodrome was just a couple of fields away and we used to go there to Mass on Sundays. Our cat would accompany us just so far, then hide herself in the hedge and wait there until we returned an hour or so later.

After a time, the airmen dispersed and were replaced by black men whom the white airmen despised. The villagers however much preferred them. They were courteous and drove their lorries with consideration down the narrow lanes.
There were many large and beautiful churches in the neighbourhood, and Father George, who was very musical, used to organise the concerts. The black soldiers would sing, and we local people enjoyed these concerts very much.

The bombing continued and we often had friends from London to stay a few days to relax from the bombing. One was a girl called Grete Kern, a friend from Clent Grove days. She enjoyed making herself free with the American boys who were always wanting things from the villagers.

'Say, have you got any eggs?'

Her reply: 'No but I've got some very nice legs!'

In my babyhood, there is already hospitality for those in need, and an interest in the wider world.

Change is coming. My father is offered a job at the Bee Research Department at Rothamsted Experimental Agricultural Station which he accepts. Our thatched cottage must be left to other occupants. We will move to Hertfordshire, a hundred miles in the direction of Hay.

I am a tiny creature when I am bundled up in my knitted frock, cardigan and woolly booties. My two months' old baby life is left behind in the cottage with its roof of thatch, the scents in the garden of cabbage and flowers, the outside sanitation and the cold-water tap. I had absorbed all its simplicity while I fed and gurgled and learned to smile. It is part of me, deeply emplaced. My mother and my beekeeper father are taking me to a new house with a boundless garden.

3 The Boundless Garden

My bare legs and arms are being scratched by the trunk of the cherry tree as I cling on in panic. "Ma ma ma…" I yell. I have scrambled up the sloping trunk which has partly fallen in a storm. The yellow cherries with the red blush are just out of my reach, the fruit that has tempted me up. "Ma ma ma…" The leaves are whirling around me, and then I hear the voice of calm. My mother reaches up and her arms go round me, circling my chubby body as she unpicks my fingers and brings me down.

"What will you get up to next, Bridgie!" she says.

My mother is always busy, and I have the freedom of this garden which goes as far as I can see from the top of the steps. There are cherry, apple and greengage trees, lots of flowers, hens, two ponds which are used by toads, and of course beehives. We are alert to nature, close to creatures, and here I have adventures. I have learned to crawl and then to take my first clumsy steps. Now I am a proficient toddler. The hens peck around freely. They are monstrously big, and as high as my chin, but I am not afraid. Neither is the hen because she is almost the same size as me. I want her, and I reach out. Quick as a flick, her head darts at me.

"Aaaaaaaaaaaah…" I howl. "It pecked me."

"Never mind, darling," my mummy says as she cuddles me. "There's no serious harm done." She is always around for the rescue.

………………………………………

The wartime household

I am a four-month-old baby when my father sends a Christmas letter to his family and friends, explaining the move from our thatched cottage to the bungalow with the cherry tree in the garden. His letter:

Early in October with much regret, we left our four-roomed cottage which in spite of its lack of mod cons we had made very homely during the twelve months we had in it.

Harpenden and district is very full, and we count ourselves lucky to have a furnished bed-sitting room – we had to store our furniture. Here Mary valiantly helps our landlady by cooking for upwards of nine people, providing nourishment for Bridget in between.

The only way to get a home of one's own seems to be to buy a house at two or three times its pre-war value; furnished rooms are difficult and unfurnished ones impossible to get. It will clearly be difficult for three people and a dog to live in one inadequately furnished room indefinitely.

Bridget Mary is a happy, square-headed straw-topped bundle of 12 lbs 9 ozs. She was slow at putting on weight, but soon after we moved to Harpenden, she started making it up fast and now looks very bonny.

I am very hopeful that 1945 will bring an end of the long drawn out and wasteful war. May we have soon a progressive government ready, willing and able, firstly to lay for ever the spectre of unemployment with a constructive full employment policy; secondly, to take strong action towards building a generous, really constructive peace and towards laying the foundation of a worldwide political and economic co-operating society.

The war has certainly been wasteful, but it is so much more than that. My father and mother must have known about the ghettos, the concentration camps, the war in the east, the invasion of the Soviet Union. 'Wasteful' seems an inadequate word, but this is a letter designed for family and friends with an inevitable range of opinions, so my father chose his words circumspectly. His friend Geoff, to whom this copy of the letter is addressed, and who served as a witness in his tribunal, is working in London where his building company is helping to repair bomb damage.

Perhaps my grandparents helped financially in the move to the house in Harpenden. My nine-month-old photos show me with a big smile and curls brushed up to the top of my head in the fashion of the day.

....

The toddler in the garden

My father is busy outside when I hear him call. I am dressed in my brown corduroy suit and playing around. "Bridget, come quickly. There's a hedgehog." I toddle along as fast as I can but it has gone by the time I get there. I am learning about creatures and natural things in this garden.

When I stand at the door of the house, I can look down to the rose bushes on the right.

A boy and a girl who live over the road have come to play with me. We decide to play shops, and for that game, we need some money. The rosebuds will make lovely pennies, so we go down to the rose bushes and pull them off, making a nice pile. We are happy at our game until my mother sees us.

"Bridget – what are you children doing! Stop that this minute!" My friends are sent home and I am in disgrace. How am I to know that rosebuds are not to be used for pennies?

One summer day, we have visitors, my Aunty Margaret and my cousin David who is similar in age to me.

"John – be careful with that wheelbarrow," warns my mother. He is giving David and me a ride around the garden.

"Off you go – into the pond," he teases and pretends to tip us in as we scream in terror and joy. Unfortunately, he tips too hard and in we go. He picks us out, and our mothers console us and change our clothes. In winter, the toads in this pond become frozen stiff and we can see them under the surface of the ice. To everyone's surprise, when the pond thaws, the toads do too, and they are still alive.

………………………………………

Inside the house

To me, the toddler, the house is large. There are some big rooms leading off a hall, and a kitchen is off to the right. One of the big rooms is my bedroom, and another my parents'.

There is an attic bedroom which is reached by a ladder.

Other people live in the house with us. There is an elderly gentleman who is a retired grocer, and a young woman called Joan Thurston, a botanist from Rothamsted, both paying guests. I have a sense of a busy household. My mother feels the need to help people who are lonely, to give them friendship and a welcome in our household.

My bedroom is painted bright yellow, and I get into trouble when I make muddy footprints on the wall from my bed. Later, when I have a new little sister, we will share the room, me in my bed and she in a cot with wooden bars.

....

Two little sisters

Helen was born in June 1946, just before I became two years old. This story is known to me from my mother's account in later years. She decided to go to hospital for the birth instead of staying at home, as she had done in the Thatched Cottage.

She regretted the choice. Attitudes to childbirth go through fashions, and in those days, hospitals were strict places. After the birth of my perfect little sister, the nurses took the baby away and put her in the infants' ward. My mother was only allowed to hold her and feed her at the appointed times, in a routine of feeding and washing every four hours. This was painful for both mother and baby.

They stayed in hospital for a week. At this time, women giving birth were treated as invalids in need of care. It was probably a good rest for many hard-working women, a welcome holiday when they were being fed and looked after, but my mother was glad when she could escape with Helen.

My next little sister was due to be born in early 1948, and this time my mother arranged to stay at home. I was three and a half years old, and at the right moment, I was allowed into the bedroom. There on the floor, beside the big double bed, was a brown wicker baby basket.

"This is your new little sister, Bridgie," they tell me. I know better than that.

"That's not a baby," I say. "That's a dolly." My new sister is named Elizabeth Rose, and we always call her Rosie.

Now we are a family of five.

....

The tragedy of my lost uncle

On 3 December 1944, while we are still in the lodging house in Harpenden, Richard, my mother's good-looking, clever brother is killed in a bombing raid far away in Thailand. The news doesn't reach us right away. For five years, very little has been heard of him since he left for the army in June 1939.

There are two surviving photos of him in his uniform. In September 1941, he sailed to Singapore, arriving in November. After the surrender of Singapore, he was taken prisoner by the Japanese and jailed in Changi camp where he was kept until June 1942. From there, he was sent north to work on the railway which the Japanese were constructing from Thailand to Burma. He was still there when my parents were married, but his whereabouts were not known at the time. In March 1944, he was moved to Thailand, still in Japanese hands. He suffered unimaginably, including loss of hearing. In December 1944, he was killed during an Allied bombing raid because he had not heard the air raid warning. It was a pointless, heart-breaking end to his life. Some of his colleagues who survived later communicated this story to his mother, my Granny Izzie.

My mother has lost her brother, and we have lost an uncle, in this war in which my father did not participate.[2]

....

Germans in our house

The Germans finally surrendered to the Allies in May 1945, about six months after we arrived in Harpenden. My parents are motivated to make peace with their former enemies.

Consequently, we have Germans in my toddler world.

Wolfgang is the first. Fancy having the name of a wolf! We have stories about Red Riding Hood and the wicked wolf, so the name makes Helen and me giggle. He is a prisoner of war, and there are several camps in Hertfordshire near where we live. Wolfgang thinks I am spoiled, and he reprimands my mother about my bad table manners. He is quite right.

Among my other naughty behaviours, I don't want to eat my crusts, and I have a trick of hiding them on a ledge under the top of the table. When eventually my mother finds out, they are covered with mould.

After Wolfgang, we have Willi Beerhorst. There is a photo in my mother's album with baby Helen two months old in her arms. The season and year are written on the back in her handwriting, summer 1946. It is a tiny wartime photo, measuring only one-and-a-half inches by two. Its ornamental border is different from the usual squared finish.

This is clearly a special occasion as there is not much money for baby photos in these frugal days. My mother has her hair done up in curls at the top of her head, with a neat parting and carefully combed curls at the side.

She is wearing a flowery cotton dress, with Helen folded up in her arms. Two other snaps taken at the same time show me playing, looking at flowers, and down on the grass. My potty is nearby and baby clothes are drying on the line behind.

Willi Beerhorst took these photos before he returned to Germany where he had them developed in this non-English style with the ornamental border. Thus, we can deduce that he took the photos and returned to Germany in the months that follow.

By summer 1948, he is well re-established in Germany as we can see from three later photos which are in my mother's album. He is smartly dressed in a suit in one photo. In another, he and his wife Wilma looked well turned out in tailored coats and wearing hats. In a third, Willi is at an easel with a scene that he has painted. The couple seem to be in their thirties or perhaps forties.

This is not a time when most people would surely have felt sympathy for Germans, and even though my father was a conscientious objector, and my mother a hospitable kindly person, there are questions in my mind as I write. How is it that the people who lost the war should look so much more prosperous than my family? How did my parents justify being so kind to people whose regime had caused such terrible sufferings? And so immediately?

What did Wolfgang and Willi Beerhorst talk about with my parents when they were in our house? Their war experiences? What they had seen, and done? Of course they were not wicked Nazis – no German prisoner of war would admit to that. Is it too soon to forgive and forget when the world is still full of traumatised war survivors? As a toddler, I understand nothing, but as I grow up I ask myself these questions. For many following years, Willi Beerhorst sends us Christmas packages in recognition of our family's hospitality.

During this phase, my parents also host a young German Jewish woman called Regina, a wartime survivor. She is pregnant, unmarried and miserable. My mother gives her lots of love and attention, and encourages her to keep the baby.

Later, Regina manages to get to Israel where she marries Gerd, and they live in a kibbutz. She will remain my mother's lifelong friend. My parents also take under their wing a little German girl called Eva Marie Valerius from Munich. There are a lot of people in our bungalow.

....

Beyond the garden

The crazy paving around our house leads to the gate, and I sense an opportunity. There is a wider world out there. I know the way to our Granny Izzie's house, and Helen is with me. I open the gate and encourage her along. There is no sign of our mother. Helen is barefooted and wearing a little shirt and shorts. It is rather slow work because her feet hurt. I urge her onward. Up the curving road we go towards the right turn to Ox Lane.

We never get there. Someone brings us back home.

Perhaps it was a policeman. Toddler that I am, I am already establishing my role as someone who leads people astray and gets them lost in wild places.

With baby Rosie in the pram and when Helen is a confident walker, our mother regularly takes us to visit our granny at Vine Cottage. As we make our way down the road towards Ox Lane, I have a great surprise. A district nurse in her navy uniform is running down the pavement on the other side of the road. I gaze in surprise. These are before the days of joggers and I don't know that grown-ups can run.

Our granny's house has a peach tree trained against the wall, and it has a cool wooden floor smelling of polish which pleases Helen. She loves us, and makes us welcome in her gentle diffident way. Helen, no more than two years old, is conscious of the cool wooden floor which smells of polish, and the quiet calm in the house. It is so different from the bustling activity at our bungalow.

Sometimes my mother takes us out of the house in the other direction. We turn left out of the garden, then up a slope near a railway line. We go under the railway bridge to the shops. I am even sometimes put on the back seat of my mother's bike, and I have a swooping ride down the hill, behind her brown headscarf. Bicycling with the wind in my hair. That's what I like!

....

Growing girls for the photo record

Our parents want Helen and me to be recorded by Poly Photos. For this procedure, the photographer sits us down while a helper with toys and antics encourages us to smile. A hundred tiny photos are quickly taken which are later presented on a single sheet, each one-and-a-quarter inches square. The snapshots can be cut up, shared with family and friends, with the ones they liked best put in the family albums.

There are three of me aged 16 months, wearing a corduroy cap and jacket, and dated autumn 1945. The photos have a brownish tint, and my outfit is the one that I was wearing when my daddy called me to see the hedgehog. In spring 1947, when Helen is nine months old, her hair is combed up into curls on top of her head.

More Poly Photos in the same year show us looking healthy and happy, Helen with her hair in bunches and me, the 'square-headed girl' with a centre parting and ribbons.

In summer 1948, Helen and six-month-old baby Rosie are posing in the garden with my mother, who looks cheerful and is wearing a dark flowered dress. The beekeeper's family has grown since the time of the thatched cottage.

....

The beekeeper's dream

Discussions are taking place in our bungalow in 1948. My mother is fully occupied bringing up three little girls and catering for the German visitors and other lodgers, but my father is not content with his work at Rothamsted. He wants to be a full-time beekeeper, and is building up his collection of beehives and equipment. Where can he do this? He needs some land, a house in the countryside, and he finds an advertisement in *Peace News* for a cottage in the county of Radnorshire, just over the border in Wales, not far from a market town called Hay.

It is a rural hideaway, with no electricity or mains water, in the hills, isolated, and with a couple of acres of land. We can keep animals. My mother has an idealistic vision of a life of simplicity, and our beekeeper father longs for independence. The cottage with its land costs £400. Our parents make a visit. When they come back, our mummy tells Helen and me that to reach the cottage, you must go along the Green Road which is covered with wild flowers. I am impressed. Daffodils, tulips and roses, that's what flowers are, and I will see them all along the road.

One day, from my bed, I say to Helen, "We're going to the New Cottage today!"

I know no such thing. Helen looks at me trustingly as she stands holding the bars of her cot, and I almost believe my own story. Every day, we ask, "Are we moving to the New Cottage today?" I am worrying that my doll's pram might not be brought along, but my mother tells me that it will be in the removal lorry with all the other things.

We don't yet know that our destiny will take us to Hay, but we are several hundred miles closer, and being drawn into its orbit.

4 Top o' Lane

The road comes to an end next to a house in a muddy farmyard. Where should the open-backed lorry loaded with furniture go now?

"Hey there. Anyone around? Where is Hilltop Cottage?" the driver calls out.

The farmer comes out of the house. He points to a rough grassy track leading to a chimney on a rooftop just visible up the hill.

"Up there. At the top o' the lane," he says.

"They don't expect us to drive up there, do they!" the driver exclaims to his colleague. But that is the destination, and so they decide to try.

Low gear, lots of revs, exhaust gases billowing, up the slope the lorry struggles, slipping backwards. On with the emergency brake. More revs, and trying again. It takes lots of stops and starts, while the contents rattle around behind.

The family at the top of the lane hear the engine, and come out to watch. What a hullabaloo! Will it get there?

Somehow it does. Everything arrives safely including my toy pram.

But my parents vow that never again will they try to get a motor vehicle, of any kind, up that hillside. The other way to get to the New Cottage is along the more level Green Road. It doesn't go all the way to the front door, but it is better than the way the lorry came from the muddy farmyard to the cottage at the top o' the lane.

That is how the cottage gets christened. Hilltop isn't much of a name. Top o' Lane it will be.

....

Top o' Lane

Here we are, the English outsiders, in our new cottage in the Welsh countryside; five of us, our beekeeper father, our idealistic mother who will soon be plunged into the reality of country life, me aged four, Helen aged two and baby Rosie about eight months old. It is autumn 1948.

Our cottage is a mile or so from the hamlet of Painscastle which is six miles from the market town of Hay. My father is renting a workshop in Hay for his bee equipment and honey bottling. We will visit it often for shopping and to go to the Catholic church on Sundays. It will be an important part of our lives. There is a weekly market, and you can get everything you might need in the town.

We have arrived at our parents' dream location, surrounded by fields of clover, hedges with hawthorn, wild flowers along the lanes, our cottage set among sheep-grazed rolling hills where there is heather for the summer honey crop. Hay is a central point for my father to process and sell his honey, with good roads to the larger towns of Hereford and Brecon, and not far from the mining towns of South Wales.

This is our new world. The images from those days, the tones of voice, the words, linger in my mind. The stories are the foundation of the child-person I am becoming, in the rural world of the Welsh border a few miles from the town of Hay.

The stone cottage at Top o' Lane is at the heart of my adventures and misdemeanours, with two-year-old Helen always nearby. We patter in and out while my mother attends to baby Rosie, seeing to every aspect of domestic life and our animals.

We enter the cottage through a porch. On the left are the pegs for the outdoor coats, and places for the muddy boots. On the right are two very important water buckets, with lids on.

The main door leads into the middle of a long room which is the whole downstairs. The air smells of paraffin and wood smoke. Immediately, opposite is a blue paraffin cooking stove. To the left is the black range called The Guid Housewife with its central fireplace and oven.[3]

Around the room is some basic furniture and some of our toys, including my doll's pram.

Across the room, an opening leads to a narrow staircase, at the top of which is a small landing and two bedrooms with sloping ceilings. One is for my father and mother, and one for my sisters and me. A tall, thin paraffin heater, unstable and a fire hazard, is there to keep the worst of the winter chill at bay.

Outside the front door, a few steps to the right, is a small stone extension which contains the Elsan. This is a big bucket, with a smaller internal bucket and a seat. It smells tarry, of some special chemical which somehow neutralises the contents. Big children like me can sit on the Elsan seat. My little sister Helen needs help, or may use the potty in the house.

Straight ahead from the front door is a path leading to a gate which is kept shut to keep the children safe. There is a rainwater barrel to the left, and a little further on a woodpile.

Directly behind the cottage is a path to the edge of our piece of land, leading to a gate. Beyond is a tree-lined streamlet called The Dingle. Water trickles down in the rainy seasons of the year.

At the top of the steep slope behind the cottage, near the upper boundary wall, is the goat shed where Annabel and Dora, our two goats, live. They came with the purchase of the cottage. In the daytime, they are tethered out on the rough pasture around their shed.

Downslope is the garden. To the left, there is an unmentionable hole with lush green grasses and weeds around, and below it, fairly safely below, is the vegetable patch. A henhouse is off to one side. At the bottom of the garden, a rough boundary wall encloses our land. It is only a low wall, with a few weather-beaten hawthorn and mountain ash trees.

....

Daily work

In this world of perhaps a couple of acres, my mother is left to look after my sisters and me while my daddy goes off to Hay in his van to see to his bees and process his honey.

Her day's work lies ahead. There is no poem about everyday life in a country cottage as there had been at the thatched cottage in Norfolk while she was expecting me. There is no time for that sort of thing.

As Helen and I play around her feet, she looks around every morning and wonders where to start.

Rosie's nappy needs to be changed. She had her first milk meal earlier, and the consequences need to be dealt with.

Water – everything depends on water. The fire in the range may have already been lit and then she heats water in a kettle. Otherwise, she heats a little in a pan on the paraffin stove.

Then it is poured into an enamel bowl, and Rosie is held in it to be cleaned before being dressed and put into her cot.

More water is heated to deal with the breakfast dishes, using a little soap or bicarbonate of soda.

Annabel, the older goat, has to be milked. Dora, the younger, has not yet had a kid and so has no milk. The problem is always what to do with Helen and me while she leaves us for twenty minutes to go the goats' shed. If she manages it before my father goes off to Hay, he can supervise, but if not, we girls are left to our own devices, either in the cottage or playing in the garden. The routine is to take her white enamel billycan to the small dark goat shed. Squatting on a stool, she milks Annabel's two teats. In good weather, she tethers the goats outside, and roughly cleans out the goat shed.

In poor weather, the goats must be fed and clean water carried to them. When this is all done, she returns to her little girls.

On one occasion, she gets an unwelcome surprise.

Left to our own devices, I have decided that Helen would look much better if she has a haircut, and Helen obligingly sits down. Finding my mother's scissors, I carefully begin to cut a chunk out of the side of her hair. I find it a big improvement. I happily cut away until our mother comes in.

"Bridget – good gracious girl – what have you done!" she cries, pulling away the scissors. Helen and I are upset. We were having such a nice game.

Most days the nappies must be washed. To keep them decent, the cotton towelling nappies need to be boiled. Every drop of water must be carried in and heated. After scraping off solid material, and disposing of it in the Elsan, the soiled nappies must be rinsed in clean water before being boiled and washed in soapy water. They must be rinsed to remove the soap more than once, and each time wrung out by hand. Then they are to be dried either on an outside line or on a clothes horse indoors. Helen and I play around our mother's feet while she does this task, and our frequent squabbles must be sorted out as she goes along. When she takes the nappies outside to peg them on the line, we want to follow, and need shoes or boots, coats or hats to be put on. This is all a huge, time-consuming task.

To reduce the labour involved, after every feed, and carefully watching for the symptoms, my mother holds baby Rosie over some old newspaper. With luck and good management, she catches the emissions as they emerge, and the newspaper can be rolled up and put on the fire. That is one nappy she need not wash. As soon as she can sit securely, Rose will be placed on a tin potty, and she will often perform the bigger job there. She is doing her Hard Work, my parents say.

Every week, Monday being the traditional day, the clothes for the family are washed. This involves larger quantities of water and a big pan to heat it up. Washing powder is new and expensive. Yellow laundry soap is used and dirty stains rubbed hard. Rinsing once or twice to remove the soap is still to be done, and the wringing out. Each time the water must be carried in, and after each procedure disposed of. There are no drains to pour it down. The bowl is taken outside and the water flung across the garden.

Bottles of milk for Rosie punctuate the day, and perhaps some breast feeding too. Then more potty training and nappy changing, before putting the baby down for another sleep. The ordinary domestic chores must be done, the floor swept and the house tidied. All this goes on with two active little girls running around, getting in the way and in my case often causing mischief. I tease and annoy Helen frequently.

"Please be a good girl," our patient mother says to me so many times that one day, in the end, she can stand it no more. She sends me upstairs to get her hairbrush.

Perfectly self-assured, I go up the narrow stairs which lead out from the centre of the room. I find the hairbrush on my mother's dressing table. It has a round, flat back, with the prickly bits in the rubber on the front. Unconcernedly I take the hairbrush downstairs and hand it over.

My mother picks me up, seats herself on her chair, and lays me face down over her knee. Then she spanks me on my bottom, many times, very hard, with the flat side of the hairbrush. This is the biggest surprise of my young life. I yell in shock and outrage. My ego has taken a significant blow.[4]

After the morning tasks are completed, a simple midday meal must be prepared. Then we girls are put down for a rest on our beds which we certainly often resist. Between settling the girls and feeding the baby, the afternoon rest is never long enough for our exhausted mother. Before she knows what, it is time to prepare tea, the evening meal, for my father coming home. This involves peeling potatoes and preparing vegetables. Daddy might bring some essential supplies from Hay, with perhaps a small piece of meat. After the meal, there is water to heat to wash the dishes. Scraps from the plates and the dish water is thrown out for the hens. The goat is to be milked again, and the girls to be washed and put to bed. In darker evenings, the Tilley lamp hisses and lights us as we go off to bed, leaving our parents to have a few quiet moments before it starts all over again the next day.

....

Water supply

Everything depends on the water supply. The cottage has been built next to The Dingle, the streamlet running down beside our garden. Before moving there, our parents thought that it would be handy for everyday water supplies. However, they discover that The Dingle dries up after periods of no rain, so other sources must be found.

For drinking water, my father must take two buckets, cross the field beyond The Dingle, climb a stile and cross a field, then climb another stile. Beyond that is a small cluster of trees, and in a dell is a square slab covering a pool of clear water.

This is The Spring. My daddy must fill the buckets and carry them carefully back to our cottage. Anyone who has ever needed to carry water knows how heavy it is. How long do two buckets of drinking water last? One day, perhaps two. It is a precious resource.

To eke out this supply, we have a rainwater barrel into which water flows from the roof. Despite it having a lid, spiders and flies and green bits and pieces collect in and around the barrel. It is lovely water for bathing children or washing hair, but definitely not for drinking or cooking.

As for toileting, our arrangement is different from most of the farms around here. Most of them have a shed at the bottom of the garden with a pit dug in it. Over the pit is a wooden box. A nice round hole has been carved out of the lid of the box making a seat for the users, and over time, it becomes smooth and comfortable. In some of these arrangements, to my mother's expressed surprise, the box lid is long enough for two holes. In rare cases, there could be three holes, two for adults and a lower one for a child. Thus, using the outhouse could be a companionable exercise. The mainly organic contents drain away into the soil.

The vegetable garden is usually a little lower down. This it is the normal arrangement for these remote country places, and just what is to be expected.

My father though is a man of the wider world, and has other ideas. He prefers a more scientific solution with the Elsan.

Also, being located close to the cottage front door, we can avoid a cold trail through the garden in wet, wintry weather.

Periodically the Elsan fills up. That is when my mother closes the door, and her mind. We children understand none of this. My father takes the bucket to the unmentionable hole down the garden, and does what he needs to do. Then he must clean the bucket with more of our ration of water and return it, replacing the essential chemicals.

Yes, water is everything. Living there teaches my mother, who teaches us, that water is precious. Not a drop must be wasted. The two buckets in the porch have important differences. One contains rainwater, and has a blue lid. The other with the green lid is strictly for drinking. This has been carried over two stiles and three fields. I am tempted to do one of the naughtiest things of my young life.

My father sometimes comes home from market day in Hay with a present for the children. We are not allowed to ask, but we always hope. One day, he brings me a yellow plastic canary. It has a pipe which you blow down, and a little place to hold water. When you blow, the air goes through the water and the bird whistles a chirrupy song. I love my canary. When the water is used up, the canary needs to be refilled.

"Now Bridget, you may fill your canary with the water in the blue bucket," my mother tells me, "but not from the green bucket." I know the rule well already but she is reminding me. I happily play with my canary, and follow the rule. But one day, when no-one is looking, I furtively lift the green lid and fill my canary. I am never found out, and it remains my guilty secret.

....

Bridget's world map

From my four-year-old perspective, Top o' Lane is at the centre of a network of pathways. Helen and I listen as our parents talk about our neighbours and the names of the places where they live. In my head is a set of images leading in various directions, down a lane, over a stream, through a farmyard and up on the hillside. This is where I am learning to find myself, in the late-1940s Welsh countryside.

Down from Top o' Lane is Middle Pentre, with the muddy farmyard. Joyce Goodall lives there. She is a year or so older than me, and she becomes my friend. She has a brother, and her mother is called Freda.

Further down the lane in the direction of Painscastle, is Lower Pentre, and there lives a formidable farm woman called Mrs Lewis. She has hens ranging freely.

If we turn left at Middle Pentre instead of heading towards Painscastle, we come to Upper Pentre, the home of a mysterious family.

The Goodalls' farmhouse is higher up and across the hillside. They are related to the family of Middle Pentre, and are our friends.

From Top o' Lane, if we follow the Green Road, we soon come to the Breeze family's farm, called The Wern. Eileen is my age. A little further on is the farm with the song-like name Bailey Bedw, the home of the Evans family.

My father is a practical man who gets along well with farmers, and my sociable mother makes friends with many of the women. We are becoming country people and share our neighbours' interest in farming and producing food from the land.

....

Children's cottage days

Joyce from Middle Pentre comes up one day to play. Helen and I are allowed to go with her, out of our gate onto the adjoining hillside where there are two small quarries overgrown with vegetation. People from the nearby cottages and farms have been throwing rubbish into them for a long time, and they are full of treasures.

We are going to make houses for ourselves. We pick out stones lying around and arrange them into squares on the warm grass which has been nibbled neatly down by sheep. We each have our own house, and carefully leave an opening for the door. We feel a primitive thrill as we claim our houses. The next thing is to get china for our house.

Among the rusty metal old stoves and farm odds and ends are pieces of broken china. These are very valuable for our houses. We pick up white oddments of plate, and now and again a cup handle. A blue scrap is leapt upon with glee. The biggest thrill of all is to find a piece showing a red rose, surrounded by little bits of green leaf, and perhaps a speck of a blue flower.

With our lovely new sets of china, we can prepare meals.

Flowers and leaves are our food and twigs are knives and forks. We are safe in our little houses with the sheep smell in the air. The ewes around are baaing for their lambs, who bleat in reply. We are children of the land, claiming our homesteads, with the safety of our cottage chimney down below.

....

Making sense of things

Joyce is a source of information beyond that of my family. I have a lot to learn. Bright blue speedwell flowers are in bloom.

"Don't pick them," Joyce tells me, "or the birds will come and peck your eyes out." She calls the flowers Birds' Eyes. I am worried and I tell my mother.

"Of course they won't," she says. There is no superstition in our household, but there is religion.

My mother regularly reads to Helen and me, and we have some books including children's bible stories. Catholics must learn about kind Jesus, and the watchful God. Before meals, as we sit around the table, we put our hands together to say grace.

"Guard bless our food and make us good. Amen." It is a short and simple grace for little ones.

However, I have been read Christopher Robin's Verses, with Changing Guards at Buckingham Palace. I know it is a guard with a big black helmet who is hearing our grace. There is much to learn, including the fact that other families do things differently.

One day, I am invited to tea with Joyce's family. We are sitting around the table. Her mother is holding a loaf of bread under her arm, spreading butter on the open edge, and then cutting off the slice before laying it on the plate. This is odd. My mother cuts all the slices first, and then butters them afterwards. But there are different kinds of manners too.

As we sit around eating our bread and butter, I need to break wind. So I do, with a loud pop. Everyone laughs. I have no idea this is funny, but I observe the reaction.

"You did it," Joyce says, pointing to her brother.

"I didn't. It wasn't me!" he denies. But they all laugh, and blame him.

I hadn't realised this would be a cause of humour, but I pick up the atmosphere. I know that I should take the blame, but I don't own up. I am learning cunning.

One day, Helen and I are very naughty and our mother has tried hard to make us behave without success.

"I've reached my wits' end!" she cries. "I'm running away!" She really does leave us, taking baby Rosie in her arms, running down the path and through the gate, up to the open hillside where we have our little houses. When Helen and I realise that she has gone, we start to cry. We are all alone. There is no-one to look after us. We are abandoned to unknowable terrors.

She soon comes back to two sombre, penitent little girls.

Nearly all the children I know live on farms. Animals are part of their everyday existence – calves, the house cow for their daily milk, dogs for sheep and to guard the farmyard, hens, cockerels, lambs in season, ewes and rams, turkeys, geese, pigs. Horses are still used on the farms, although tractors are appearing. Our postman delivers our letters on horseback. There are wild ponies grazing on the hillside above the cottage.

We are a little different from the farm families, our animals being goats. Annabel is the mature one, whitish grey, with a long beard and hairy coat. The young Dora is frisky, and Helen and I are a little in awe of her.

One day, our mother tells us it is Dora's birthday. We know about birthday cards, so we decide that we will each make her one. When they are ready, we carry them up to where she is tethered in the garden. She stretches out her head as we hold them to her, snatches them one after the other and eats them.

"Mummy, Dora has eaten the cards," we wail.

"Never mind, darlings. Goats eat all kinds of things. She must have loved your cards," she consoles us.

Annabel is pregnant. A female kid would be very welcome, but a male has no value. There is a strange atmosphere in our house one day. I feel it but I don't understand. My mother is deeply upset. When the kid was born, a male, it had to be disposed of. There was no kind way to do it in those austere days. My father took on the unenviable job, and probably the blame.

He is the one who has to do other indelicate jobs. One day, he comes home dangling a dead rabbit that he had been given. This will make a delicious pie. The furry creature has to be skinned and gutted. My father sets to work. The smell of its flesh penetrates the room, and there is a ripping sound as its coat is torn from the skin. Our cat rubs herself ingratiatingly around my mother's legs, purring noisily as she waits for some bloody scraps. This incident causes my mother to dislike cats ever after.

One day, my daddy comes home with a cardboard box which he places on the living room floor.

"Cheep cheep cheep" comes from inside. To our joy, there are a couple of dozen day old chicks, yellow and fluffy. We will have our own supply of eggs. As they grow up, they are put in a henhouse in the lower garden. I learn that chicks which grow up to lay eggs are called pullets. Thus with a goat who supplies milk, our eggs and our vegetable garden, supplemented with delicious honey, our little home is providing a good portion of our food.

Our hens, however, have properties quite beyond the normal.

At Eastertime, our mother tells us: "On Easter Sunday, hens lay chocolate eggs!"

Really? Helen and I go out in a state of great excitement. Tucked among the woodpile we discover big eggs wrapped in coloured paper. Our hens have laid them. Nothing could be more natural.

My mother is very proud of her young hens. Old Mrs Goodall, our neighbour, comes to visit one day, and she says, "Would you like to see my pullets?"

We are in the process of baking a cake, and I am helping by stirring it. I am told I can go on stirring while they go down the garden. Then I have a good idea.

I really like sugar. I think the cake will taste much nicer if I add some more, which I do. And I go on mixing.

When the grownups come back, my mother puts the mixture in a tin to bake in the oven.

I begin to worry. When we eat the cake, everyone will know about my naughty behaviour because the cake will be so sweet. But no-one notices. In this way, I have learned that I can sometimes get away with bad behaviour.

....

Country neighbours

We are going on a walk to visit our neighbours, the Goodalls. My father and mother take turns carrying Rosie, while Helen and I trot alongside. Beyond us, on a round hilltop on the skyline, is a circle of pine trees inside a stone wall. This is called The Roundabout. We turn to the right, past our little houses next to the quarry, and along the sheep-nibbled turf. Helen and I cross the streamlet with big jumps. There we see an apple tree, bearing pretty red and yellow apples, some fallen on the ground.

"It's a crab apple tree," our parents tell us. Apples, food, growing on a tree? We can't eat them. Are they poisonous? We know about poisoned apples from the Snow White story.

"They are not exactly poisonous," my mother tells us. "But they will give you a tummy ache."

We pass an ominous building called The Ruin, an overgrown stone structure with broken walls, not much of a roof, lots of nettles around, and shaded by dark trees. People have lived there, people who have gone away. We know nothing about ghosts or spirits, but we feel the haunting emptiness.

When we reach a long farm building, we are invited in by Mr and Mrs Goodall who are a generation older than our parents. The room is dark, with low brown beams. The grownups have lots to talk about, while Helen and I play around, cautiously.

We breathe in the smoky wood atmosphere. There are sides of bacon hanging from the beams, and we hear the story that sometimes mice run around on them. When it is time for tea, kindly Mrs Goodall cuts up and cooks some mushrooms for us, freshly picked nearby. This is a real treat.

We little girls aren't sure about this at all. They are long and slimy. I whisper to Helen when no-one can hear, "They are snakes!"

There is another family whose house we pass by, but don't go in. We only go there once. The children, of whom there are many, peep at us out of a darkened window. The father has a big black beard. His eye roves as he talks. His wife is a shadowy figure. The children don't go to school. Hearing oddments from our parents' conversation, we have the feeling that strange things happen in that household.

The Evans family from Bailey Bedw are our friends, and they have two children, Betty and Malwyn. My father has made a wheeled cart for Malwyn. One day, we all go on a big expedition along the path across the round hills of the Begwyns, two women, four children and baby Rosie. As we go along, it starts to rain. Helen and I make a miraculous discovery. We can put our faces up towards the sky, open our mouths and get a free drink. Surely, this has never been thought of before.

The Roundabout is on our right as we follow this path.

One day later, I learn the word 'landmark'. My mother looked up at the hilltop where the trees of the Roundabout stand in their circle. They aren't there. Someone has chopped them down.

"How could they do that?" she says. "To destroy a landmark! This is vandalism. To cut down those trees!"

This is what I hear, and this is what I learn.

....

Painscastle

The Painscastle of my world is not much more than a farm and a few small houses. It has a public house with no sign outside, for which there is no need when anyone who is likely to go there knows where it is. There is a post office and a shop.

When we first moved to Top o' Lane, my parents visited the post office. In the dark, little room which serves as both post office and shop, my mother bought the important stamps, and then looked around for the merchandise, butter, jam, biscuits.

The small, stout post office woman shakes her head. "Would you like some margarine or some candles?" she asks. That is all she has for sale.

A post office, an informal public house and a school. These are the amenities of Painscastle in our world of 1948.[5] I am now four years old, and ready to start at the village school.

························

The village school

"Off you go now, Bridgie. Be a good girl and go straight down the hill. Don't stop along the way," says my mummy as she ties up the strings of my bonnet. I am warmly dressed with my winter coat, thick stockings and square woolly hat which frames my face. I set off on my sturdy four-year old legs down the lane to Middle Pentre. I am all alone, dispatched with a little wave by my mother. I know the way, and this is what country people do.

At the bottom of the lane, I meet Joyce Goodall. She is in charge and I am aware of her seniority. We follow the farm lane past Lower Pentre, between stone walls and skimpy hawthorn trees. When we arrive at the proper road, we have to act cautiously. The woman, as old as in our fairy stories, lives there with her turkeys. Gobble gobble. They might run out at us. She often comes out, stares at us and makes some obscure grown-up comment. We get past her in relief, go round a bend, and then the Big Steep Hill is facing us.

Joyce being older takes it in her stride. For me, it is a mountain and my pace slows down. When we get to the top, on our right is a derelict cottage among the scrubby trees.

"A witch lives there!" Joyce reminds me every time we pass.

As Joyce herself isn't really scared I don't worry too much. Whereas the turkey woman is real, we never see anyone here.

Rounding the corner, we come to the village of Painscastle. There is a farm, the post office and a cottage or two on each side of the road. At the end, facing us is the school.

The walk has taken about three quarters of an hour. Two little girls, unattended, facing the weather, the turkey woman and the witch, arrive without harm.

The school has two classes, the Infants for me and the Big Class for Joyce. Hers is a room of mysteries and secrets not accessible to me.

My teacher is Miss Jones. She is young, pretty and kind, with a smiling face and fair curly hair. Her desk is in the front, and we children sit on wooden forms. They are long benches with desks fixed in front. The older, cleverer infants are at the back of the room. I am at the front.

Windows make the room bright, but they are too high for us to see out. Children must attend to the work in front of them.

On the first day of school, I am presented by Miss Jones with a reading book. I already know how to write the alphabet in big capital letters, so I think learning to read will be easy. She sits with me, and shows me a picture of a Japanese woman under a parasol. She reads out words. I am to read after her. After a while, she leaves me with an older girl and I go on repeating as well as I can. It is totally mystifying.

At writing time, we are given slates, real Welsh quarry slates of the kind that are put on roofs. They are smooth, dark grey and cold. Using sticks of chalk, we practise forming our letters. It is very economical because we have dusters to erase our writing, and then we can start again. Pencils and paper are reserved for the Big Class.

The way I write my letters is wrong. Being urban educated people, my parents thought they'd give me a good start and teach me the alphabet before I started school. But modern schooling methods have changed, and the teacher tells me that I must write in lower case. Capital letters are to be left until later, and when they learn this, my parents are duly mortified.

Just before playtime, the cook opens the door.

"Hands up for cocoa!" she says, and notes down the number. "Now, hands up for milk!" she says.

A few minutes later, she brings in the warm drinks on a tray.

I always choose cocoa. One day, I decide to choose milk, which is unfortunate because I don't like it.

As soon as we've finished our drinks, we are allowed out into the playground. But on this day, I don't want to drink my milk, so I sit there. After a while, Mr Gwilliem, the headmaster from the Big Class comes in.

"Bridget, why haven't you drunk your milk?" he asks.

What am I to say? I simply have no good reason. So I improvise.

"A spider walked over it," I say.

Given an impossible question, this is my curious invention.

He probably smiles but he lets me out.

We learn to sing:

> Jesus bids us shine
> With a pure clear light,
> Like a little candle
> Burning in the night.
> In this realm of darkness
> We shall shine
> You in your small corner
> And I in mine.

There is no Welsh taught or spoken in the school, but we learn the word *eisteddfod*. In the summer, a marquee is erected in a field for the event, at the edge of the village. We are just a little school, but the teachers do their best. The school choir performs, and I being so young have only a short poem to recite. On the day, with my parents in the audience, I do my piece, but rush off dramatically after reciting only the first verse.

Out in the playground, girls on one side, boys separated by a wall on another, are the outhouses. These are two cubicles with earth closets inside and holes made in the boards upon which we must sit. Beyond the outhouses is an overgrown hedge which is full of tunnels made by the girls leading into little play areas which are our 'houses'.

The other girls don't always like me. I speak in a funny way. I've been brought up by parents who are different from theirs, not from around here, and I have a big opinion of myself. One day, feeling left out, I go back into the classroom.

"They won't let me play with them," I complain.

Miss Jones is eating orange and lemon sweets, jelly slices. Feeling sorry for me, she offers me one. Then she takes me outside and asks the girls to let me play. They are obliging enough. But oh the pleasure of that orange slice, juicy, acidic, sweet!

Sometimes it is raining and we can't go out to play. Then we must entertain ourselves in the classroom or the porch. Miss Jones is free at playtime too, and she has an entrancing hobby. I watch her fingers fly back and forth, round and round, as the wool flicks over the long needles. This is called knitting. It is something my mother cannot do.

In the porch, the girls sometimes play a thrilling game. We line up with our backs to a wall. One girl stands against the opposite wall, not looking at us.

"What time is it, Mr Wolf," we chant.

"Two o'clock!" the wolf says. We all tiptoe two steps closer to her.

"What time is it, Mr Wolf!" we chant again. She chooses the number.

"Three o'clock." The tension builds up as we creep three steps closer.

"What time is it, Mr Wolf," we call out again, tiptoeing and bending slightly backwards because we are very close and we know what is about to happen.

"Dinner time!" Claws raised, the wolf turns and attacks us.

We run in a state of primal terror before the bite that kills, back to the safety of our wall. But the wolf grabs the slowest one of us, who will take her turn to be Mr Wolf.

In the playground, Miss Jones teaches us circle games. We hold hands in a ring. One child is outside the ring, holding a handkerchief, and she circles us while we chant:

I sent a letter to my love
And on the way I dropped it
Someone must have picked it up
And put it in their pocket.

She drops the letter behind one of us, and when that person realises she chases the other round the ring, who is racing to the empty space. This is an exciting game which is only played at school.

Sometimes, we have Physical Training in the playground. Once, as we are leaping up and down, legs-and-arms-out, legs-and-arms-in, I see my mother approaching the school along the village road. Rosie is in the pram and Helen walking alongside, and I run out of the line to see her. I am still only four years old and have a lot to learn.

Unusually, while we are sitting at work in our classroom, we hear a distant rumbling noise outside. The headmaster comes into our room, and escorts us quickly into the playground. We look up towards the sound in the sky and there, moving along, is an aeroplane, something we have never seen before. This is news to take back to tell our parents.

When it is time to go home, Joyce and I retrace our steps.

Sometimes she has a penny, and she knows that she can buy an Oxo cube at the public house, the dark interior of which we bravely penetrate. If I am lucky, she might let me have a lusty lick or two at its salty shape.

Joyce and I are walking back along the lane, past Lower Pentre one spring day. The hens are coming into full lay, and are allowed to run freely. They are known to lay their eggs in hidden corners, away from the henhouse.

Out springs Mrs Lewis. "You girls have been stealing my eggs!" She glares at us. "I'm going to tell your mother, Joyce. I'm going to tell your mother too," she says, pointing at me.

Two baffled children look at her. What does this mean? Have we been stealing eggs? Because she is a grown-up, and says I have, I am puzzled and anxious.

When I get home, I fearfully tell my mother. Perhaps she will be angry with me.

"Darling, of course you haven't stolen the eggs. Where would you put them?" she says, reassuring me. But I am worried. Why would she say I had stolen eggs? From then on, it is frightening to walk past Mrs Lewis's farm gate.

On our way home, after we reach Middle Pentre where Joyce lives, I must do the final stretch up the hill to our cottage by myself. Near the farmhouse, there is a clump of holly trees with good hiding places under the branches. Joyce decides to show me a new game. We take holly leaves and play 'doctors'. This game is so absorbing we forget the time.

"Bridget, where are you?" I hear my mother call. She has left my little sisters in the cottage while she comes looking for me. Without understanding why, I know this is not a game about which to tell my mother, but she senses something.

After this episode, she decides that a change needs to be made. Instead of walking down the hill to join Joyce, I am to go along the Green Road to the Breezes' farm. There I will join Eileen, who is similar in age to me. The family has a hundred-acre farm, large for this locality, and a little black Ford car in which her father will drive us both to school.

The new routine means I must leave our cottage and go up onto the open hillside. Then I will turn to the left, walk along a field, and then one more, before heading down to the Breezes' farmhouse. Another terror has to be faced. Big gobblegobble turkeys flap their pink wattles at me. I hesitate and back off.

"They won't hurt you," says Mrs Breeze. "Pay no attention." The trouble is that their beaks are level with my face. They are monsters. I struggle by.

Eileen and I sit in the back of her father's car. I am four-and-three-quarters years old and it is summer. We can see the tall, pinkish-purple foxglove flowers growing between the stones of the walls on either side of the lane. There is a matter of prestige to be sorted out here. We must count them, and whoever has the most foxgloves on their side of the car is the winner.

At other times, we compare whose father is the richer. "Mine is richer because we have a car," Eileen says.

"No, mine is because my daddy has a van!" I reply. "I have more money than you," says Eileen.

How can I answer that? I don't have any money of my own.

"No, you don't. I'm richer than you!" is the best I can do.

I tell my mother about these conversations. "I had no idea children of your age even think about such things!" she says.

The days go by in this way, with the walk between our cottage and the Breezes' farm. One time, it is more frightening than the gobble-gobble monster turkeys. I leave home in the usual way, and a little way along, out of sight of home, I see ahead of me some giant creatures. They are much taller than me, big, wide, hairy creatures with great long legs. They are pulling at the grass with long white teeth, right in my pathway. What am I to do? I stand transfixed, not daring to get closer. I stand, and I stand, and I stand. Mr Breeze must have left for school. I stand some more. The wild ponies graze here and there, paying no attention to this bonneted, frightened little girl.

In the end, I turn around and go crying back home.

"Bridget, what are you doing here?" My surprised mother dries my tears. She dresses Helen, cleans and tidies Rosie and puts her in the pram. We all walk down the hill past Middle Pentre and on to Painscastle where she deposits me, very late, at school.

The long journey to school is acknowledged by the headmaster in my spring school report: "She is a very plucky girl to travel the distance she does at the age of 4 years."

My little sister, Helen, aged only three and a half years, is allowed on a couple of occasions to come to school too. She sits in the 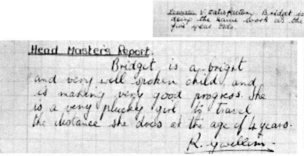 Breezes' little black car and can see the ponies out of the window. She tastes the watery cocoa and plays with the girls in the dens in the hedges. Our first introduction to school life is rural and gentle.

Going to Hay

"We are going to the market in Hay today," says our mother.

This is a big excitement and doesn't happen often. My father usually brings essential items of food home in his van in the evenings. But occasionally, to have a day out where she can talk to other people and make her own choices, my mother decides we will go to Hay.

Down the hill, we walk to the Hay road. We wait near the bridge where the turkey woman lives until along comes the green country bus, and we climb excitedly up the steps through the open doorway. All the seats inside are filled with farm women, baskets of eggs on their knees and in the gangway.

Market day is their day out too. Those with babies who can't be left behind have them wrapped in shawls.

When we get to the bridge over the River Wye in Hay, we all pile out of the bus because the bridge is so unstable that it can't take more than one ton in weight. We walk over to the other side, the farmwomen with their baskets, those with babies having tied them onto their backs. The bus meanwhile drives over, empty of passengers. Some get in again for the final stretch.

Once arrived in town, and finding that doing her errands in time for the return bus is tricky with Helen and me alongside, my mother has a good idea. There is a field with a fence and a gate, not far from the shops. It is peaceful enough, with only a few lambs in the far corner. We will be safe there. She tells Helen and me to play there quietly, and she will be back soon.

Not long after she leaves, the lambs trot up. They aren't new-borns with long dangly legs, but big strong ones. They come right up to us, and butt us with their woolly heads. Down we fall, onto the grass. We get up and try to run away, but they keep butting us down.

We start to scream. We yell, and we cry, and yell some more. A woman who lives over the road hears us, rescues us and takes us to her house. When our mother returns, she finds that her girls have disappeared. Panic! We are soon brought out and reunited. Nothing could ease Helen's and my hurt feelings. When we are told that those assertive creatures are pet lambs, used to being fed by people and quite harmless, we know better. They were tossing us, just like bulls do.

The same routine with the bus and the bridge takes place on the return journey, everyone carrying their purchases, and the farmwomen with their egg money in their pockets. When we finally reach our stop, my mother must encourage tired little girls along the last mile to the cottage.

Going to market is a big undertaking and doesn't happen very often.

Another reason for going to Hay is to attend the Catholic church. Every Sunday, we are made as clean and tidy as possible, and get into the van for the journey. My father has created a wooden bench inside the back of the van for Helen and me. Rosie is on my mother's knee in front. We are a Catholic family and going to attend Mass on Sunday is an obligation.

The van drives along the Green Road, not filled with daffodils and roses, but dotted with small yellow celandines in spring and tormentil in summer, lovely indeed to my mother. It is six miles to Hay. We soon reach the narrow single-track hard road, and the van trundles along.

"Are we nearly there?" we call out over the noise of the engine.

"Won't be long now," says my mother,

"When will be there?" we complain a few minutes later.

The journey seems to take such a long time, as we bump and rattle around in the back. My father speaks to us sharply. "That's enough noise." Children are not allowed to complain.

Sometimes a farmer with a flock of sheep is moving along the road. We need to wait patiently as he and the dog guide the sheep into a field.

In Hay, we join the small Catholic congregation, and after Mass, we clamber into the van again for the ride home. One day, my father suddenly tells us: "Do you know there is a mill in Rhos Goch? A water mill?" he said. This is in a hamlet not far from Painscastle.

A water mill is quite beyond my comprehension. It is his tone of voice which makes an impact. We children cannot know, until years later, his understanding that this is a historic remnant of a bygone age.

....

The mystery of Eva Marie Valerius

In Harpenden, we had been hosts to two German prisoners of war. We also took care of a German girl called Eva Marie Valerius. There is a mystery here. I know almost nothing about her. She appears in my mother's album in a picture dated summer 1948, which is just before we leave Harpenden. The ornamental border and the quality of the photo tells us it had been sent from Germany.

In the photo, she looks seriously, directly, into the camera. Her hair is carefully styled into a heap on the top of her head. Below neat side partings hang two tidy plaits, and there is a locket around her neck. She is eleven years old.

I don't understand the circumstances in which Eva Marie joined our family. She moves with us from Harpenden, and there is a photo of her with my sisters and me at Top o' Lane.

Why have I not mentioned Eva Marie Valerius in all the stories about our life in Top o' Lane? Has some subconscious resistance pushed her out of my mind? Has she such a nondescript personality that she has made no effect on me?

How is it that she wasn't with me when Joyce and I went to school? Or was she, and I have pushed it out of my mind? Didn't she play games with us? Where was she when my mother went out to milk the goats?

Unanswerable questions all. And yet, Helen has this story, an image which has stayed in her mind from when she was less than four years old. "There was someone with long plaits sitting on the sofa next to my mother, and I was jealous of her for that. Not that I had words for that feeling at the time."

In her handwritten booklet, About the Houses, written in the year 2000, my mother records:

> Bridget and Eva Marie Valerius went to school in Painscastle. They set off with Eva in tears, Bridget full of smiles. They returned with Eva in smiles and Bridget in tears – their experiences of school were so different from what they expected. Eva returned to her parents in Germany in 1950 – rather to my sorrow, for I would gladly have adopted her.

If that had happened, I would no longer have been the privileged eldest child, and my self-confidence would doubtless have taken a blow. I was told later that Eva Marie had come in a programme to help German children who had suffered in the war. If she had been Jewish, I would have been made aware of that. Photos which date from summer 1949 in my mother's album show that she was still with us, a tall thin girl playing with Helen and me beside the river.

Snow on the hills

The autumn winds of 1949 are chilly at Top o' Lane. Our family has lived there for a year, one short year.

For my mother, who as a girl had lived in the town, with servants and modern comforts, moving to this cottage in remote Wales had been a dream. Although there are times when the fresh grass-scented air and the view across the hillside fills her with delight, most of the time she has been labouring to keep the children fed and clean, and doing it in isolation. Every morning, after my father leaves for his workshop, after I have been dispatched to school, and the postman on horseback has delivered a letter if there is one, the silence and the loneliness would fall. Helen and Rosie are beloved, but they are not adult company. The endless repetitious chores have to be done. But worst of all are the long hours without company, day after day.

My father would come home at the end of a hard day to an exhausted and sometimes tearful wife. There are chores waiting to be done. He must collect the drinking water, maintain the vegetable garden, skin a rabbit.

Two adults, inside the walls of this little house, sometimes comfortably together, but at other times ill at ease. There are tensions and arguments, tears and anger. A change is being discussed.

This is prompted by my mother's awareness that she is expecting another baby. The snow is falling, bringing the wild ponies down from the hill. Winter is to be gone through, but a decision has been made. In a narrow street in the centre of Hay are three ramshackle adjoining houses, and my parents manage to acquire them.

We have been participating in a way of life that is fast disappearing: horse transport; walking miles to school; quiet lands with isolated families and women supporting themselves with their poultry; an aeroplane being a reason to take children out of the classroom.

The day comes when my daddy drives the van for the last time along the Green Road towards Hay. My mother and Rosie are in front as usual, and Helen and I, the two big girls, are in the back. We have belonged, briefly, to the life of rural Wales. The cottage of Top o' Lane, the Dingle, the goats and the hens, the green hills and the winding lanes are being left behind. Rosie is too young to know, but Helen and I have taken it into ourselves. This time will always be with us.

The street in the market town of Hay is our destination.

A meagre living

"Everyone was poor in those days," my mother once said to me in later life. Were the farming families, who were our neighbours, really poor? That depends on how we understand poverty.

Around Top o' Lane, a small family farm like that at Bailey Bedw might be 30 acres, compared with the larger Breezes' farm of 100 acres. Most farms would be run on a low cash economy. An important source of income was from annual lamb sales. Wool sold after shearing in the summer would bring in a little more. A few beef or dairy animals raised in the fields could be sold in the auction market at Hay, for fattening up in the rich grasslands of Herefordshire.

The women weren't given housekeeping money, so they earned their own. They did this from poultry, producing eggs from their hens during the summer months, selling chickens for the pot, and fattening turkeys, perhaps some geese, for sale at Christmas.

Cash was needed for essential items: petrol for the tractors and small cars that were beginning to appear. Coffee, tea, flour for baking and sugar had to be paid for. Shoes, clothes and wellington boots likewise were a big expense. Luxuries like toilet paper were yet to be considered worth paying for. Cut up squares of old newspaper was more like it.

The farms had resources which by-passed the need for cash. Many would have a pig or two for bacon and fat. The families could eat their own eggs. There would be a vegetable garden with staples of potatoes and cabbage, sufficiently lower down from the outhouse. The big leaves of the rhubarb patch could be found in most gardens. On the more fertile fields, wheat, barley or oats might be grown. The harvested grain could be sold or ground at the mill. Turnips were a source of winter fodder for the stock. A cow or two could be kept for milk for the house, and butter might be made and sold at the market in Hay. A rabbit would appear at times for the table.

As late as 1940s, and around the time we moved there, Mr Evans of Bailey Bedw took wheat by horse and cart to the water mill at Rhos Goch. Mrs Evans baked bread from their flour in a brick oven inside the house.

My father produced honey from his bees, and perhaps a little was shared or bartered. Mushrooms were a free source of food, and hazel nuts could be collected in good seasons. Basically though, it was a pastoral landscape. Grass grows readily, animals eat grass and people earned their livelihood from their animals.

(Includes notes taken after a random encounter with Malwyn Evans near Bailey Bedw in 1990)

5 The Family at 3 Market Street

"Just look at the size of this key," says my mother on the day we move into our house at 3 Market Street in spring 1950. It is made of iron, six inches long and weighs over a quarter of a pound. We  three girls, Rosie aged one-and-a-half, Helen aged three, and me aged five, cluster around her as she opens the door, turning the heavy key with a click.

I am entranced by the ornamental coloured glass panes in the door. When I look through, everything outside is coloured red or blue or green. I turn around and join my little sisters who are exploring our new house.

....

Ramshackle house

A great hole lies in the centre of the floor in the first room. We look down into what seems the bottom of the world. This room will be our playroom, and my father will soon get that great hole mended.

Up a step from the playroom is the kitchen with an ancient fireplace. This will be our main living room. Beyond that is the scullery with a cold-water tap running into a white ceramic sink. After using it, all you have to do is pull out the plug and the water actually drains away by itself. There is no need to carry water and throw it away after use as at Top o' Lane. It will be much easier to wash the new baby in a bowl in the sink than in an enamel bowl as formerly.

Beyond the narrow scullery is the yard, with the outside toilet called the Lav. It has a high-up water tank and a chain, so is a big improvement on the Elsan.

The yard leads out into the back lane where we look over the wall to a real castle.

A door off the kitchen leads down into a room which my mother immediately christens the Sitting Room. Like the playroom, it has big windows directly onto the street. She will be able to bring her piano here, and her writing desk, neither of which were in the cottage at Top o' Lane.

Stairs lead up from the kitchen to three bedrooms. The floors slope down towards the windows overlooking the street where we can see the pillars of the butter market to one side and the stone building holding the Catholic church on the other. Our house is very old, with the upper floor extending over the lower as in history books. My father has plans to convert one of the bedrooms into a bathroom. After washing in front of the fire, in a tin bath, at Top o' Lane, this will be a great convenience.

(Photo 1960)

I shall be going to a new school, and Helen will soon follow.

Our lives in Hay will take root. Our beekeeper father has his workshop nearby, and my mother is preparing for the birth of her new baby. There is not much time to make domestic improvements before the arrival of the new baby, but we adjust to our new life, attending the church over the road on Sunday, and playing with our new neighbours and friends.

....

New babies

"I'm taking you for a holiday," our father suddenly tells Helen and me. "You can go and stay with your Granny Annie for little while." We are only five and three years old. What is a holiday?

We arrive at the wooden arched doorway of a house with a big garden in front, where our father leaves us with his mother. Granny Annie has different ways from our own house. For one thing, we are always being asked to wash our hands. At our house, that is almost unknown. The Lav has no washbasin. The nearest would be the kitchen sink, and who is going to chase us to that all the time. But here, we must wash hands before we eat, and after we eat, and every time we use the toilet.

Our Granfer is almost blind. He is kind, and he sits in his chair most of the time, smoking his pipe. It is many years since he has had little girls running around.

Every day, after we have had our breakfast, we are sent out to play in the garden so that Granny can get on with the housework. We look around, but we haven't any toys, and we don't know what to do.

"I don't know. Make a daisy chain," says Granny. We do that, but it only takes a few minutes. Then we sit about, wondering.

There is a school next to the house. The decision is made that we should go there to keep us occupied. We are country children, and awkward, in strange surroundings, and we don't fit in.

"Aaaaah!" I am screaming. It is bedtime, and the bed I am sharing a bed with Helen has clean shiny cotton sheets. I needed the potty, which is tucked under the bed, and I have slipped on the sheets smashing it into smithereens. A sliver of china has cut my leg, and blood is pouring out. Granny comes rushing in, taking me into the bathroom and applying a sticking plaster. Every day after that, she needs to change it, and I object because I know it hurts. "No fuss now, Bridget," she says, and rips it off with one rapid sweep. Complaints are not allowed. My mother would take it off, bit by bit, gently.

When the few days are over, our father takes us back to Hay. We find that we have a new brother called Richard.

Slowly the house is being improved. The hole in the playroom floor is mended, and the room is full of our toys. There is a broken black telephone, a wooden rocking horse and the round back of a padded chair which you can sit in and roll sideways, back and forth. We girls don't like tidying up and anyone visiting our house must pick their way through the clutter of the playroom. My father's mind is elsewhere, and my mother just can't keep on top of the mess we make.

The kitchen has been painted primrose-yellow and is the centre of the household. The ancient fireplace has been replaced with a more efficient Rayburn, a small Aga-like stove. When it is fired, it provides hot water and heat. The washed clothes can be dried above it in bad weather. There are iron hot plates on which pans can be placed for cooking. After the paraffin stove of Top o' Lane, this is modern indeed. The kitchen is warm when it is lit, and on cold days, we can be washed in front of its heat.

A table large enough for the family fills the kitchen, and we girls sit side by side on a long bench. On my right is the green door to the scullery, which is how I learn Right from Left.

The scullery has a gas stove too because fortunately Hay has a gas works. This is useful for cooking when the weather is warm and the Rayburn does not need to be lit.

When Richard is a year and a half old, another baby is on the way. We girls know about babies. My mother has one growing inside her tummy, and her friend Mrs Galsworthy likewise. They sit and chat about things as we children play around. One day, our Catholic priest, Father Brady, is visiting. Rosie touches his big round belly, and asks him if there is a baby inside. We wonder why the grownups are laughing. That is where babies come from after all.

"You girls are going for a holiday in a caravan," my mother tells us one day. This is very exciting. We know about caravans as we have been to the seaside. But this time, we are going to stay in Whitney, a hamlet a few miles from Hay. Mr and Mrs Biddle have offered to look after us. They live in a house on a bank overlooking the River Wyc. Thus, eight-year-old Bridget and six-year-old Helen are once again put gently out of the way to allow my mother to give birth in relative peace.

Once we have looked round the caravan, we are pleased to see that Mr Biddle has put a tent up in the garden in which we may play. The only trouble is that it begins to attract daddy-longlegs and spiders, and we won't go in it. Oddly, they put cheese in scrambled eggs, which is very tasty. These grown-ups are trying their hardest to keep us content. But in the middle of the night, in our dark caravan, we are scared and begin to cry. The rain is beating down on the roof, and a dark shape looking like a ghost comes in. It is Mr Biddle holding a raincoat over his head. He reassures us, and we soon go back to sleep.

Everyone is relieved when it is time to send us home again where we find we have another brother called Stephen. There are now five of us.

....

The Beeman's family

"Bridget, would you like to feed the baby?" my mother often says. I snuggle down in the Woolly Chair near the warmth of the Rayburn, and little Stephen folds himself into my arms. I hold the bottle of warm milk slightly tipped so that he doesn't suck in any air. He looks at me, the source of his food, with adoring eyes. He smells sweet, and I nuzzle his silken hair.

Slowly his tummy fills and he becomes sleepy. I hand him back to my mother, and she tucks him up in his pram. With luck, he'll sleep now for an hour or two. I do love him.

The house is becoming quite respectable, and suitable for visitors. The sitting room has been painted orange. This is the tidy room, a place of retreat for my parents. My mother's piano is here, the bookcases and a sofa and chair. From here, her music is often background to our games. As we grow older, she draws us round to sing songs from her Oxford Song Book or the Children's Hymnal. We might do an action routine from her teaching days:

Down in the tall grass one summer's day,
Tommy and Betty stepped this way…

She plays as we high-step it round the room.

The walls of the Lav have been whitened with distemper which is a cheap kind of whitewash. Izal Germicide toilet roll is coming into vogue, and adds its disinfectant smell. It has to be paid for, and so my father cuts up newspaper squares of the right size 'to economise'. In use, we must place one piece of Izal on top of the newspaper.

One of the bedrooms is now a bathroom, the other the boys' room, and our parents' room has been floored with cool brown Lino. Helen, Rosie and I like to play Divers, stripping down nearly bare and sliding from the big bed around the floor.

My father has organised the attic into three bedrooms, one each for Helen, Rosie and me. When the bedrooms are being constructed, and nearly ready, we girls are allowed to choose our own wallpaper. We turn over the pages of a big book of patterns. Helen chooses a delicate floral pattern with pink and blue flowers and leaves arranged in regular circles. I go for big roses. Rosie chooses nursery rhyme characters.

In the corners of the stairs up to the attic, big white moth pupae sometimes incubate, and I am terrified to pass them. I get up and down with great leapings.

The stairs' window looks out the back, over the yard, to the castle. That view is my early landscape painting.

Helen's and Rosie's rooms have skylight windows. Mine looks out of a small dormer window, onto the roof of the old butter market opposite, now an egg-packing station, and over the rooftops where the pigeons coo. My mother likes their soothing sound, but my father thinks they are dirty creatures. We girls feel a moment of shivery silence when the subject comes up.

At the end of the day, Helen, Rosie and I are always put to bed before we feel tired. Thus, we linger awake. Helen often sees a ghost peeping round her door. I have a different problem. No sooner are we settled than a spider appears somewhere in my room and I scream in terror. Up the two flights of stairs our tired mother has to come to dispose of it. This night. Next night. Every night. In the end, Rosie and I swap rooms as she doesn't seem to mind the spiders.

The rooms are joined by a small landing, and the plasterboard walls are thin. With the doors open, we can talk to each other, and my job is to entertain Helen and Rosie with stories about adventurous girls.

The worst thing about being the oldest of the three girls is that I have to empty the potty. It is a long way down to the Lav, so a white enamelled-metal potty is put on the landing. We must squat on this to do what we need to, but being little girls we often overspill. Thus, there is usually a puddle on the floor, and I always make a big fuss about having to carry the potty down the stairs, avoiding the white moths.

One day, we find two thin ladies sitting on the sofa talking to my mother. They have come from an orphanage in Hereford. A little while later, Johnnie Gaughran joins the household. He is the same age as Rosie, now six, our new foster brother.

Johnnie looks very different from Richard and baby Stephen. He is dark haired, mischievous, a charming little ragamuffin.

My mother is conscientious; of that, there is no doubt. She has achieved her lifelong ambition to have a family of six. But despite her good intentions, and her kind heart, she can't control her new child's behaviour. We all get slapped from time to time but Johnny gets more because he is often naughty. When my father puts him over his knee and spanks him with a slipper, my mother chokes and swallows back her tears.

Sometimes our little brother Richard is naughty too, and he is treated the same way. We are used to it. Slippering naughty children is often featured in our comics. My father thinks it will teach us to behave. That is the current way of thinking. Spare the rod and spoil the child.

Johnny is a handsome little fellow, and we get along in a rough and ready way. Too rough at times. I am a brash, bossy big sister, and one time when I am escorting Johnny along the street at a school midday dinner break, he is misbehaving. I am giving him some wallops.

"Just you stop that this minute," calls a woman walking on the other side of the road. "I'm going to tell your mother on you. You leave that boy alone." This reprimand stings, and rightfully. He is our foster brother, but I in particular am not always kind.

Justice is uneven. Johnny wets the bed frequently. My mother is usually kind, but one time she seems to snap. Perhaps it is the endless washing and drying of sheets, the making of the bed, the bathing that must be done every morning. She has chalked a circle on the playroom floor around Johnny and is dancing around mocking him, while Helen is watching in dismay. The little girl is so upset that she runs upstairs to him afterwards and gives him her treasure, a precious threepenny piece.

....

Next-door neighbours

"Good morning, Mrs A," says our neighbour at No 2 Market Street. She is outside her door, getting ready to go to the shops with Peter, her youngest, hanging on to her coat.

"Good morning to you, Mrs O," replies my mother. The two women use the shortened version of their surnames which is the way married women normally address each other. "Are all the children well, and off to school?"

"Thank you, yes, Mrs A. Lorraine had a bit of a cold, and Christopher was complaining because he doesn't want to go. Terry never makes a fuss, and they've all gone."

Mrs Ottowell, our neighbour, like my mother, has five children. She has some news. "Tony is coming home on leave for two days soon, and so the whole family will be together."

Tony is in the army doing his national service which is still obligatory for healthy young men aged between 17 and 21 years.

"That's good news," says my mother. "It will be busy in Market Street, with all eleven children running around." She begins to hatch up a plan to ask my father to take a photograph of them all.

The Ottowell family are living in the house tucked between ours and my father's workshop at 1 Market Street. They are from somewhere far away, and speak with a London accent which sounds a little outlandish in Hay. Mr Ottowell is a builder, but he is not working because he has an illness which we children don't understand. My father and he together had turned our attic into the three bedrooms for Helen, Rosie and me.

Richard, Peter, Rosie, Helen, Bridget, Christopher, Lorraine, Terry, Tony;
Stephen in pram

Sometimes, but not often, we go into each other's houses. The attraction at 2 Market Street is the pole in the middle of the front room, which we can hold onto and swing round, leaping from the steps which go down from the kitchen. Our houses are old, historic and unstable, and this pole is supporting the upstairs floor.

....

Living with bees

Terrible screams suddenly burst forth from the street outside our house. Rosie comes running.

"Bridget, come quick, quick. A bee has stung Roddy!"

Tears running down his face, crying in fear, Rosie's little friend shows us the pointed sting still embedded in the skin near his thumb.

"A bee, look, it stung me." Panic stricken, and shaking, the boy rubs the sting which pushes the venom more deeply into his hand, and makes it hurt more. His screams become even louder.

We girls put our arms around him, and lead him, still crying in pain, to his house just down the steps and round the corner. "Roddy – what a fuss! What has happened?" his distraught mother cries. We tell her, and then she waves us goodbye and takes him inside. His family's cure for all ills, TCP, is applied generously, and he is put in a cool room to rest until he feels better.

The story soon spreads among Roddy's family and friends. "It's Mr Ashton the Beeman. One of his bees stung our Roddy. He keeps them bees around the back of the house. How dangerous it must be for those little children, living with bees everywhere."

But we hardly ever get stung. Roddy was just unfortunate. It was his hand all sticky from sweets which had attracted the bee, and he must have made an unintentional movement which caused it to sting. We know about bees, and we always have a jar of delicious honey on our tea table.

The house at 1 Market Street is my father's honey workshop. Inside he extracts the honey from the combs ready for bottling. Some of the honey has been produced in 6-inch square wooden frames and is nicely sealed in the comb. This won't be bottled, and gets the highest prices. It takes special management to produce honey this way.

"How would you girls like to earn some money?" our daddy asks Helen, Rosie and me one day. Of course, we would. We never have enough money for sweets and comics.

Inside his workshop, he has all his one-pound glass honey jars to wash and rinse. Five-year-old Rosie is big enough to help. We have to carry the washed jars outside and put them in a wooden crate. We are not allowed to put the labels on the jars, but we like the red dragon and the motif: Ashton's Welsh Honey. We are the Ashtons. That is our family.

The crates hold twelve jars by twelve. We know from our times tables that the sum is 144 jars. My father teaches us that 144 is called a Gross. The number system based on twelve is still used then.

When all the jars are crated and drying, we each get the reward of a twelve-sided threepenny bit. We call it 'thruppence', and it is written as 3d, the *d* standing for pennies. This is a good reward, and we feel grown-up because we have been paid for doing a real job.

There is a sack of dark brown sugar lying open in my father's workshop. Its big molasses-tasting crystals are given to the bees when they need an extra feeding during the winter and in early spring before the pollen and nectar is ready on the flowers. We can dip our fingers into it when no-one is looking. But if my father tries to put it on the kitchen table, for us to use on our breakfast cereal or bread and butter, my mother demurs. It is for bees, not for children.

We can go out through the back of his workshop which leads into the yard and the back lane. There are piles of scrap wood and items which will come in handy. This is where my father does his carpentry. Most of his bees are out on farms, but occasionally, he keeps some here as poor Roddy found out.

L to R:
Richard,
Helen and
Johnny

In this town of shopkeepers, traders and artisans, each trade has its character which permeates their houses and their children. The smell of melting beef dripping comes from the fish and chip shop, of beer and cigarette smoke from the public house, of cut flesh and blood from the butcher's, of coffee and cheese from the grocer's, of ink and stamps from the post office, of leather from the shoeshop, and of clean cotton from the clothiers. But my father is a beekeeper, and we have the nicest smells of all.

When he sits us on his knee, his clothes and his arms smell of honey. The fragrance of beeswax is in his hair and on his hands. It is the cleanest and loveliest smell, and it all comes from those little creatures, the bees. They make all this food for the us, the lucky children of the Beeman.

…………………………………

Houses and friends

Christine Jones is my best friend and we are playing 'up the garden' on a sunny afternoon. On one side of the path is the neat vegetable patch belonging to her neighbour. On her family's side, there is a rather weedy patch of vegetables, lots of junk, and a strong smell of tomcats. We are seesawing and balancing on some old bits of wood.

'Up the garden' is our playground. Branches from an old unpruned pear tree overhang the bottom end. The Jones family and their neighbours have long narrow plots running behind their small town centre houses. These have an ancient ancestry, probably dating back to the twelfth or thirteenth century. Hay's old town wall bounds the narrow ends of the garden. Our horizons are limited and such information doesn't concern us. Bumblebees buzz around us, a cat steals between the runner bean poles and our bare legs are warm in the sunshine.

Suddenly, blood, blood, is streaming down my leg, making my white sock all red. A sharp nail on some wood has pierced my skin. A kind neighbour runs down with me to the surgery, leaving a trail of bloody drips. The doctor stitches up the wound with a needle and thread. It is just like my mother doing the darning, and he clips off the thread with a pair of scissors. It won't be long before we are back playing in the garden.

Christine's house is one of a pair of cottages separated by an arched passageway. On many a day, I go up a few steps, through the passage, and come out into a weedy, open cobbled yard. On the left, as far as the street front, lives Mrs Gaughan. She wears a flowery apron, and has no time for nonsense from little girls. She gives me suspicious looks. Mr Gaughan keeps the tidy vegetable garden. Attached to the back of her house, and facing into the cobbled yard, is yet another property, lived in by a simple woman and her brother. They are often standing in one of the two doorways, looking around. No-one ever peeps into the darkness behind.

Christine's door is on the right. Mrs Jones is usually sitting behind the table which faces the doorway. Calm, rotund, overweight, she looks out onto the world from behind that table. To her rear is the fireplace. This good woman has had about ten children. Most are well grown and left home. Rose was to have been the last child, but then another baby appeared on the scene, nearly a decade later. She is my friend Christine.

"Let's play the piano," I suggest one day. We go into the dark sitting room to the right, where a tiny window faces onto the street. Christine has had a few piano lessons, and she tinkles out a tune on the instrument, mightily impressing me. There is a brown shiny sofa and a couple of chairs. This room is tidy. It is the best room, and consequently hardly ever used.

A narrow winding staircase leads up from the sitting room to three miniature, low ceilinged bedrooms. We have no reason to go up there as a general rule. The front bedroom is where Christine's mother and father sleep. The two back bedrooms are separated only by a door, which means that Christine's brother must pass through her room to go to bed. The upstairs is tiny, decent, close. Friends may come by to sleep with Christine as she becomes older, including me. We will fit into the bedding as it is, and talk our teenage fantasies into the night.

Washing clothes in this tiny house is infrequent. The scullery leads off from main downstairs room. It is merely a narrow corridor with a pottery sink and a cold water tap. This is where all body washing, all clothes washing, and all dishwashing must be done. Next to the sink is one towel used by the family for all purposes. Clothes, sheets, everything, when they are washed in the sink, must be taken up the garden and hung out to dry. In this house, this calm, uncomplaining woman has raised ten children, and is still responsible for two.

Up the steps into the garden is an outhouse under a tree. There is no effective door, but there is a lavatory bowl with a tank and a dangling chain to pull. It never works. The contents seem to drain away. Mrs Jones relieves herself here, as does everyone in her household, and as Christine and I do. The expression 'up the garden' means going to the toilet.

Over twenty or thirty years, Mrs Jones has had baby after baby, fed them and watched them grow in this tiny house. When the weather is cold, she lights the fire behind her table. The staple food is potatoes cut into chips and cooked in beef dripping, with its dominating fatty smell. There is a kettle for tea for the grownups, and sometimes coloured fizzy pop for Christine. If Mrs Jones has a big white loaf, she cuts it in slices as she holds it under her arm. But usually these days the bread comes sliced and wrapped. Each piece is spread with a thin layer of margarine and a smear of red jam. This is the height of luxury to me, because in our house, I am used to my mother's sensible food.

Poor as they are, this family is deeply rooted in the life of the town. Mr Jones has worked at the local gasworks for years, for ever. He wears a grey cap, and his clothes and complexion are the same colour. He has well defined and classical features, and like Mrs Jones, he goes about his life with a smooth demeanour. In the evenings, he often escapes domesticity by going out to his chosen public house where he sits over half a pint of cider.

Mrs Jones, with Christine centre and Dorothy Highway. (Photo 1960)

Mrs Jones earns a few extra pounds each week by running a 'club'. She has a catalogue with every kind of article in it for sale. Clothes. Shoes. Kitchen odds and ends. Her customers may choose an item for a few pounds, and then they come to her house and pay a few shillings a week until it is paid off.

For this, she gets a small commission. When she is old enough, Christine helps by taking the cash to the post office and buying a postal order, which her mother then dispatches. The 'club' enables people with limited resources to buy a fresh new garment from time to time.

One day, Christine arrives at my house to play wearing trousers. I am very surprised. That has never happened before. I didn't know girls could wear trousers, so this is quite revolutionary. We always wear woollen skirts in the winter and cotton dresses in summer, and will do so for some years yet.

"Mummy, Christine didn't come to school yesterday," I inform my mother one day, "because her sister has had some babies."

"That's a strange reason for her not going to school," my mother replies. "What do you mean, has had some babies?"

"Rose has had twins. Christine is an auntie," I tell her.

The story emerges. Christine's sixteen-year-old sister has given birth to twins, and the chaos in the family was such that everyone forgot about Christine going to school. Thus, my friend aged nine, is an auntie. What makes it even

79

stranger was that an even older sister had had a baby before Christine was born, so she is already an auntie to someone older than herself. Now she is twice an auntie.

This all seems perfectly natural to me, although exactly how babies come into the world I don't find out for quite a long time. Something about coming out through a hole like a belly button, I think.

One of the twins dies shortly after birth. The healthy baby is called Suzanne, and before too long, she is deposited with Christine's mother who brings her up as her own. Suzanne treats her grandmother as her mother, and Christine as a big sister. There is acceptance and tolerance. That's just how things are.

I find Christine very clever. She teaches me some French. "Polly voo fransay," she says, and I am impressed. I try it on my mother, who tells me it means "Do you speak French?" I will hear several languages in Hay, but that is my first exposure to French.

Mrs Jones has definite ideas about housing. "They should pull that old castle down, and build houses for people," she tells me one day. "What is the use of a heap of old stones like that?" It is an idea that strikes me. I am after all an ignorant child.

My sister Helen, younger than me but of more delicate sensitivities, sometimes comes to Christine's house. She recoils from the circumstances, the cramped kitchen, the cooking smells, the difficulty of keeping bodies clean. My father knows the family, and understands how decent people must sometimes live in difficult conditions. I absorb it all without questioning.

Dorothy Heighway is my friend too. She lives in Brook Street, a minute's walk from my house. A small terrace house on the corner, the door as in 3 Market Street, opens straight from the pavement into the room. The house is small and probably damp and her father is recovering from tuberculosis.

"Are you coming out to play?" I often ask. She has permission and no-one worries about where we are going. Dorothy will be back when she is hungry.

We wander down Chancery Lane which is opposite where she lives. Some of the poorest families in Hay live in these single-storey cottages. Chancery Lane? What chancery?

Where does that name come from? There is a lawyer's office at the bottom of the street. Perhaps that is the connection.

A girl in one of the cottages once borrowed one of my storybooks, and when I get it back someone has drawn with a blue crayon all over the pages. In our house, this would never be permitted. My mother has to try to explain why this has happened. It is to do with education and poverty. I must learn this, and I must not feel superior. It is puzzling.

"Let's go to the bars," Dorothy suggests one day. There is no children's playground, but we can find our own. Behind the castle is a triangle of grass surrounded by round metal railings where we can practice somersaults. Some are low to our knees, but we can get a good roly-poly on the higher ones. I like to swing from my knees, upside down, because I am practising being a trapeze artist for when I grow up.

Gillian Coombes is my friend too. She has two little sisters, like me. Her father is a butcher on Castle Street. The big attraction is her house. She lives in the castle, and I can visit her whenever I want. Her father is the caretaker, and an open stony track leads to their house.

I often walk up to the back entrance and knock on her door.

The interior is warm and friendly. Gillian's sisters Julie and Jenny are tumbling around, and they have a dog called Jess. All those 'J' sounds. Gillian is allowed to come out. Sometimes we go with her red scooter down to the hard pavements and streets in the town where she may let me have a ride. Often we just stay in our playground, the castle garden.

This is where Boadicea, queen of the Ancient Britons, fights the Romans and defeats them. We climb onto the huge iron lawn roller, and then we leap off. We are heroines, and our horses pull our chariots as we drive the wicked Romans away. We win the battles, vanquishing those invaders from foreign lands, just as the English invaded Wales, and the Welsh always drove away the Saxons. Our teacher has told us the stories, and we don't worry if our history is a bit confused.

When we tire of this game, we wonder if we dare climb the tumbling steps inside the overgrown remains of the castle gatehouse. This is strictly forbidden because it is dangerous. We decide we will because no-one is there to see. We wriggle past the bush with white, orange-scented blossom and creep up the steps, peeping down as we go. There is the dungeon full of tangled bushes and thorns. We know it is a dungeon. What else could it be? If we fall down there, we will be lost forever. No-one sees us, and we don't fall, but we know if Gillian's father finds out we will be in serious trouble.

Enclosing the edges of the lawn, which Gillian's father keeps smooth and green, are trees and rhododendron bushes. They create good hidey holes. We look down over the street below, a back street where no-one can observe us. There goes a gypsy woman with her hair plaited in loops over her ears.

Her long skirt is swinging, and she carries a basket with goods to sell.

"You fool!" Gillian shouts at her from behind the bushes. "You fool!" I am very worried about this. "Gillian, you shouldn't say that," I tell her. I have learned from my mother that he who calls his brother a fool is worthy of the fires of hell. It is not just about my brothers, but it applies to my friends too, and to everyone. Gillian will burn in the flames with the devil poking her eyes out with his nasty sword. When I tell her this, she just laughs.

Helen has a friend who is a little different. After school, Lecky Adams is collected by car, the only child we know who is treated this way. Sometimes

Helen and I are invited to her grand house which is half a mile out of the town centre. There are well-tended gardens surrounding it, and there is a wonderful rotating seesaw. Helen slips comfortably into this sophistication, enjoying the surroundings and comparing it all with the old broken toys in our playroom.

The Welsh habit of naming people by their place of work or their trade applies to some of her other friends. Ann the Fish and Chips and Pat the Half Moon are cousins, and by our standards very privileged. Ann, with a beautiful head of fair curls, carries the aura of her parents' chip shop around with her, and always seems to be in the teachers' good books. Pat has lots of dolls which in our more abstemious family seems the height of luxury. Helen and I have only one doll each.

Pat has the trick of slipping some unpaid-for sweets into her pocket, scandalous behaviour which shocks my sister. Yet they share some mischief. Their teacher Mr Pound is in the street. Helen and Pat hide behind a car, and feeling very daring, they call out: "Mr Pound of Sugar!" Hell doesn't break loose. He just chuckles and goes on his way.

………………………………………

Coming to tea

"Mummy, please can Christine stay for tea?" We don't want to stop playing together. I often have a slice of white bread with margarine and jam put into my hand at her house, which we eat as we run out to play.

But at our house, at five o'clock, we have an organised sit-down meal. The bread is sliced and buttered on a big plate. We all sit round the table, girls on our bench and the boys on their higher chairs. Our plate, knife and cup are set out for us, with an extra one for the visitor. First, we must all say grace, hands together. Our little guest sits quietly and takes this in.

"First piece plain," my mother reminds us when we finish grace. We must take a slice of the buttered bread, in which the limited ration of butter is partly mixed with margarine, and eat it by itself. We must learn to appreciate our blessings. After that, we may choose from whatever savoury items are on the table: Marmite, my favourite, or cheese, perhaps sardines or some cheap sandwich meat. After that, we may have jam, homemade full of chewy plums, and much inferior in my view to the red smear at Christine's house. There is always honey, rich golden honey, with the odd bee's leg or wing inside.

"Nothing wrong with that," my father says. "Just pick it out." This is the honey which doesn't go in the jars which he sells.

The bread is crusty and fresh from Maddy's the baker, sometimes brown, sometimes white. We are allowed to eat our fill. For drinking, there is a big jug of water poured into cups for the children. The grownups drink tea with milk.

"Please can I get down?" This is the ritual request before we leave the table. We can't just run down as we please, and we can't come back either once down. Off we go to play, leaving the grownups to finish their tea in peace.

Bread and water. The basic stuff of life. We have it every day, and we love it.

....

Are we poor?

My mother tells me in later life: "Everyone in Hay was poor in those days."

My sisters and I soon find our place among the others of our age. Some are more deprived than us, and Helen and I learn that we are 'well brought up'. We are not spoiled with sweets and we eat sensible food. We must obey our parents, and rudeness is not tolerated. This does not mean that we are always good. My mother wrote in her 1953 diary:

> Oh dear, what a terrible day! It started with the children's bickering before seven a.m. and seemed to go on all day… John vexed, so I was crying again… We set off for a party in Brecon. Party very noisy and baby yelling. Very miserable, as always hate all parties. Nuns very nice and interested, and kept telling me how wonderful I was, which restored my flagging spirits a little.

By the time she writes this, I am nine years old, Helen seven, Rosie and Johnnie five, Richard three and Stephen not yet one. We are a handful indeed, and rows between our parents are not uncommon. Here we are, a lively healthy bunch of children with slightly unconventional parents who don't always see eye to eye, being brought up in Hay in the decade after the war.

The greatest influence on our daily lives is unsurprisingly my mother.

6 My Mother the Housewife

"Rosie, would you like to stir in the sugar?" my mother asks. Five-year-old Rosie happily clambers up on the stool next to the Rayburn.

Today, we are making 16 pounds of raspberry jam. The fruit has been placed in the bottom of the pan, without water, and is gently heated until it dissolves into a juicy mixture.

My mother hands Rosie the wooden spoon, instructing her to hold the pan securely while she pours in eight pounds of sugar. A peaked mountain of white sugar settles in the dark red mixture and the juice slowly seeps upward. It is a lovely combination of dark red, pink and white. Then Rosie uses the wooden spoon to stir the white mountain into the red juice, round and round, feeling the crispy crystals at the bottom of the pan. Gradually they all dissolve and the jam comes slowly up to the boil.

Now we must wait because the jam must be left to bubble until it reaches setting point. That takes such a long time. The smell of jammy fruit invades the kitchen, and we are impatient.

"Is it ready yet?" we ask. Our mummy removes a spoonful and puts it on a plate to cool. Then she blows on it.

"Not yet," she says. She is waiting for ripples to appear on the surface of the cooling jam. More minutes go by, and there are several samples on the plate. Finally, my mother decides the setting point is reached.

She puts the big pan on the table, and pours the slippy-sloppy jam into the 16 gleaming empty jars. When this is done, we can have what we are waiting for.

"Richard, you can lick the wooden spoon," she says. Rosie and Johnny are given spoons to scrape out the pan with its pink sugary sediments stuck on the sides. And then, Helen and I are allowed to spread the test samples from the plate on some bread and butter. At the end of this, we are all sticky messes with pink lips and cheeks, the glory of jam making.

Post-war housekeeping

My mother has achieved her lifetime ambition to have six children. She is a writer: of letters, of nature notebooks, of autobiography, poetry and diaries. Her 1953 diary survives. It is a large week-to-view Boots diary which cost two shillings and sixpence, and she has made 233 entries out of the 365 days of the year. It's a rare picture of a family and domestic life in Hay during the years following World War II.

It is intimate, practical and of course subjective. As it tells of her daily activities, it sometimes records incidents which I have held for decades in my own mind. Mainly, however, it describes the daily life of a housewife in Hay in 1953, how she coped with the frugalities of post-war Britain, and the ups and downs of family life.

As a child who had grown up in a privileged household with servants, she is now doing the work of the nanny and the maids who looked after her as a child. She is a housewife. She has learned the skills and crafts of housewifery through trial and error, through experience in her jobs before marriage, and from books. Being a housewife carries some positive status.

Housewives are managers. A married woman, who has children, must know how to cook, how to wash and iron clothes, how to sew and mend, how to keep the house clean and tidy. All these are craft skills which must be learned, and there are right and wrong ways to do everything.

As a mother, she must take care of the developmental needs of babies and growing children. Her husband has expectations which she must meet. As he is the breadwinner, she relies on him for money to do her job. She needs budgeting skills, and in those years often, she needs to manage without sufficient money. It is an exhausting never-ending round of chores, with little financial independence.

In the decade since the end of the Second World War in the UK, life is gradually becoming easier although ration books from war days are still in use and money is tight.

My mother plans out her daily work in a kind of New Year's Resolution list in her diary:

Up at 7 am	
7–7.45	Housework
7.45	Cook breakfast
8–8.30	Breakfast
8.30–8.45	Make beds
8.45–9.30	Wash up – tidy kitchen
9.30–9.50	Catechism
10 am	Children to school
10.30	Snack
11 am	Baby in pram – shopping – cooking
12.15	Dinner
1 pm	Washing up
1.15	Children to school
1.30–2.30	Rest
2.30–3.30	Walk
4.15	Tea
5–6	Play with children
6 pm	Richard and Stephen to bed
6.30	Johnnie and Rosie to bed
7 pm	Cocoa and biscuits for B. H. R. and J.
7.30	Johnnie and Rose upstairs
8 pm	Bridget and Helen upstairs.

It is Saturday. "Come along Bridget and help me make the beds," she says. We go upstairs. There are five beds to be tidied, and sometimes the sheets and pillowcases to be changed. Grumbling a little, I take my place on one side of the bed, and with her on the other, we straighten out the bottom sheet, shake up the pillows and straighten out the top sheet.

"First the tail and then the head, that's the way to make a bed."

I am expected to help make neat hospital corners with the flat cotton sheets. Some of the sheets are 'sides to middle'.

Because the cotton sheets wear out in the middle first, their lives can be extended by being cut lengthways in half and the strong unworn edges being stitched together. A good housewife knows how to do this. It means that we lie on a seam in the middle of our bed, but that is a small price to pay for such economy.

The blankets are placed on top of the sheets, with hospital corners too, and if it is cold weather, a feather eiderdown is put on top. These all made from fine natural materials, cotton, wool and down, which seven decades later will be considered luxuries.

My mother and I make the parents' double bed, then the boys' single beds and finally the baby's cot. We girls must make our own beds in our attic, except for sheet changing days. And on those days, a pile of sheets and pillow cases are taken downstairs to be sent to the laundry in winter because they cannot be washed and dried in bad weather. This is another expense from the weekly budget. In summer, my mother saves the money by washing the sheets in the scullery sink and drying them outside.

"You can go and play now, Bridget," she says when the beds are made. She turns her attention now to washing up after breakfast.

There is hot water if the Rayburn is lit, and she likes to say, "There is no hardship to washing up as long as there is plenty of hot water." In warm weather, when the Rayburn is off, a kettle on the gas stove is used. Not all the houses of my friends have a hot water supply like ours to help wash greasy pans and dishes, or to do the laundry.

On school days when the beds are made and the kitchen is tidied up, my mother says to my baby brother Stephen, "Time to get you in the pram, my little man." Richard is too young for school, so he will hold hands alongside as they go round the shops. They are two bonny fair-haired little boys, Stevie with his ready smile and earnest Richard with his chubby legs, and they attract friendly comments. Once back home, she puts Stephen in his playpen and prepares the midday dinner, the main meal of the day.

....

Dinner time

"John, dinner's ready," my mother calls every day when he is working in his bee workshop at Market Street.

Rosie, Helen and I come home from school for our dinner. We sit on our bench-for-three at the table. If one person gets up, the others must be careful or the bench will over-balance and tip into the air. Richard and Johnny are on the other side of the table and baby Stephen is strapped in his high chair.

We can be fidgety and quarrelsome. Our parents have a seat at each end, and when my father comes in, often late to my mother's annoyance, our behaviour improves.

On Fridays, we aren't allowed to eat meat. This day, it is smoked haddock, peas and potatoes.

I pick at the fish, and manage the peas, but I don't like lumpy mashed potatoes and I have let them get cold which makes them worse.

"Stop fussing, Bridget, and eat your food," my father says. Somehow I get the potatoes down. Then it is pudding time. Everyone happily eats up their sweet milky rice pudding.

Except me!

"Please can I get down?" Helen, Rosie, Johnnie and Richard say, one by one. The older ones run off to school. My father goes back to his workshop after saying to my mother, "Bridget stays there until she has eaten her pudding."

My mother clears the table and goes into the scullery to do the washing up. I am left sitting sulkily by myself. I sit and I sit, and the room is quiet. Defiantly, daringly, I decide to run away to school and slip out. This is risky. A hard slap on the leg is a warranted punishment, but by the time I come home after school the matter has been forgotten. It has been a rare challenge to parental authority.

When we all go out, quiet descends on the kitchen. My mother looks at the mountains of washing up waiting to be tackled. Three first-course saucepans and their lids, cooking spoons and potato masher, chopping boards, mixing bowls, pudding and custard pans and jug. Then there are six sets of plates, knives, forks, spoons and cups, and six pudding bowls. It is all to be scraped clean, stacked, washed, rinsed, dried and put away. All by herself. Thank goodness for a supply of hot water!

Next, baby Stephen must be toileted, changed and put down for a nap, and a rest hour fitted in to her daily schedule.

....

Feeding the family

We are well fed, healthy children. In her diary, my mother has written out weekly menus, which may not always be followed but show what she aims for:

Mon	Shepherd's pie. Apple Charlotte
Tues	Egg and chips. Baked Suet pud. Treacle
Wed	Haddock. Suet Pud and apples
Thurs	Liver. Ground Rice
Fri	Spaghetti & Tomatoes. Spotted Dick
Sat	Sausages. Semolina
Sun	Roast beef. Plum & Apple [6]

These menus contain basic health-giving ingredients and knowledge of cookery. The main course assumes potatoes and vegetables served with the meat. She knows that a balanced meal consists of three parts: a protein food which is meat, eggs, cheese or fish; carbohydrates sourced normally from potatoes; and vitamins and fibre which are in the vegetables. All her planned meals take this into account.

Potatoes are a staple. She cooks them in a variety of ways, boiling, mashing, roasting and our favourite which is chips. To make them, a pan with a solid lump of beef dripping is placed on the Rayburn to melt. We children like to watch as the big white lump slowly softens and turns into golden liquid. This is magic indeed. When the fat is the right temperature, the chipped potatoes go in with a sizzle. We can't eat them too often. When the fat cools down again, at the base is a salty, brown layer which can be spread on bread for a delicious treat.

Every midday dinner has a second course. We love the suet puddings in which the shredded suet has been mixed with the flour, eggs and milk, the whole thing steamed in a bowl for an hour over a pan of water. Sometimes currants are added and then it is called Spotted Dick. At other times it is made with treacle, a golden syrup which drips through the cakelike mixture, or bright red jam. These puddings are always served with custard, a sweet yellow sauce made from Birds' custard powder and milk.

Often she makes pastry. She gently rubs the fat into the flour with her fingers, then adds water before kneading it into a paste and rolling it out. Treacle tart, apple pie and jam tart are all served with custard sauce. The pies are cut conveniently into eighths, one piece for each of the six children and my mother and father.

Sweetened fruit appears regularly, apples and plums in particular, served with custard. There are the rice and semolina milk puddings too, which I don't like, but are still popular in the family. Specialities appear: apple Charlotte with its crispy top layer and apple crumble which is simpler to make as there is no pastry to roll out. My favourite of all is bread and butter pudding. For this, an egg, milk and sugar mixture is baked with the bread, and perhaps raisins or jam added.

This is food for royalty, surely. Many of the ingredients are locally obtained, particularly the fruit, meat and eggs. Rabbit, chicken and beef for the stews come from the butcher in town, and the vegetables from the greengrocer. My mother sees herself as a plain cook, but she pays close attention to nourishing her family on a minimal budget. It is a shame that we children, me in particular, are what she calls 'the fussiest children on earth'. I don't like the main course of meat, vegetables and mashed potatoes. I especially resist meat, but I also fuss over carrots, turnips, sprouts and cabbage. Soon, I can hear my mother saying to her friends, "Bridget is the only vegetarian on earth who doesn't like vegetables!"

....

Baking skills

One Saturday in August, she described her cooking. "Began baking after dinner. Made 24 buns, one fruitcake, one plain cake, one sandwich cake, a treacle tart and a jam tart. All turned out well." This was all done in the afternoon, after cooking and clearing up the midday meal. And after the baking was finished, there would be more dishes to wash, which she doesn't mention. She goes on: "Then went upstairs and polished attic and stairs so was very tired after." The entry ends: "Washed my hair after tea, then Bridget's and Helen's. Bathed the little ones and washed their hair too."

It all seems such a lot of work.

She also at times bakes bread, using all the skills that yeast-based recipes require, and which explains the 24 buns.

In the days when basic ingredients are still rationed, skilled housewives can turn their hand to bake with whichever of the basic ingredients of flour, fat, eggs, sugar and milk they have in the house, used in simple proportions.

Thus, if my mother is short of eggs, she can make pastry with flour, fat and water. If she is short of butter or margarine, scones only need one portion of fat to four of flour, and a little milk to mix. There are two main possibilities for cakes, which require fat, flour and eggs. A rubbed-in fruitcake only needs half fat to flour, but a sandwich cake needs equal fat to flour made in a creaming method. If she has no butter or margarine, a sponge cake can be whisked up with eggs, sugar and flour.

My mother uses her ingenuity to bake something tasty for tea with whatever she has available.

In the single baking session described above, she makes a yeast-based recipe, two different cake-making methods and then two pastry-based tarts. This kind of cooking is called 'batch baking'.

The trick with cake making is the way the fat is blended with flour. The rubbed-in method is used for recipes which have a maximum of half fat to flour. The fat is cut up into small pieces, and then lightly rubbed into the flour with the fingertips until it looks like breadcrumbs. Other dry ingredients are added, and then the egg and enough milk to make a firm consistency. For the richer sandwich cake, using equal fat to flour, she uses the creaming method. The fat and sugar are firmly creamed together around the sides of a bowl with a wooden spoon until light and fluffy, and then the whisked eggs and flour are gently added.[7]

Pastry for the treacle tart and jam tart is started off using the rubbed-in method. Thus at the beginning of the session, she would separate the mixture to be used for the cakes and the pastry.

When she rolls out the pastry and cuts it into shapes for tarts, there is usually some oddment left over. Any child nearby may be invited to roll it out and make shapes of people, or snakes, or balls, and currants added for eyes. These creations go in the oven too.

Sometimes she bakes scones which can be made quickly, which is useful when unexpected visitors arrive. Most go in the oven, but Welsh cakes and girdle scones can be cooked on the Rayburn's hot plates, or in a pan on the gas stove.

At another baking session, she recorded: "The Rayburn decided to heat well, and I made a lovely sponge sandwich, fairy cakes, a treacle tart, apple pie, lots of biscuits and a big fruit cake."

We have a record of my mother's baking from her diary, but many Hay housewives are skilled cooks. Rosie's friend Roddy loves his mother's apple pies, sliced and eaten with custard, and suet puddings made with treacle. For him, the best pudding of all is jam roly-poly, layers of suet pastry rolled out, spread with jam, rolled up again and steamed for what seems hours.

Our mothers can put their hands to savoury dishes too.

Sometimes they use meat left over from Sunday dinner to make pasties on Monday, or if they can afford the meat, and have the time, they may make steak and kidney pies. It is always possible for children to spit out the kidney bits, and even I, the evolving vegetarian, love the pastry and gravy.

Everything is made from basic ingredients. Ready rolled-out pastry or cake mixes are unheard-of. These meals may appear stodgy and sugary, but we are active children, running around outside for hours most days, and many of our parents do hard physical work. We use up the calories. Overweight children are rarely seen.

"John, would you cut the cake please?" my mother asks at Sunday teatimes. He cuts it into eight neat sections. It is a sandwich cake with jam in the middle and a dusting of icing sugar on top. We often go out for the afternoon, and enjoy our tea when we come home. Having eaten as much bread and butter as we like, we are ready for our Sunday treat.

My father's favourite is a plain fruitcake made using the rubbed-in half-fat-to-flour recipe, with sultanas or currants added. Sometimes the cake is varied with grated coconut. It is important that there is always a fruitcake in the tin for him. It is a man's cake.

....

Budgeting and ration books

Saturday is the day my father hands over the housekeeping money. The allowance must be stretched out, and by the end of the week, things are tight. On Fridays, Catholics are not allowed to eat meat. One particular day, my mother writes in her diary that abstaining from meat has been abolished in honour of the feast of the Holy Apostles. "Not that it makes much difference to us as I'm always broke on Fridays. It was boiled eggs and apple and custard for dinner."

Rosie is watching my mother one day as she looks underneath the two candlesticks on the mantelpiece. She has hidden two silver half-crown pieces, one under each candlestick, because she needs some extra funds.

"I'm using my emergency money," she tells Rosie. This is a secret which she shares with my little sister. No-one else must know because my mother doesn't believe in putting temptation in people's way.

One day Rosie watches her mummy and daddy eating their eggs at breakfast time. She wants one too, so our mother cut hers in half and gives some to her, which Rosie thinks is so kind. Even eggs can be in short supply at times.

When she goes shopping, my mother must take the ration books. There are brown ones for the two grown-ups and six green ones for the children. Having Johnnie gives us the benefit of an extra ration book. When we go to the shops with my mother, we watch the shopkeeper using his scissors to clip out the stamps for each allowable item from the book.

All the meals my mother planned in the year of her diary have had to take account of the rations available. Like everyone, she has had to cope with wartime regulations since January 1940, when meat, tea, margarine, cooking fats and cheese were rationed. In 1941, jam, marmalade, treacle, syrup, eggs and milk were added. In 1942, sweets, and then in 1946 bread, were rationed. However, by 1953, my mother's diary year, bread, jam, tea, sweets, cream, eggs and sugar are no longer rationed.[8] Although we children know that ration books are something to do with the war, and grown-ups are always complaining about them, the war feels long-ago and remote.

On 2 May, my mother writes: "Got our new ration books after breakfast. May it be the last we shall ever require. Did shopping after and spent all my money as always." By this time, people had used ration books for thirteen years. She will have to wait until 1954 for butter, cheese, margarine and cooking fats, and meat to be taken off the ration.

Thus every time she bakes or cooks, using these basic ingredients, she has to work out not only what is affordable but what is available.

I love butter and dislike margarine. One ounce of butter per person per week doesn't go very far, so my mother cuts both fats into little cubes, softens them on the Rayburn and mixes all together. But I can tell the difference. The margarine is a more yellow colour, and Rosie watches me picking out the buttery bits whenever I get the chance.

There is no surviving record of how much housekeeping money my father hands over on Saturdays to my mother.

However, we do know that in 1953, my father had a mere £300 from honey sales. From that, he would have expenses, and thus perhaps he would hand over £4 or £3 each week. The housekeeping income is supplemented by family allowances from the new welfare state, without which life would have been run on a shoestring. It is disbursed on Tuesdays at the post office which is in the next street down from our house.

"Behave quietly, children. Not so much noise," she says as we fidget in the post office lines. Roddy lives above the post office because his father is the postmaster, and he is often playing around. He is very attracted to our little sister with her fair curly hair. My mother agrees that she may run outside and play ball games with him in the square.

Helen and I meanwhile look in awe at the three tellers behind the counter who stamp the booklets and tear out the pages before handing over some useful cash. I am the eldest, and the first child gets no family allowance. However, my mother is awarded eight shillings each week for Helen, Rosie and Johnnie, her three school-aged children. Twenty-four shillings, which is one pound and four shillings, goes a long way to help paying for food until Saturday's housekeeping comes in. One Tuesday, she writes:

> I dashed out to the shops during the morning and bought a good stock of food. I find it more economical to buy a lot of food at once and then keep away from the shops. Also to have only two shopping days a week – Saturday and Tuesday.

A useful monthly cheque comes in as a payment for the expenses of Johnnie, our foster brother. After the arrival of her cheque on 31 January, she sent off at once for a new piece of linoleum flooring for the kitchen, and discovered that there was a sale at Galsworthy's clothing shop:

> Bought very recklessly a lovely grey jumper suit and pale blue rayon summer frock, 25/- each. Now all I need is a very firm foundation garment which must be my next buy.

This is the corset which we children call her 'corsnip'.

One Saturday, when the cheque arrives, she has a feeling of plenty. A farmwoman from the nearby village of Dorstone in England calls at our house, with some nice things to sell. My mother extravagantly buys a chicken and a bunch of flowers for one pound. The chicken can be roasted on Sunday, the cold leftover meat eaten on Monday and a soup made from the bones on Tuesday.

"Helen and Bridget, come along my dears," she says one time, feeling rich with her newly arrived cheque. "Time for us to get some new shoes." Excitedly, we all go down to Mrs Jones the Clock Tower's shoe shop. We girls get some fresh, leathery-smelling T-bar summer sandals, and my mother treats herself to a white pair. We skip and jump with an extra spring all the way home.

She orders her groceries the same day, and the delivery arrives with an extra half pound of ham which was not put on the bill. "Had a tussle with my conscience. Should have sent it back, but couldn't." This is such a tasty, unexpected treat, and is delicious on bread and butter for our tea. But in the end she writes: "Eventually decided to pay for it on Monday." After all, she knows that God is watching.

....

Making ends meet

Keeping on top of all the tasks is so exhausting that my mother decides she must engage some help to be paid for out of the weekly budget:

> Mrs Prosser came in the morning, and cleaned all the upstairs. We both got on well. I'm really feeling the benefit of having her, and the house certainly looks better.

This day in the April school holidays describes her daily life and the management of her budget:

> A fine sunny day, so did a lot more washing, curtains, chair covers, winter scarves, gloves, bonnets etc. Started the girls cleaning their own rooms which they did well, then Mrs Prosser came. Was glad to see her except financially. Started the day with £1 note – hurrah – no money worries this week. Then had to pay 8/10½ for three weeks laundry, 5/- to Mrs Prosser, 2/6 for fish, 3/- for flour, so am now stony broke till Saturday.

There are 20 shillings in the pound, so anyone who knows how to calculate in pounds, shillings and pence can work out that she is left with one shilling and thruppence-ha'penny to last from Wednesday until Saturday.

Sometimes she makes budgeting extravagances:

Decided to put Baby into Paddi-Pads, a form of disposable napkin in plastic pants. It will cost 5/- a week, but how well worth it.

Shopped in the morning – rashly bought a chicken (8/6d) and had two laundry bundles, so came home with one shilling and fourpence ha'penny which must last until Tuesday.

Jumble sales are a big help in clothing the family. There is a Women's Institute Jumble Sale at the Parish Hall at 2 pm on 25 July. Bargain-hunting mothers are queuing when we arrive with the baby in the pram, and we are all part of the rush when the door opens, everyone pushing and shoving. Children in prams and pushchairs are parked at the side of the hall while the women rummage and shake and pull out a pretty dress or a warm jumper or a shirt for the boys. Jumble sales have tables for everything: clothes sorted accorded to age and gender, toys, bric-a-brac, shoes and boots, cakes, books and magazines. It is worth the struggle, and my mother loads her purchases into the pram:

I got some wonderful bargains. A cloth Humpty Dumpty and rattle for Stephen's birthday tomorrow and a carpenter set and model car and caravan for Johnnie's birthday. Also flowers, cakes, gooseberries and magazines.

The little boys are as happy with their presents as if they came from expensive toyshops. The cakes are homemade and delicious. The flowers will brighten up the kitchen. And all this for pennies. Jumble sales have an important part to play in household management in 1950s Hay.

……………………………………

Clothing the family

"Open it quickly, Mummy. Come on." A parcel has been delivered by the postman. We cluster round as our mother carefully unties the knots. String is not to be wasted.

"Look at this," she says, removing the tissue paper. "A dress for you Bridget, and another one, for you Helen. And here is Rosie's."

Our Granny Izzie is a skilled home-dressmaker, and she has been busy. We each have a white, cotton square-necked dress with puffy sleeves and a full skirt. We will look so beautiful.

"We must have a photograph of this," my mother says.

We happily put on our dresses and clean white socks under our new T-bar summer sandals. She combs our hair, a middle parting for Helen with a ribboned bunch on each side, and mine and Rosie's with two side partings.

We stand in the sunshine at the edge of the square to have our photograph taken. The resulting tiny 3 inch by 2 inch photo is proudly put in the family album. It is a modest little picture demonstrating our frugal life style, like nearly all the photos from these years.

Our granny regularly sends us homemade clothes. Once it is a set of navy blue skirts held up with H-straps over the shoulders, and another time tartan skirts for winter. She has made dresses of checked cotton and others with fairy-wing sleeves.

We have richer relations. My mother's cousin Pamela has two daughters, Eliza and Theresa and a son Simon. She sends us clothes they have grown out of.

"What lovely party dresses!" says my mother as she opens one of their parcels. She tells us this crinkly material is taffeta, which is a lustrous silk, and indeed the dresses are pretty. Mine is green and Helen's is yellow. I admire my green one, but I refuse to wear it except for dressing-up games. It is too smart, and not like anything my friends have.

One day, a parcel comes from my mother's cousin Letitia. That is a real help. It contains two pairs of shoes for Richard, and frocks and skirts for Rosie.

Another time I am sent a winter coat, warm and beautifully tailored, but it has a velvet collar. I refuse to wear it because the velvet gives me the shivers. "Oh dear, I suppose I can't force you to wear it," my mother says.

Passing good quality clothes from growing children to younger ones helps everyone, and we girls receive a series of attractive cotton dresses in a range of styles: gathered with smocking, full skirts, sometimes with white Peter Pan collars, and in winter warm skirts often made of woolly tartan. My mother doesn't knit, but we inherit woollen sweaters and cardigans with Fair Isle patterns, either from richer relations or my mother acquires them at jumble sales.

Johnnie has a clothing allowance which is included in my mother's monthly cheque from the orphanage. As he grows out of his new clothes, they come in handy for Richard and Stephen in their turn.

Friends who have fewer brothers and sisters than me are often dressed in shop-bought clothes which look fancy to us, and Christine's mother purchases brand new items for her from the 'club'.

Are we smart and in the fashion? My mother keeps as tidy as she can. At one time, blazers that look like school uniforms are in vogue, and all of us except baby Stephen are wearing them in a photo taken on one of our holidays. With her fashion-consciousness, Helen thinks we look like the Beano comic characters, the Bash Street Kids.

....

Mending and laundry

Clothes get torn, and wear out. Every good housewife needs to know how to repair clothes to keep them in good order and so they last longer. Hems must be turned down or up as the garments move from one growing child to another. Holes in socks must be darned in matching coloured wool pushed through the big eyes of darning needles. The wooden darning mushroom is placed under the hole inside the sock. Using a pattern of little stitches going one way, and then at right angles in the other direction, a tapestry of darning wool fills the hole. My mother does her mending dutifully, if rather roughly to her growing daughters' critical eyes.

Tiny holes in the cotton sheets can be mended with neat, skilfully manoeuvred patches, which are real works of art and can be done by specialists at the laundry. For less skilful menders, a simple darn with white cotton thread does the job. The mending basket is always sitting on the windowsill to be brought down on a quiet evening when our mother listens to the radio.

The kitchen sink is the place where all the clothes and linen items must be washed. Monday is the traditional official washing day. When we are not at school, we children are used to piles of clothes on the floor, a sweating struggling mother and the steamy smells. Our babies' nappies must be boiled to keep them white and hygienic, and a copper boiler in the scullery heats up the water. Once boiled, the nappies are pulled out of the hot water with wooden tongs, and put through the hand-turned set of rollers called the mangle. They go through two rinsings and manglings with cold water in the sink. Finally the cotton squares are pegged out on the line on good drying days, and are the mother's flags of honour.

White and light coloured cottons are washed in the sink, and the dark colours last. Each hand-washed item must be rubbed, scrubbed on the dirty places, swished up and down, rinsed and mangled. People who don't have a mangle must wring out by hand.

Wool clothing requires special treatment, and thus wool garments are not changed more often than necessary. In order to avoid shrinking, the water must be lukewarm, and the item moved gently up and down in the soapy mixture. Then it must be squeezed but not harshly wrung out, and rinsed once or twice in water of the same temperature. That is not the end.

Good wool hand knitted jumpers must be rolled in a towel and dried flat.

Anyone who can afford it will send the bed linen out to a laundry. This is another expense to come out of the family budget. Poor people are unlikely to prioritise sheet changing, but my mother and father have come from homes and worked in institutions where this is important. Manoeuvring soaking-wet, heavy cotton sheets in and out of the sink, mangling them through the roller, rinsing and mangling again, is a heavy job.

A Monday diary entry records: "Another nice fine day. Baby slept upstairs until 12, so this leaves a lovely long morning. Did a big wash including sheets which I'm now doing myself for the summer season."

On a fine windy day, seeing all the washed clothes blowing in the breeze is satisfying. On wet winter days, it all has to be dried indoors, with the misery of damp clothes dripping around the kitchen table. A January entry gives an example of my mother's difficulties. "A horrid, cold, foggy day. Washed a big wash, but did not hang it outside as a pure waste of time. I tried to put out a few jerseys but icicles came down from them."

On one October morning, my mother had begun the washing before breakfast. The children had to be got off to school before she could finish. "The girls started their knee-length woollen socks today, and I had to make them a pair of garters each. Johnnie managed to wet himself and I had to change him. Richard had a vital button off his trousers, so was panting by the time they were finally waved off to school. After that I finished a big wash, counterpanes, towels, nappies, hankies etc., which took most of the morning."

Once washed and dried, the items have to be ironed, a task which usually follows the next day. Electric irons are beginning to come available, but still in

100

the 1950s, my mother was using two alternating flat irons. One is on the Rayburn plate heating up, while the other is being used as long as it stays hot.

Cottons need to be damp-dry and ironed at a hot temperature. Woollens must be pressed under a damp cloth, using a heavy upward and downward movement to avoid shrinkage.

Handkerchiefs have had special treatment. They must be soaked overnight in a salty solution, and then scraped clean before being boiled. This is not a job for delicate constitutions. Paper handkerchiefs are not yet thought of, and if they had been the idea of using something once and then throwing it away would have been considered the height of extravagance.

"Can I iron the hankies?" I often ask my mummy. I am allowed to do this if I am careful. I lay out the hankies neatly, one on top of the other, so that the top one helps to iron the one beneath. At the end, I have a sweet-smelling pile of square folded hankies.

Finally, all the clean, ironed clothes must be aired to ensure they are fully dry before being put away. In the days before washing machines, doing laundry is a weekly task that my mother, like every woman in Hay, must know how to do.

....

Summer time

"Oyez oyez" comes the cry, accompanied by the ringing of a handbell outside our house. The town crier has an important announcement to make. "The water will be cut off from 10 o'clock this morning until 3 o'clock this afternoon. It will be cut off from 6 o'clock this evening until 7 o'clock tomorrow morning." He rings the bell again, calls out, "God Save the Queen", and marches off to make his next announcement.

It is July, and the weather has been so dry and hot that the level of water in the town's reservoir is very low. But there is a pleasant and romantic solution to our drinking water needs.

"Rosie, you take the billycan," our mother says, as she assembles all of us with jugs and bottles. "We'll get our own fresh water." We children parade along Castle Street and down the hill towards the Swan Hotel, behind which is a spring of clear fresh drinking water. We can play and splash each other under the cool overhanging vegetation from which this water is magically emerging. We carry the heavy jugs of water carefully home.

On the last day of August, my mother writes a thankful entry in her diary:
After dinner, heard the glad news that the water supply is now back to normal. What a relief.

The good weather is producing a bumper crop of fruit, and my mother like many others must get busy with jam making and bottling if we are to eat fruit in the forthcoming winter season.

We live near the orchards and fruit fields of Herefordshire, and in season, the produce can be cheap. These are the jams and bottlings she recorded in her 1953 diary. The standard abbreviations for pounds in weight is 'lbs', which is equivalent to 454 grams:

5 June	apricot jam
11 June	gooseberry jam
24 June	bottled gooseberries
29 June	8 lbs of raspberries from lady from Dorstone
11 July	2 lbs of raspberries from the lady from Dorstone (4 lbs total)
16 July	19 lbs blackcurrant jam
26 August	6 lbs of yellow plums made into jam (24 lbs total)
27 August	12 lbs of dark red plums for 7/6d (24 lbs total)
27 August	blackberry and apple jam
29 August	24 lbs of plum and apple jam, plums at 6 pence a pound (48 lbs total)
2 Sept	bottling blackberries. Stoning 24 pounds of plums for bottling.

Jam needs one pound of sugar to one pound of fruit. Thus from the above record where she mentions the quantities, we can calculate 116 one pound jars, and obviously it is much more than that. Perhaps 150 jars, all lining the larder shelf, and numerous bottles of preserved fruit.

In the entry for 2 September, she writes: "Bottled some jars of blackberries in the morning and set to work stoning 24 pounds of plums for bottling after dinner. Johnnie and Rosie helped, and Richard hindered. I'm getting to hate the sight of fruit. Johnnie filled a jar with stoned plums then smashed the jar so that all had to be thrown away as the plums were full of splintered glass."

Sugar is still rationed until September 1953, but with six children and two adults with ration books, my mother is able to ensure we have fruit for winter. She will serve it with custard as a simple pudding, make it into fruit tarts, and provide us with jam to spread on our bread and butter at teatime.

In our larder, there is also a row of bottled gooseberries, blackberries and plums. Bottling is a more complicated process than jam making, involving large Kilner jars with lids and seals which must be sterilised. The jars are filled with fruit, and then topped up with a sugar and water syrup. When the seals are in place, the jars are sterilised in the oven for an hour.

There are well over a hundred jars of jam for us to enjoy through the next months, of a quality that seventy years later is a top-priced luxury product. At teatime, we take it for granted as an everyday food. To me, the cheap red spread served at my friend Christine's house, in a jar with a colourful label, seems a shop-bought treat in comparison.

....

Our Granny might move to Hay

Granny Izzie always remembers our birthdays. The person with the honour of the day is allowed to open the parcel, wrapped in brown paper and string with red sealing wax on the knots. This way we know that no-one has been able to get inside to steal our presents. Our granny always includes Kit Kat chocolate biscuits for each of us. As well, and importantly, she sends a five shilling postal order for the birthday recipient, which costs tuppence on top of the cost, and sixpenny ones as consolation presents for the rest of us, the cost for them being a ha'penny. A sixpenny postal order, cashed at the post office, is enough to buy a decent bar of chocolate.

What a wonderful Granny she is! "Now girls, you must write your thank-you letters," my mother tells us, which, with an internal complaint, we obediently do.

She and my mother write to each other weekly. Letter writing, in the days before household telephones, is the way they keep in touch. She sometimes joins us on our annual holidays and we feel we know her well.

Having first lost her husband from a heart attack in 1939, and then her only son Richard at the end of the war, she lives quietly alone in London.

Unfortunately, my father has somehow offended her, and she won't come to visit us in Hay. My mother arranges to meet her in Hereford one day in June 1953:

> Dressed up the boys and arrayed myself in my new blue and white dress and white hat with roses on it. Flatter myself, I still look quite attractive when dressed nicely and with help of a little make-up. Much enjoyed glances from members of male sex.

They have a pleasant day, but my mother returns alone with the boys, hot, tired and discouraged. Then, surprisingly, things change. The next day she records:

> Tried to effect a reconciliation between John and Mummy – he wasn't having any. Then all of a sudden, she appeared in the doorway, and he rushed forward and 'said his piece' very nicely and all ended happily, much to my joy and relief.

Later in summer, on my birthday, my mother takes Helen, Rosie and me by steam train to meet Granny Izzie in Hereford. Now all being peaceful, she returned to Hay to stay with us.

The big question is – might she move to Hay? First, they look at a house called The Laurels:

> I've always liked the outside, but it is very rambling and unsatisfactory and needs a lot of doing up. We went to see the solicitor re price, which is £2000. He also told us of a place called Mill Cottage, £800, which we went to see. Very sweet in its way, but badly placed and very tiny.

Our Granny Izzie soon returns to London with no progress made on this visit. Perhaps she will look again in the future.

....

Bedtime

"But Mummy, I'm not tired," I often complain. It is 8 o'clock and our exhausted mother wants us settled down for the night. A normal day of feeding, cooking, dishwashing, laundry and shopping has worn her out. At 6 o'clock, she had undressed and washed the boys and given Stephen his last bottle for the day. She prepared our bedtime snack of cocoa and biscuits at half past six, and then Rosie and Johnnie were told to get ready for bed.

"Up you go girls," she insists. We reluctantly make our way up to our attic rooms, and it is my task to tell my sisters exciting adventure stories until they fall asleep. There is a light on the landing which sheds a beam onto my bed, by which I can read for as long as I want. This would be strictly forbidden if my mother knew, as it would 'ruin my eyes'.

Downstairs, she is perhaps listening to the radio while she irons or does her mending. Somehow, she usually finds the energy to summarise her day in the diary. And in this, she sometimes reveals surprising feelings.

....

My mother and her babies

Considering she has given birth to five children, my mother doesn't like babies. In one of her diary entries, she describes her morning routine, which includes baby's bath and feed. This results in her comment: "How happy I will be when they are all older."

Another time, she is even more frank:

I feel very discouraged sometimes to think what a bad mother I am. How I dislike babies and how thankful I shall be when Stephen is three. And how fervently I hope and pray I shall never have another baby. How glad I am when the last one is in bed and I can retire to the sitting room to sit quietly alone, to think my own long thoughts, or read or listen to the wireless.

The next day she writes that after taking the children for a stroll: "I don't hate them so much today, luckily." Both entries seem to indicate a state of exhaustion. Her diaries are dominated by domestic activities, housework, cooking, shopping, and, on Sundays, churchgoing. Out of over two hundred entries for 1953, I count less than twenty which mention baby Stephen, and many of these report that he was fretful, sleeping badly and hence disturbing her nights, or that he was 'yelling'.

My mother is the church organist as well as the cleaner, and she needs peace to be able to play properly. On the feast of St Joseph, the service is in the evening, and she tries to leave the baby at home in bed. But Stephen doesn't want to be separated from his mother 'and screamed like mad so I had to take him with me. Mrs Jones took him so I could play the organ, but he yelled'. The situation is saved when her friend Mrs Dilys brings Helen and me into church and we are able to play with our little brother and quieten him. On another occasion, when our baby misses his afternoon sleep, his routine is upset and 'he was so overtired that he yelled all evening until 11pm'.

It is her choice of this word 'yelled' that seems significant. She could have chosen 'cried' or 'wept' and added words like 'brokenheartedly' or 'inconsolably'. 'Yelling' seems to imply that the baby is doing it purposefully, and making demands on her that she dislikes.

There is one entry which mentions him affectionately. She arrays him in 'finery of pale blue corduroy coat, white socks and blue shoes. Discovered he could stand leaning against my legs. He was very pleased with himself. It's hard to remember he is nearly one'.

And on his birthday a few days later, she writes: "Our little Stevie's birthday." The word 'little' seems to add a touch of affection.

All this seems strange. Her ambition was to have six children, which she has achieved. It seems odd to suffer through three years before a baby qualifies as a child.

Mentions of Richard, two years older than baby Stephen, are also infrequent and likewise tend to be negative. Rosie's birthday is in January. During a frantically busy day, she 'tore round the shops to get Rosie a cake etc., with Baby in my arms and Richard tagging along'. Poor Richard. It makes him sound like an appendage.

On the February half term holiday, my father is taking Richard and Rosie by coach to visit our Granny Annie:

> I'm somewhat disgusted to think how pleased I am to have a few less to cope with for a few days. Richard is at a very difficult stage just now, and gets very bored when children are at school.

Richard is not yet three when she writes: "Spent a sleepy hour in the afternoon. Richard climbed up on my knee and fell fast asleep in two minutes so I could not move for an hour." He is still a needy toddler who loves to snuggle up

with our cosy, curvaceous mother. It is a rare affectionate mention of this little fellow.

As for Johnny Gaughran, who completes her lifetime ambition to have six children, other than concern for teaching him and Richard their morning Catechism, he features only a few times in the diary, and then often negatively.

One time, Johnnie spends a few days with Mrs Dilys at New Forest Farm. On his return, my mother writes: "I was glad to see him again, and I think he was glad to be home. He stayed there long enough for them to discover his faults, so he got some good tickings off."

We know very little about Johnnie and the troubled background from which he probably came. We may wonder what his many faults were, and how would they be dealt with in the present age, compared to 1953 where tickings-off and slippering seemed the way to correct him.

Helen sees his face as always unhappy, and wonders in later years why he was with us. But he has his happy moments. My mother takes us to the circus, and 'Johnnie was in fits of laughter at the clowns'. He enjoys riding on Mrs Dilys' horse Beauty at her farm, and he shares our holidays at the seaside.

There is one appealing comment in her diary. Johnnie can't go with Rosie and Richard when my father takes them off to Granny Annie's for a few days. He says, "I'll stay at home and keep Mummy happy."

Also, my mother is careful to bring him into the arms of the Catholic church. Although he is only six years old, he becomes an altar boy. As the oldest of the boys in our family, this role carries status. When we sit in our family pew on Sundays, he is at the procession of the priest going to the altar, proudly carrying the crucifix. During the service, he rings the bells at the right moment.

My mother's diary is private, and she can be honest when she writes it. Yet it is not shut away with lock and key. The mere fact of writing means that she knows it might be observed, but she is a natural writer and has a need to express herself. Without this diary, which shows her strengths and fallibilities, we would not have this rare picture of domestic life in Hay in 1953.

7 Strict School

"The Welsh and the Saxons are getting ready for a big battle." Miss Davies, our teacher, is telling us our afternoon story. We in the Infants class at school already know who the Saxons are. They are those English people who always wanted to conquer the Welsh, which is who we are.

"The Saxons thought they would trick us," she goes on. "They saw the uniforms we were wearing. So they decided they would make the same uniforms as us, and then we wouldn't know who the Saxons were. But the Welsh saw their trick. They went into the woods and picked leeks, and put them in their helmets. This way they knew who the Welsh soldiers were, and so they wouldn't attack their own side. Then they fought the Saxons and drove them away. The Welsh won the victory. And that is why the leek is the emblem of Wales."[9]

Our school in Hay is in Wales, just. Hay is at the focus of three counties. In the 1950s, it is in Brecknockshire, the county town of which is Brecon. Radnorshire is on the other side of the bridge which crosses the River Wye. Herefordshire is over the Dulas Brook, just a very short walk from our school, and that county is in England.

Miss Davies is deeply Welsh. It is she who tells us stories about Boadicea who attacked the invading Romans. A woman, a queen, holding the reins on her horse-drawn chariot, her daughters beside her, drives the enemies away, and so she is my heroine.

Afternoons are story time. "Once upon a time, there was a woman so strong that she was a giantess, and she decided to build a castle in Hay," Miss Davies tells us. "Her name was Moll Walbee. She got to work and built the castle in one single night. But then, she stepped on a sharp stone and hurt her foot. She was in a rage, and she threw the huge stone all the way over the river to the little place called Llowes. If you go there, you can see the stone in the churchyard to this day."

This is another story of a strong woman which lodges itself in my six-year-old mind.

....

The children walk to school

On every school day in the first years of the 1950s, young children are tumbled out of their houses and into the narrow streets of Hay. We skip along the narrow streets, running up and jumping down from steps outside front doors. We squabble and shout to our friends. The littlest ones are only five years old, and sometimes they are holding the hands of big sisters who have been given responsibility. But at other times, those big sisters just leave them and run to their own friends, and so the youngest must find their own way. Boys kick balls and chase each other. No-one expects boys to look after the little ones. The children can hear the few cars and vans that are driving around and learn to keep out of the way.

Some of the children have come out from their shopkeeper dwellings above their businesses, or behind them in houses with hidden gardens. Others emerge from behind the doors of the cramped unhygienic cottages of Chancery Lane and Brook Street. Those from the New Houses in the Gipsy Castle estate on the edge of town have further to walk, passing the church and then up the hill past the castle. Some from that side of town go to the church school because it is nearer.

Children like us from the town centre houses go down Bear Street where I meet Christine. Lower down we join those from the English side of town. The girls from the castle follow its outer walls to the Bull Ring, and then walk down Bear Street.

The son of the butcher at the bottom of Bear Street slowly heads in the same direction, doggedly, because he hates school. Cousins from the chip shop and the Half Moon pub join children making their way along Lion Street, where some of the youngest drop off at the Church of England infants' school.

The two streets come together by the blacksmith's where the anvil is often ringing and sparks flying, and a horse may be standing with one leg raised while its shoe is hammered in place. Other children work their way up from the station side of town along Heol y Dwr, the street with the water channel alongside.

We spend five years of our childhood in Hay County Primary School next door to the police station. On arrival, we play in the big playground until the whistle blows. The terrifying Mr Davies, our headmaster, organises the hundred and fifty or so unruly children into 'Lines'.

We all know which line we are in, Infants in the front, graduating to the oldest from Standard 4 at the back. We run to the wall to be the first to put our hand on it. All those from the same class line up with their right hand on the left shoulder of the person next to them. Soon we are in five neat rows. We stay silent or risk a stern rebuke.

"Hands Down!" he orders. Like well-trained soldiers, we drop our hands. "Left Turn. Forward March."

One row at a time, Infants first, we march into our classrooms where we stay until morning playtime.

....

Daily lessons

With varying degrees of willingness, we must all learn to read and write, do arithmetic, and recite our times tables. These are the occupations of the morning after the first half hour for religious instruction and singing hymns.

We have graded readers, peopled by Dick and Dora.

Reading is easy and fun once the basics are learned. Those of us who find it easier are put beside those who struggle, to encourage them. For spelling, we have lists of ten words we must learn, followed by spelling tests. For some of us that is easy, and for others impossibly difficult.

Handwriting practice takes place every day. In the Infants class, we write with slates and chalk, which are given out by Christine and me, who are monitors. Sticks of chalk break easily, and being horrid little girls, we are careful to keep the long unbroken sticks for ourselves, nice ones for our friends and lastly the broken bits and pieces for the boys we don't like.

Even worse, one day we sneak a few pieces of broken chalk in our pockets, and on the way home at dinner time, we stop outside the house of a boy in our class, Robert Pugh the Limited. The walls of his house are made of shiny glazed brick, perfect for writing on with chalk. We squat down and start to write with our ill-formed spelling: "Robert Pugh the Limited is stupid." Absorbed in our task, we don't notice Miss Stephens coming up behind us.

"Bridget, Christine, what are you doing?" Two guilty faces peer up at her. "Give me that chalk at once. I am going to report you to Miss Davies the minute I get back to school."

Christine and I are haunted with the idea of a fearful punishment. She goes in to her house, and I continue home. Afraid to go back to school after eating my dinner, I say, "Mummy, I don't feel well."

"Oh well, dear, I suppose you'd better go upstairs and rest," she says. I spend the afternoon worrying, but I must go to school again the next day.

"What did Miss Davies do?" I ask Christine when I see her. It is something of an anti-climax because either Miss Stephens forgot, or Miss Davies decided to let the matter drop. Our naughtiness has no consequence other than leaving an impression of dangerously bad behaviour on my young self.

Just before break, the milk comes round. The tiny glass bottles hold a third of a pint. They have a round foil cap, and the milk has cream on the top. Many of the children are not well nourished, and the milk is good for them. But drinking it is optional, and I choose not to.

After milk, Miss Davies tells the Infants that they may go to do their Business in the Offices. The boys go to one side, a place we girls never enter. Our side has cubicles in each of which is a wooden board with a hole in the middle. Naturally, none of us wants to sit on the board, so we squat on it, one foot on each side of the hole. This inevitably means that we can't aim well, and they are unpleasant places. There is no flushing system. From time to time, someone flushes next door in the police station, and water runs along the drain underneath all the boards, removing the waste to some unknown place.

At one time, the toilets must have been so bad that the whole school was subjected to a strong lecture. "You must sit on the seats," says our teacher. "Squatting is not allowed. Your dirty feet get all over the seats." But we never do. For those of us who go home at dinnertime, it is better if we can wait.

We are sitting in Miss Stephen's Standard 1 class one morning when the lady who cleans the school comes in, goes to the teacher's desk and whispers something. Miss Stephens turns to us, looking shocked.

"Children, I have some very bad news to tell you," she says. "The King has died!"

What is that? Our king? We don't know much about him, but this is obviously serious. There he must be, lying on his bed, dead, with his crown on his head. On the way home for midday dinner, five-year-old Helen is walking with me up Bear Street.

"Helen, do you know the King has died?" I say. My sister is unimpressed and laughs at the news. With my superior older sister self-righteousness, I tell my mother.

"Mummy, the King has died," I say, "and I told Helen and she laughed!"

"Oh my goodness me," she says. She had no idea. "But darling, don't worry about it. Helen is just a little girl."

One day, I tell my mother that I can recite the twelve times table backwards. I am in Standard 2. "That is a very curious thing to do," she says. We regularly have to chant the tables, the easy ones like times-two, times-five and times-ten, and the much harder ones like times-seven, times-eight and times-nine. Our brains become the equivalent of calculators. Put in the figures and the answers appear. Nine times seven? Out pops the answer 63. Eleven times eleven? One hundred and twenty one. We have only the vaguest understanding of what we are doing, but the rote learning fixes the answers in our minds.

Miss Williams is our teacher in Standard 2. A diminutive spinster who takes no nonsense, she wears brown gaiters buttoned up to her knees, a dark blue dress and a brick-coloured cardigan. She wears the same clothes day after day, week after week, like most of the grown-ups in our lives. What they wear becomes part of their character.

....

Afternoons

Our dinner time breaks last for one-and-a half hours, long and leisurely. Some of the children go to the canteen, a short walk away, whereas those of us who live nearby walk home. There is just time enough to amble along, to be welcomed by our mothers and often the fathers too if they work close to home. Midday dinner is the main meal of the day, the shopping and cooking having been one of the main morning occupations of the mothers.

In the afternoons at school, our work is less strenuous.

We learn singing. In Standard 1, I boast to Miss Stephens that I am a good singer. Probably my mother has told me this. The teacher tells me to come out to the front, and I sing the first verse or two of a song we all know. She then calls out Kathleen Gibbons, who has a famously lovely voice, to do the last verse with me which much improves the performance.

Miss Stephens is a kind teacher, but she has adequately punctured my vanity.

We have twice weekly radio programmes, *Rhythm and Melody* on Tuesday and *Singing Together* on Thursday which we prefer. We sing along with the children's choir on the radio, holding our little printed books with the words and pictures. We learn English, Irish, Welsh and Scottish folk songs: *In the Garden where the Praties Grow, Kelvin Grove, My Love's an Arbutus, Rio Grande, It was in the Broad Atlantic.* The tunes and words will dance along in our minds for ever.

Girls learn useful skills. In Standard 1, once a week in the afternoon, we are taught to knit. Using white string on big needles, we must make dishcloths. *In, round, over and off.* We follow the pattern of the plain knitting stitch. We often get into impossible knots, and then must line up by Miss Stephens's desk until she patiently undoes them. In between undoing knots, she reads us stories. When left-handed Rosie gets to this age, knitting is a terror she never overcomes. Her hands want to do it backwards; her brain is being scrambled up.

In Standard 2, we will learn to sew. While we are still in Standard 1, sometimes one of the bigger girls from that class is allowed to bring her needlework achievement to show us. She has made a pair of knickers, cut out from flowery cotton, hemmed and threaded with elastic. This is certainly a useful garment, and none of the teachers seems to find it odd that the girl goes from one class to another holding up a pair of knickers in front of the boys. We don't dare to giggle in the classroom but wait until after school. Next year, I'll be making them myself.

When the time comes, the Standard 2 needlework class is taken by the headmaster's wife, Mrs Davies, and she is formidable. Every girl must learn to sew, which starts with the basic stitches of tacking and hemming. We are given a piece of white cotton, folded ready to be tacked. First, we have to thread the needle. Holding the eye up to the light, we lick the end of the thread and do our best to push it through the tiny eye. We are eight years old, and many of our fine motor skills are still developing, making this agonisingly difficult. Once the needle is threaded, we must begin to tack, which holds the cloth in place before the real stitching begins. We use red thread for tacking, and make a double stitch to start. Then a long stitch and a short gap, long stitch and short gap, on we go to the end, trying to keep it all straight, with a double stitch to finish. We line up to see if our finished work will be approved by the teacher.

If it is passed, then we go on to the hemming stiches. Hems are at the bottom of girls' dresses and boys' trousers. In our homes, extra lengths are made into big hems on the clothes of growing children so that they can be let down an inch or two as the child gets taller. Later, the hems can be put up again for the younger children who inherit the items, and down again as they grow. It is an important skill because clothes are expensive.

Hemming stitches must be so small that they do not show on the outside of the garment. First, we must thread the needle again, this time with white cotton. A double stitch is made, as always, and then we push the needle in to pick up a little thread from the front of the garment and onto the fold, pulling the two sides together. Slowly, laboriously, we work our way along.

If we get in a muddle, which is frequent, we join the line at the teacher's desk. None of us likes doing that, so we sit feeling silly and delay for as long as we can. The worst of all is losing the needle. If our clumsy fingers drop it, it may disappear into cracks in the wooden floor.

Ruth Watkins from Callamellin farm sits beside me. No-one uses the Welsh name of her farm which is Cae Nant y Melyn because it is much too difficult to pronounce. She has lost her needle, and is terrified to tell Mrs Davies. What can she do?

She gets a pin, and somehow manages to tie the thread round the head of the pin, which she yanks through the cloth.

"I've done one stitch with this awful old muggins," she whispers to me. I think this is the funniest thing I have ever heard, and her curmudgeonly tone echoes down the decades.

Eventually, I too learn how to make knickers and take them round the classes. They are such good quality that I wear them for years.

Mr Pound is our teacher in Standard 3. He is new, and he is kind. He has given out books with brown Beacon emblems on the front. They are for our geography class, and have stories about children from other lands. There is a boy who lives in Italy, where the grass is brown. Brown grass? Impossible.

Everyone knows grass is green.

Our school atlases open at a map of the world. Countries fascinate me. Mr Pound shows us the oceans, the great continents, and we learn where we live, where London is, and England and Wales. But dominating more than anything is the bright pink colour spreading across the two side-by-side pages. This is the British Empire. The great expanses of Canada, Australia and New Zealand, and many countries in Africa, the far east and dots of islands in the oceans. We are taught to be proud of this, and chant on our special holiday:

Empire Day
24th of May
If you don't give us a holiday
We'll all run away.

We have no idea of the significance of what we are learning, of inequalities, conquest, injustices and that for example at this very time, over a million native Kenyans are being herded into concentration camps where children are dying of hunger and disease. My parents, my father in particular, read the newspapers and must know something about this. We are absorbing the British Empire version of history as it is taught in the 1950s.

We think the name Mr Pound is funny, and unusually he is a teacher we are not afraid of. Some friends and I devise a little rhyme: "Mr Pound Found, while he was sleeping Sound on the Ground, a big Round Hound." We think this is hilariously funny, and put the note on his desk one playtime, before tiptoeing away. He doesn't mention it. Perhaps he is glad that our rhyming skills are developing.

....

We must learn Welsh

In Standard 3, we are taught Welsh. Hay is not a Welsh speaking town. Most of us never travel much, the furthest away being Brecon or Hereford which are English speaking, and most of the children don't like Welsh. What is the point of learning these strange words for things?

Mr Jones is our Welsh teacher. He draws a picture on the blackboard of a river with some birds flying around, and children playing. We are taught *plant* for children, *adar* for birds, *afon* for river. We learn to count, *un, dau, tri, pedwar, pump, chwech, saith, wyth, naw, deg.* And some curiously un-useful little phrases:

Y *mae pensil ar y pot ink.*	The pencil is on the ink pot.
Y *mae pot ink ar y llyfr.*	The ink pot is on the book.
Y *mae llyfr ar y desg.*	The book is on the desk.

We learned about mutations from d to dd, f to ff, c to g, m to v, and how to pronounce the Ll sound at the beginning and in the middle of words.

I like Welsh, but I am the only person I know who does.

The class is uninterested and endlessly naughty. Mr Jones gets so annoyed that he throws chalk at the culprits, and when he gets really angry he throws the duster. He is not having much success at developing a love of the native language in this class.

....

Discipline

Mr Davies, the headmaster, teaches Standard 4, the top class. By this time we have all been well trained in Reading, Writing and Arithmetic. His job is to get us ready to take the Eleven Plus exam. We are taught composition, which means writing in good English; comprehension which means reading and answering questions about what we have read which always seems obvious to me; and a careful cursive handwriting.

We line up by his desk for our English writing to be checked.

"Bridget, do you see what is wrong with this sentence?" he asks on one of my submissions. I look and I can't see any errors, and I say so.

"Have another look," he says crossly. I still can't find any errors. He is annoyed and speaks to me strictly. I go home for midday dinner very upset.

I tell Mr Ottowell, our neighbour at 2 Market Street my sad story. "Poor Mr Davies is probably angry because he suffers from appendicitis," Mr Ottowell tells me.

Poor Mr Davies? It is me that is suffering a humiliation.

But Mr Ottowell has a good idea.

"I suggest you say you are sorry," he advises. "If you do, I expect he will not be angry with you anymore." This is a surprising suggestion, but I decide to do as he says. I apologise to Mr Davies, who smiles. After that, he no longer seems to have appendicitis pain, and I have learned a lesson in diplomacy.

He is, however, a strict headmaster who stands no nonsense in his school. These are the days when physical punishment is normal. One boy, otherwise inoffensive, is always late for school. Mr Davies finally has enough, and we are obliged to watch Geoffrey putting out his hand for the teacher to give him two whacks with the cane. We cringe, and are awed into silence.

On one occasion, I am late for school too. I don't get the cane, or even a reprimand. I tell Mr Pound that my mother has been combing my hair for nits. "All right, Bridget," he says. "That is not an excuse. That is a Reason!" He knows that dealing with headlice is an ongoing problem.

....

Nit nurse

"Stand up children," says our teacher. "The nurse is ready for you."

At the front of the class, we stand in a row.

One at a time, she riddles through our hair with her fingers, scritchy scratchy. She is looking for headlice or the nits which are their eggs. Parents will be informed if she finds them, and then we must get a smelly mixture to spread on our heads, followed by regular combing to remove the nits which are stuck hard onto the hairs.

"Have you all got a clean handkerchief?" she asks next. Those few of us who have must hold it up like a little flag. Several of us often have long yellow drips hanging from our noses, and her task is to improve the situation.

"You must ask your mother to give you a clean handkerchief every day," she impresses upon us, "and if you haven't got a handkerchief, you can use a piece of clean rag."

....

Games

The best part of school without doubt is playtime, fifteen minutes in the morning and afternoon with a long midday break for dinner.

I am at the centre of a group of girls who are my friends.

We have decided to play Cross the Water, so we put our arms round each other's shoulders making a line, which we call Joining On. We parade the playground chanting: "Who'll Join On for playing Cross the Water?" One little girl who doesn't fit in my self-selected group of friends wants to Join On. She is a thin, undernourished child with ragged clothes who wears cheap black cotton shoes without socks even in the coldest of winters, and has the reputation of not having knickers.

"I'm not playing if you Join On," I say spitefully.

"What's wrong with her?" retorts Maureen, a small girl with long brown hair. "She's just as good as you are Bridget Ashton and if not better!"

I am taken aback. I am used to being the biggest, the cleverest, the oldest of six children in my family, and top of my class for lessons. Now this brown-haired diminutive Maureen has chastised me on behalf of one of the least advantaged children in our school. It is a quick and acidic retort. I thoroughly deserve it, and it is a lesson for life.

The girls' side of the playground is always full of activity.

Often we have a long skipping rope, with a girl holding each end, rotating it, and making shapely moving arcs. It goes tap tap tap as it hits the ground. We line up on tiptoes, bodies moving in readiness, getting into the rhythm of the rope:

All in together girls
This fine weather girls

Then we chant: "January, February, March, April, May, June, July, August, September, October, November, December." Each girl 'runs in' on her birthday month into the arc of the rope.

There are other games. Onesie, Twosie, Threesie, Foursie.

Round and round goes the rope. There is a skill to turning. The rhythm must be steady, with the turners working in time. It is easy to 'run in' when the rope turns in our direction.

Thus, Onesie is easy, and we need to make only one jump before 'running out'. Then, the whole line turns around for 'Twosie'. This requires much neater footwork as it is easier to catch your foot on the rope from this side. Next, we line up for 'Threesie', and so we go on until no-one is left in. Then we change:

Blue bells, cockle shells,
Eavy ivey over

We sing this in a one-and-two-and, one-and-two-and, rhythm, the rope swaying from side to side in gentle arcs. Like flowers, like shells, pretty footwork is needed. We skip in time, big jump, gentle jump, big jump, gentle jump.

But suddenly, the rhythm changes. The shock of it! The rope changes to turning round and round, and the rope goes faster and faster:

Mother's in the kitchen
Father cuts the meat
Baby's in the cradle
Fast asleep.
How many sweeties
Can you eat?
One, two, three, four…

Snap snap snap snap goes the rope on the hard surface until someone trips on the rope, and we have to start all over again.

We play *The Big Ship Sails on the Alley Alley Oh*. One girl puts her hand on the wall, and the rest of us make a chain, passing through the arch. Which ship? Which Alley? We don't think about it, but we like the chant:

The big ship sails on the alley alley oh,
The alley alley oh,
The alley alley oh.
The big ship sails on the alley alley oh,
On the last day of September.

The captain said, 'It will never, never do,
Never, never do,
Never, never do.'
The captain said, 'It will never, never do,'
On the last day of September.

The big ship sank to the bottom of the sea,
The bottom of the sea,
The bottom of the sea.
The big ship sank to the bottom of the sea,
On the last day of September.

Just outside the school gates is the street called Holy Door where we have a special game. It doesn't matter that the street sign spells it Heol y Dwr which means Water Street. We like the shallow channel of water which runs parallel to the street because we have a special game here which we often play on the way home from school.

"Please Jack, may we cross the water?" we chant. Jack is on one side of the channel with her back to us. "You can if you are wearing…red!" says Jack.

We quickly look at our clothes, our dresses, cardigans, socks, shoes. Be quick – anyone who is wearing red jumps over the water and the first one to touch Jack plays that part next time and chooses the colour.

After one school holiday, we come back to find an outdoor climbing frame in our playground. Three ropes are hanging on the metal A-frame for climbing. Now we are all sailors. There is a rope ladder too, and most exciting of all, a swinging trapeze. Now I can really practice being a trapeze artist for when I grow up.

One problem is that by turning upside down, the boys can see our underwear and tease us. But not only girls can be embarrassed. Emlyn Evans was swinging on the bars when his trousers fell down, and he was the son of a chapel minister!

Boys mostly get on with their own games, marbles, cricket, kicking a ball around. Balls tend to go over walls, to the police station on one side or a neighbour with a garden on the other. The neighbour is so annoyed about this continually happening that she charges a penny for returning the ball. In revenge, the boys have one advantage over the girls, and they aim their personal waterpipes over the wall when no-one is looking.

On one occasion, an aim is actually successful, causing huge disruption, a complaint to the school and the eventual upgrading of the boys' toilets.

At 3.30 in the afternoon, we are released and make our way back through the streets, going home for our tea. No parents come to collect us because it is taken for granted that we are capable of finding our own way. The one exception is Helen's friend, Lecky Adams, who is collected in a car because she is rich, and lives out of town.

....

After school

On one day, unusually, my mother arrives after school to see the teacher, pushing baby Stephen in the pram. This cannot be good. She is having a quiet discussion with Miss Stephens while I am left outside.

Next day I find out the reason.

"Children, I want you all to put your hands over your eyes," Miss Stephens tells the class.

She takes me out to the porch where I am required to put on my orangey-pink National Health glasses. I definitely don't like this, and I have so far refused to wear them. But I can't oppose my teacher. She picks me up and carries me into the classroom. All the children have their hands over their eyes, but I know they are peeping between their fingers, and I am bound to accept this humiliation.

One day, I come up with a good idea to break the monotony of the classroom. If any child has found an item of value, for example a handkerchief, they are allowed to take it round the classes, saying, "Has anyone lost this handkerchief?" I tell my teacher that my mother has lost a ten-shilling note, so she permits me to go round from room to room saying, "Has anyone found a ten shilling note?"

This is a significant amount of money, and around this time, my mother meets Miss Stephens in the street.

"Mrs Ashton, I do hope you managed to find that lost ten shilling note," she says. My mother is puzzled and asks for the explanation. When she realises I have entirely invented the story, I am in trouble.

"Bridget, we will go straight to church and you will confess your sin and say sorry for telling this lie," she says.

I am humiliated in front of Elspeth Beattie, my friend who is coming to play with me. Elspeth has to wait while I am taken up the stairs to church and obliged to kneel down and make my confession. It hadn't been such a good idea after all, and it was my bad luck that my mother met the teacher that day.

One after-school visit to the teacher concerns my little sister Rosie who has just started in the Infants class. My mother has modern ideas about education.

"Rosie is still very unsettled at school," she writes in her diary in September 1953. "Most reluctant to go, and hysterical outbursts getting more and more frequent. I think this left-handed business is at the back of the trouble, and Miss Davies is much too keen on persuading her to use her right. I went to see her after school, and after a lot of pleasant talk in which she agreed to everything I said, without anything being settled, I managed to persuade her to leave Rosie alone for the time being to use which hand she likes."

Rosie is proud of my mother's intervention on her behalf. Most of the time, however, the grown-ups are content to let the teachers take complete charge. From 9 in the morning to 3.30 in the afternoon, parents are free to get on with their daily work. While we are in school, we are under a disciplined rule, and yet at the same time there is a kind of freedom. There are no walls hiding us from passers-by as we play in our playground, no office staff in a room with a buzzer to check visitors, and no after-school activities to lengthen the day. When the bell rings at half past three, off we all run to play on the way home, working up a good appetite for our bread and butter tea.

8 Only Catholics go to Heaven

"Mummy, do you know Jesus had brothers and sisters?" I ask her one dinnertime. I imagine Jesus sitting around the table just like we do, with all the children saying grace and learning good table manners.

"Where on earth did you hear that?" She was aghast.

"My teacher told me. And he said that Joseph was Jesus's real father, and God adopted him."

My mother is horrified. This simply will not do. Mr Pound is our new teacher for Standard 3, and I am being taught these untruths.

This most unpleasant shock must be dealt with. She writes in her diary: "This is an ample illustration of the truth of Father O'Reilley's remark that 'error creeps in'."

She goes down to school the very next day and accosts Mr Davies, the headmaster.

"Is this doctrine part of the religious syllabus, or merely Mr Pound's private interpretation?" she asks.

Mr Davies tries to alleviate the tension.

"Mr Pound certainly should not have said those things," he admits, "but he is a new teacher and I don't want to upset his confidence by criticising him after his first week at school."

My mother writes in her diary that this is all very well, but she is not reassured. She will watch out attentively in future. Soon she records: "Have definitely decided not to let any of the children attend scripture classes in future, and will try to teach them a little myself – but alas – it's easier to make good resolutions than to keep them."

....

Children of a Catholic mother

My sisters and brothers and I are in the curious situation of being brought up as strict Catholics in a town of Protestants and non-conformists. My mother had converted to Catholicism when she was in her teacher training college in 1940. She is glad to be in Hay where she can participate fully in St Joseph's church activities and bring us up correctly.

We absorb a few basic facts. One of the most fundamental is that only Catholics will go to heaven because we have the one true faith. This means that our friends are not so lucky.

"Mummy, does that mean they will go to hell?" I ask.

She gives us a waffling answer because she is a kind person. "I don't really know dear. God will decide." That is the sort of thing I am told, with in-between places called Limbo and Purgatory. It leaves me uncertain, and worried.

On Sundays, when I watch people in the town make their way down to the parish church, I look at them and wonder if they are good. They seem to be all right, but they can't be as good as us.

After the incident at school, my mother firms up her decision that we are not to attend religious instruction lessons any more. This is quite acceptable to Helen, Rosie and me because we miss the first half hour of school. Whereas everyone else must start with religious instruction at 9 o'clock, we need not be there until 9.30. However, we don't get away with it altogether. We must take Catechism lessons on Saturday as my mother had found it too exacting to do this herself. Mrs Biddle, her Catholic friend, is our teacher.

The Catechism gives structure and certainty. The question and answer format is in a little red book which has all the rules for good Catholics. My mother is guided by question number 201, which tells her that the duty of parents towards their children is to provide, instruct and correct them, and to give them a good Catholic education. She regrets that there is no Catholic school in Hay, so on Saturday up the steps we go to the room serving as the Catholic church, just across the road from our house.

Of the 370 questions and answers in the Catechism, we must learn those which are within our understanding. The constant repetition of the first two will stay in our minds permanently:

Question 1. Who made you? *Answer:* God made me.

Question 2. Why did God make you? *Answer*: God made me to know Him, love Him and serve Him in this world, and to be happy with Him for ever in the next.

We repeat these two every session, and they become imprinted. Some of the later concepts are harder:

Question 17. What is God?

The question is easy but the answer is not. "God is the supreme Spirit, who alone exists of himself, and is infinite in all perfections." I don't think I ever get that one right. The answer to another one sounds almost scientific. It is easy to recite:

Question 20. Had God any beginning? *Answer*: God had no beginning: He always was, He is, and He always will be.

There are two questions which concern our immediate lives:

Question 21. Where is God? *Answer*: God is everywhere.

Question 22. Does God know and see all things? *Answer*: God knows and sees all things, even our most secret thoughts.[10]

Thus, we learn that, wherever we go, God is watching. He is like a big parent hiding out of sight. Even if we think bad thoughts, he knows. When I am unkind to my sister, or feel annoyed about having to take the smelly potty down the stairs, God knows. When my mother has smacked me and I smoulder with resentment, he knows the bad things I say to myself about her. There is no escape. We are trapped because we are often naughty.

But in reality I don't spend a lot of time thinking about it. There is an element of vagueness, of uncertainty. Yes he is probably up there somewhere behind the clouds, but I am busy and active, and I can't see him.

One day, Mrs Biddle is really shocked. Helen and I are getting fidgety at our Catechism lesson. In our bathtub at home, we have a game where we poke each other in our round little tummies and say, "Binkers!" This is our word for bacon. We giggle as we Binker each other in our Catechism class. Mrs Biddle reprimands us. We are not sure why, but she tells us, "You shouldn't do that, Bridget and Helen. It is very immodest."

What does that mean? My mother just laughs when we tell her. She likes our chubby shapes, and Rosie in particular has the nickname Rosie Posie Plummy Tummy. She doesn't think that God the Father would be upset by our childish game. Why, he might even find it funny.

Father Brady, the kind priest, comes sometimes to our Catechism class to ensure we are making progress, and here he is testing five-year-old Rosie on her Catechism.

"Rosie, can you answer this question? Who made you?"

That's an easy one. Rosie answers confidently: "God made me."

"Good girl. Now, why did God make you?"

"Um, um, He made me to know Him and love Him…" And she falters, trembling.

Father Brady supplies the rest of the answer and reassures her. He knows there is plenty of time for Rosie to learn her Catechism, and my little sister's burden is lightened.

....

St Joseph's Roman Catholic church in Hay

"Shall I show you the church?" I ask Christine. My friends are somewhat in awe of this church with its intriguing incense smell, and from which we emerge at times wearing pretty white veils and dresses, looking like bridesmaids.

The door to the church is only about ten big steps and a jump across the road from our house at 3 Market Street. Two upstairs rooms are rented for the church from the local council, underneath which are the public toilets and a storage area with old tables and other junk.

We go up the wide wooden staircase. My mother is doing some cleaning, so we can go in. At the top of the stairs is a landing with two brown doors, one of which has a curious peephole. A round wooden circle of wood can be slid sideways from the inside to check for intruders. I have been told that this comes from the time when the room belonged to the secretive Masons.

Christine looks at the statues of the Virgin Mary and St Joseph one on each side of the altar. Do we worship them? I know from my Catechism, and from what my mother has taught me, that they are there to remind us. The Catechism teaches us that "we do not pray to relics or images, for they can neither see, nor hear, nor help us" and "they relate to Christ and his Saints, and are memorials of them".[11]

There are several rows of pews which my mother is busily polishing.

"What are you girls doing here?" she asks. I tell her that we've just come to look around. I show Christine the organ, which is actually a harmonium but we don't use that name. My mother is the organist. To play the hymns, she pumps the two foot pedals up and down, and uses the stops to make the sound she wants.

As well as being a cleaner and organist, my mother has taken the role of unofficial caretaker, and her tasks include unlocking and locking every day. A Catholic church must be open as much as possible to enable prayer at any time. The main church is in Brecon, fifteen miles away. The priests come on Sundays to serve Hay and the surrounding area's tiny Catholic population. We live so close to the church that my mother is able to be helpful.

Catholics are different, and other children feel this. Rosie's six-year-old friend Roddy knows the Catholic church is up the stairs, near where they play with their balls in Castle Square. It is mysterious, forbidden and he feels fearful about what lies inside. He has seen photos of the Pope, which give him the feeling of something dark and sinister, menacing and frightening. He has picked up the idea that priests check up on your behaviour. But things are not entirely negative. When he was a baby, his mother and Mrs Madigan, her Catholic friend, would push their babies around in their prams together. And Rosie is adorable. We can't be all that bad.

....

Remember to keep holy the Sabbath day

"Hurry up girls and get your clothes on," our mother calls, to get us out of our beds. Every Sunday, she has to get six children up, washed, dressed and hair brushed. Baby Stephen has to have a fresh nappy pinned in place. Those of us who are not receiving Holy Communion are allowed to have breakfast of cornflakes with sugar and milk which are put on the table. Then it is all to be cleared away so that the kitchen is ready for the priest to come for his breakfast after Mass.

For my mother, this is all to be done on an empty stomach.

Catholics who want to receive Holy Communion are not allowed to have eaten any food, nor drinks of tea or coffee, and not even a drink of water. But then, on 18 January 1953, she records in her diary: "Heard the glad news that the Pope has ordained that everyone may drink water before receiving Communion, and some other people including mothers a nourishing drink."

We are ready, finally, and we cross the road and go up the stairs to our church. Sometimes my father comes too. He is not a Catholic, but he is a sympathiser. We file into our pew, which is filled with our father, mother, me, Helen, Rosie, Johnnie, Richard and baby Stephen.

We are the largest family of children in the church. Sometimes Edith Stanton is there with her father who is a tollgate keeper, or the two Keylock boys, Norman and Nigel, sons of the butcher. Like us, they are from a mixed family. Their father is Catholic, but their mother is not. The arrangement, I have learned, is that any daughters will follow their mother, and the sons their father. There are two Gallagher boys, Gerry and Shaun, older than us, who are sometimes present.

Our brother Johnnie is the youngest altar boy, and he takes his turn leading the priest to the altar, holding the long brass pole with the crucifix. He kneels on the right of the altar, moving back and forth as the service continues. His duties include making responses in Latin, which he parrots totally without understanding, holding the vessels for the priest to pour the wine and the water, pouring water over the priest's hands and ringing the bells at the consecration of the bread and the wine. Then he must hold the container for the little round circles of bread which have been consecrated into the body of Christ as the priest places one on the tongue of the communicant.

We have all been thoroughly trained in the routine of the Mass. But, oh, it does go on so long. On and on. As we know, we are in God's house, and especially if our own father is in the pew with us, we must behave ourselves. The different movements of standing, kneeling and sitting help a little, but it is hard to be still for such a long time. For those of us who have taken our First Holy Communion, which includes Helen and me, this breaks the monotony a little as we line up at the appropriate time with the adults. Then with bowed heads we return to our pew, knowing that Jesus is inside us.

We are not always well behaved in church, shown by these two diary extracts:

All toiled to church at 9.15. Very hot and exhausting. Father O'Reilley preached a sermon on the trials of married life – amply illustrated by the screaming infants of the congregation.

128

All to church in good time, but children very badly behaved and sent them to bed for an hour afterwards as a punishment.

My sisters and brothers and I learn that Catholics have the true faith, and we accept what we are told. Our missals have the Latin language on one side of the page and the English translation on the other. As we get older we can look at some of the easier, more familiar phrases, and absorb some of the language:

In Nomine Patris, et Filii et Spiritus Sanctus.
Pater noster, qui es in caelis.
Sanctus, sanctus, sanctus.
Credo in Unum Deum Omnipotentem.

Benediction sometimes follows the Mass. That is a relief because we can enjoy some singing. My mother plays the organ:

Adoremus, in aeternum, sanctifimuum, sacramentum.
Genitori, genitorque.
O salutaris hostia.

These evocative tunes bring ancient times into our lives, and the mystery of singing in a secret language links us together in our special superior religion. The scent of incense from the swinging thurible sends our messages up to God in heaven.

After Mass and Benediction, we are hungry. One of the alternating priests, either Father Brady or the younger Father O'Reilley, comes to our house for breakfast or Sunday dinner. Good Catholics must support their priests and this is a duty which my mother enjoys.[12] Other local Catholics often join our family after the services. My mother has made our house a sociable Catholic home.

....

First Holy Communion

When I am 6 years old, I am considered to have reached the age of reason. Before I can make my first Holy Communion, I must make my first Confession. The Catechism instructs us that 'children are bound to go to confession as soon as they have come to the use of reason, and are capable of mortal sin', and that is generally supposed to be about the age of seven years.[13]

My mother has decided that I am ready by August 1950, just a few days after my sixth birthday.

At the back of the church is a double wooden confessional constructed out of two small, narrow cubicles, one side for the priest and one for me. I have been taught what to do, and I go into the darkness and kneel down. There is a grid between the priest and me, so we can't see each other's faces. I repeat the words I have learned: "Bless me Father for I have sinned. This is my first confession."

I have prepared a list of sins.

"I was disobedient to my mother," I say.

"I was unkind to my sister," I say next. I am pretty sure to have done both of those sins.

"I told a lie," I go on, totting the sins up mentally. "I was greedy," I say without going into details.

That is probably enough. The priest forgives me. "I absolve thee from thy sins, in the name of the Father, and of the Son, and of the Holy Ghost." He then says, "For penance, say three Hail Marys and one Our Father."

I leave the cubicle and kneel down in the church to say my penance. Now my soul is clean, and I can make my First Holy Communion.

First Holy Communions are a special event. On the day, I look adorable and innocent. I am wearing a lovely white dress made by my grandmother, and I have a transparent veil on my neatly combed hair. I've been given a white children's prayer book with pretty pictures inside, and my own rosary. Everything is in place. Edith Stanton is making her First Holy Communion with me. At the right moment during the Mass, we are primed to go to the altar. We kneel down and the priest comes forward. Edith is first.

She closes her eyes and opens her mouth. Placing the white wafer on her tongue, the priest says, *"Corpus Domini nostri Jesu Christi custodiat animam tuam in vitam aeternam. Amen."*

Now it is my turn. I open my mouth and receive the host, the body of Jesus Christ, but I know everybody is looking at me and I react shamefully. I run away from the altar, back to my mother. I have disgraced her in front of the whole congregation.

It gets worse. Later, at our house, the visitors are sitting around, the two Mr Grants from the newsagents, the priest, Miss Chappell a headmistress and Mrs Biddle our Catechism teacher. I am still being very naughty. I run up and down the stairs making a noise, and don't obey when I'm told. My mother is mortified.

"Bridget, I am so ashamed," she says. "Go straight to your bedroom." My initiation into this important sacrament of the Catholic church has been completed, but the omens are not good.

In June 1952, Helen makes her First Holy Communion. She receives a holy water stoup as her gift. This is a container for holy water into which fingers are dipped before making the sign of the cross. Helen and I regularly take communion after this. In 1953, my mother makes 39 Sunday diary entries, and she records that I participated 9 times and Helen 13 times.

Probably my behaviour begins to improve.

....

Sin and the little child

Helen, aged under eight years old, has been tempted by the pennies stored in my mother's box for keeping change for the public telephone. She takes two coins when no-one is looking, and sneaks down to Bryant's shop in Bear Street where you can buy a tuppenny ice cream cone. She licks it up and thinks no-one will ever know. But back at the house, she has ice cream all over her face. My mother guesses what has happened, and looks in her money box.

"Sit down here with me, Helen," she says, pointing to the sofa. Helen always longs for cuddles from my mother, but this time is different. "Don't you know that it is wrong to steal? People who steal are called thieves."

Of course, she knows. The temptation had been so strong.

Tears are forming in her eyes.

"Now you can put the sin right if you confess it to God, who will forgive you," my mother says. "Next time, when you go to confession, you can tell the priest, and all will be well."

But my sister is ashamed to tell Father Brady that she is a thief. At her next confession, she doesn't tell him. This sensitive little girl now knows that she will go to hell where she will burn in flames for eternity. Every time she goes to confession after that, she makes the situation worse by omitting to own up to the sin. When she takes communion, she knows that Jesus is in her body, the body of a thief. She cries in her bed, night after night, year after year.

Helen, left, on the day of her First Holy Communion.
Back row L – R: Father Brady, Miss Chappell, our mother and Mrs Biddle.
Children include Rosie, Richard and Bridget. Two other children names unknown

....

Catholic festivals over the Year

"Bridget, today is your saint's day," my mother tells me on 1 February. We are all named after saints. Saint Brigid is Irish, and that explains why her name is spelled differently from mine. I am given a colourful picture card to put in my prayer book.

Saints' days are noted in my mother's 1953 diary. Saint Helen's is on 18 August and Saint Rose's on 30 August.

Richard is named after my uncle who died in Thailand in the war, and his saint's day is 3 April. Saint Stephen's day is the day after Christmas. We are taught that we honour saints, and we may pray to them, but we don't worship them. However, our own homely saints' days are not particularly high on the annual round of Catholic festivals. Shrove Tuesday, which we all know as Pancake Day, is very important. We have the excitement of watching my mother toss them before we eat so many that we never want to see another pancake again. For some of the grown-ups, Lent follows and this means a much stricter eating regimen. My mother notes in her diary:

No Mass this morning – however fasted and abstained with fair rigour though had to have a small piece of bread extra morning and evening.

On Ash Wednesday, the priest marks a cross of ashes with his thumb onto our foreheads as we kneel at the altar. The ash is made from last year's burned palms left from Palm Sunday.

The ash is to remind us that we are dust, and to dust we shall return. When we go outside after Mass, with the cross of ash on our heads, we children are self-consciously aware that we are part of a select, holy community.

Palm Sunday inserts some interest to the repetitiveness of the weekly Mass. "Palm Sunday, all to Confession and Communion. Lent draws on towards its close," my mother writes. We are all given a cross formed out of a frond from a palm leaf. I imagine that they grow in this shape on the tree.

Easter rituals are disturbed in 1953 when my mother decides that the outdoor lavatory needs to be freshly distempered.

We go to Brecon for the Maundy Thursday service without her while she finishes her job, finally completing it on Good Friday.

Lenten fasts are almost over, and she cooks 'a good fish dinner' before taking us all to church for the Stations of the Cross at 3 o'clock on Good Friday. Stephen, the baby, who is now eight months old, is taken along. On the walls of our little church are fourteen scenes representing Jesus as he is taken from his condemnation by Pontius Pilate along the way to his crucifixion.

This is a brutal story for small children, but we move along, one station at a time, the scenes holding our attention. The bloody imagery, the falling, the lashings, the stripping of the cloth which tear his skin, the driving in of the nails to the living flesh, and his slow eventual death. Even though we know he will rise again from the dead in three days' time, this is heavy stuff.

There are some redeeming features among all this. On Maundy Thursday, Helen, Rosie and I go out to collect flowers for an Easter garden all by ourselves while my mother whitewashes the lavatory. We bring home moss, twigs, celandines, violets and wood sorrel, a lovely collection of greens, browns, gold, violet and bright white which our mummy will help us to arrange. Three crosses of sticks, for Jesus and the two thieves on Calvary, are pressed into the moss. We make a tomb with a few stones, and arrange the flowers, and it is beautiful.

Among all of this activity is my father's reaction to the distempering of the lavatory. She writes on Holy Saturday: "Row with John in the morning on the subject of my whitewashing the lavatory which he said was silly."

133

The same day, she records being up until 10.30 pm 'baking bread, icing cake, arranging flowers, making jelly and blancmange, etc etc.' She is preparing for a Sunday feast with Father O'Reilley and other guests.

Jesus rising from the dead on Easter Sunday is a relief. We go to Mass, and on that rainy day in April 1953 my mother records that we are 'arrayed in summer frocks and straw hats'. But what about Easter eggs? Surely, they are the most important part of Easter for hungry, sweets-obsessed children?

Her diary doesn't mention them.

In June, we girls go to Brecon to the parent church for a Corpus Christi procession. We like this because we are dressed up in our attractive white frocks and veils, and are given a scented bunch of flowers to carry. We little girls parade along the streets to the statue of Jesus in the garden, following the tall boy in front who holds the crucifix, and behind us the boys wearing white shirts and red sashes. I expect we were told that the words Corpus Christi mean the body of Christ, but it is the procession which means most to us.

The adults in the procession will know that the feast originated in 1264 when 'St Thomas Aquinas created a feast focussed solely on the Holy Eucharist, being the Body and Blood, Soul and Divinity of Jesus Christ'.[14] There is a 1950 photo in my mother's album of nuns dressed in black, and men and women kneeling alongside.

But in 1953, unfortunately, she didn't go:

Row with John at breakfast time. It seems too much to try to please God and John. Tears again, so couldn't go to Mass. Corpus Christi procession but couldn't face it. The girls went and I took the boys for a walk.

By the end of the year, the four weeks of Advent lead us towards Christmas. My mother guides us into making an Advent ring. We go out into the wintry fields and collect ivy and holly which we weave into a ring. Four candles, one for each Sunday of Advent are fixed into the ring. We light first one, then two, then three and on the fourth Sunday all four candles. The red candles are all four different heights, the first being the shortest, all the way up to the fourth which is newly lit. The big day is coming closer and we are impatient.

In the church, during Advent, the altar cloths and the priests' vestments are a sombre purple. The crib is assembled as the day approaches, with Mary and Joseph, the shepherds, the ox and the ass in the stable. The manger is empty. Baby Jesus won't be added until midnight on Christmas Eve.

Helen and I are allowed to attend midnight Mass as we grow older. Woken out of our slumbers, we are dressed warmly before we cross the road. Having hung up our stockings, we are looking up at the sky for Father Christmas. In the crib, we see that Baby Jesus has been born, and is holding out his arms to us all.

Going to midnight Mass completes our Catholic Christmas duty. Back home, we are once again in bed, but before we go to sleep Helen whispers to me, "Did you see Father Christmas and his reindeer?" I am not sure. "I saw him through the windows of the church," she insists. And with this, we slide into slumber before the excitement of opening our stockings in the morning.

The annual rituals of the Catholic church thus guide the lives of my sisters, my brothers and me. The combination of attractive ceremonies, pretty dresses, processions, music and incense keep us immersed in the Catholic faith, mingled with the brutalities of the crucifixion story and the burden of sin.

Being children of a religious minority in Hay, the other churches and chapels of the town are forbidden to us. Even entering them is seen as putting ourselves in the way of temptation. Thus, there are times when there is a dilemma to be faced.

"Mummy, can we go to the carol service?" we ask before Christmas. Our school plans to join the children's event at the parish church of St Mary's. With some hesitation, our mother gives us permission and thus we join in with *Hark the Herald, Once in Royal David's City, Away in the Manger* and the other familiar carols which we know.

In Hay, there are the chapels, some of which host musical performances. Welsh choirs are an established tradition, and my mother wants to go. At times, she takes us too, so in this way we get a glimpse of their plain interior. Some of my friends belong to the Girls Friendly Society and go to weekly meetings at the Baptist chapel. I really want to go too, as it is the closest thing I know to being a Brownie, but I am not allowed. "Why can't I go?" I ask my mother. Her answers are not convincing. The organisation is connected with the Protestant church, and is forbidden to me. Our Catholic God is watching.

At school, we have a tiny library in a box, and some of the books have been around for decades. It is here that I find Enid Blyton's *Tales of Ancient Greece*. Thus, I learn that there are other older gods, from faraway lands, and that there is more than one way to look at things.

One day, I am walking along the cobbled path outside Gillian Coombes' castle home. I consider the question: "What if I say I believe that Zeus is God?"

This is very daring and I don't actually say it. It will take a few more years to summon up the courage. Hell and damnation are a bit too close, but I am beginning, only beginning, to ask questions.

....

The sacrifice of the Mass

We know that Mass is a sacrifice. It says so in the missals which Helen and I are able to read, and we can see the pictures. Jesus sacrifices himself for us so that we can go to heaven when we die. This is a difficult concept. We accept, learn and may perhaps understand later.

Our Old Testament picture books, which we are also allowed to look at to keep us quiet during Mass, show Abraham about to kill his son Isaac, and then instead he kills a ram. God seems to want sacrifices. But what happens next? After the ram is killed, it is roasted and the smells go up to heaven. In those ancient days, the priests and perhaps people too must have eaten the roasted ram.

In our missal is one section which harks back to those desert sacrifices. The chalice of wine is offered to God 'humbly begging of Thy mercy that it may arise before Thy divine majesty with a pleasing fragrance, for our salvation and that of all the world'. The Latin words, *cum odore suavitatis ascendat*, mean 'arise with a pleasing fragrance'.[15]

The smouldering incense in Mass and the music of the Benediction also reach up to God. With ecstatic music, mystical language, pleasing fragrances sent heavenward, and the body of Jesus inside us, we children who understand little are swept into a realm of spirituality.

9 Being Ill and the NHS

"Time for Licky, girls, as soon as you have washed yourselves," says our mummy.

It is bath time at 3 Market Street. When we are fresh and clean, Helen, Rosie and I stand up in the water, our mouths open. Our mother holds up a squarish bottle filled with a golden oily liquid which we like. One after the other, she gives us a spoonful of this cod liver oil, and we lick it down. She has learned that any spills are easiest cleaned up in the bathtub.

From this, we get our Vitamins A and D.

Next, out comes the orange juice bottle with the same flat shape. This is even tastier and is our source of Vitamin C. We are being brought up to be as healthy as we can possibly be.

....

The new National Health Service is looking after us

One or two of my friends have ricketty legs, slightly bowed owing to malnourishment. The father of another friend is recovering from TB. And many children have grey rotting milk teeth. Despite these defects, most of us rollick around in Hay, apparently healthy enough as we play and go to school. What we do not understand, unlike our parents who have known pre-war health care and war-time privation, is that for the first time in history we children are being looked after regardless of the state of family finances. This is owing to our new National Health Service.

In July 1948, when we still lived in Hertfordshire, my parents, along with every other household in the United Kingdom, received a government leaflet in the post telling them about the new universal health care system.

"It will provide you with all medical, dental and nursing care. Everyone — rich or poor, man, woman or child — can use it or any part of it. There are no charges, except for a few special items. There are no insurance qualifications. But it is not a 'charity'. You are all paying for it, mainly as tax payers, and it will relieve your money worries in time of illness."[16]

My father is a Labour Party man, and approves of the new laws. Some of them had begun during the war, stimulated by the 1942 Beveridge Report which focussed on Want, Disease, Ignorance, Squalor and Idleness, all of which can still be found in 1950s Hay. But times are changing. Among other blessings has been the Family Allowances Act of 1945 of which our family is a beneficiary.

Even though there is still some evidence of malnutrition among people we know, things are improving. The 1941 Vitamin Welfare Scheme for children is still supplying children with the cod liver oil and orange juice which we take in our bath. With the National Health Service Act of 1946, our medical needs are being taken care of.

"Time to go to the clinic," my mother says, putting baby Stephen in the pram. She has washed and changed him to make the best impression. He is to have his weight and progress checked, and she will stock up on nourishing food supplements while she is there. The clinic is in the town council offices, at the bottom of the hill next to the clock tower. He passes all his tests and then she gets big round tins of National Dried Milk which is free for babies like Stephen, and the cod liver oil and orange juice for all of us. The dried milk is tasty, and we enjoy being given spoons of it when our mother prepares Stephen's bottles.

We can also use the town doctor's services without worrying about the cost. Several times, I have told my mother that my fingers feel funny.

"I have made an appointment with Dr Trumper," she says finally. She takes me down to the surgery in Market Square.

There is no appointment system, so we look around the waiting room to see who is before us.

"Bridget is a vegetarian," she tells the doctor. "And she eats nothing but bread and butter."

"Well, there is plenty of goodness in bread and butter," he tells us. "She is a healthy little girl, I can see that. But there could be a shortage of Vitamin B. I will give you a note that she must have Marmite, which you can get in the clinic."

From then onwards, at teatime, I spread the Marmite thinly on my bread and butter. I find it delicious, and I don't have funny fingers any more.

Thus, our National Health Service is providing us with foods containing vitamins A, B, C and D, milk at school for our general health and National Milk Powder for the babies. It will take a while for this good nutrition to fully penetrate the households of all my friends in Hay, but the steps are in the right direction.

....

The dentist

Tooth care is also ready for improvement. The connection between sugary food and tooth decay seems barely understood. All the children I know, myself included, are obsessed with sweets, and we love puddings and cakes. Home teeth cleaning is in its infancy. Many children have their smiles ruined by black rotting teeth. Although most of the damage at our age is in milk teeth, it can spread to permanent teeth if not corrected.

We line up at school when the dentist arrives. "Open wide," he says. One by one, our mouths are inspected, pick, poke, scratch. His report is passed on to parents who then can make appointments with their dentist who provides free treatment for children through the National Health Service.

My mother has not yet quite brought us to the point where our teeth are cleaned every night. She often gives us slices of apple in the afternoon, which she assures us clean our teeth. Then one report from the school dentist contains bad news.

"Helen, darling, this letter says that you need to have a tooth taken out," our mother says one day.

Helen doesn't like the sound of this.

"Mummy, I don't want to go. Why do I have to go?" she asks?

"Don't worry dear. The dentist won't hurt you. He will put you to sleep, and you won't feel a thing."

Put her to sleep? What does that mean?

Helen is taken to the surgery in a dark stone building in Lion Street. She is seated in the chair, and there are two canisters nearby containing gas. A big rubber mask appears in front of her face, and is placed over her nose and mouth. A swimming blurry feeling comes over her. When she wakes up, feeling sick and dizzy, the tooth has gone. As she goes home, her tongue feels the bloody gap in her mouth.

The procedure was probably worth it for her dental health in the long run. Helen was two years old when the National Health Service was established in 1948. At that time, around 75% of the adult population had no teeth of their own, and dental health in the UK was worse than in Germany which had lost the war. We children can't understand these things. All we know is our own discomfort. Among the millions of artificial teeth which were fitted after 1948 are those of my mother.

In her July diary, she writes:

Had toothache all morning, in the tooth next to the one I had out last month, and was half distracted. So I plucked up my courage, which ebbed exceeding low, and went to Mr Foster Fairy in the afternoon. He said there was an abscess and the tooth must come out, so out it came without much trouble. Now I have lost two front teeth and must have – horrors!!

Antibiotics are an expensive rarity in 1953, and root canal treatment which might have saved her the teeth is not yet a consideration.

By October, her mouth has healed sufficiently to collect the dental plate. "Horror of horrors!!" she writes. "I've always dreaded the thought of the thing, but contrary to usual experience it actually was even worse than the thought of it. I can't eat, can't talk and feel fifty. It seems odd that I can eat, talk and enjoy life minus two teeth, but plus two can do neither. It cost me two pounds, six shillings and thruppence which I could ill afford, but lucky I suppose to have it."

The money is nearly half of one week's housekeeping money, and she is thirty-two years of age.

....

My mother is ill

It is springtime, and my mother is sneezing, coughing and wheezing. As she prepares our bread and butter, she reaches out for her handkerchief, sneezes again, puts the food on the table and collapses into her chair.

Six young children eat their food tentatively. She is almost in tears, and gasping for breath. We watch her over the next few days. What do we do when our mother, the centre of our existence, our food, our bath time, our daily organiser, is falling around us?

She can't drop everything. We must be fed and got ready for school, and fed again. Then there is church to go to on Sunday which is a holy obligation. We are all reacting and sensing the withdrawal of authority. When she spends time in bed, "Johnnie took advantage of my absence by getting into every devilment imaginable and earned three beatings," she writes.

Johnnie was put over my father's knee and whacked, fortunately only through his clothes. Yet three times in one day seems excessive. What could he have done to warrant such a punishment?

Next day, she totters down to Dr Trumper's surgery. She has a strange set of symptoms. Partly it is hay fever which causes shortness of breath, but there are stomach and urinary infections.

The doctor tells her that rest is the only cure for the stomach disorder and she should come back to see him if she is not better soon. How can she rest? "Just managed to get through the day by resting frequently on the sofa." We active children see this as we run in and out. My mother, lying on the sofa? What is this?

She writes on Monday: "Did a bit of washing and ironed it."

On Tuesday, she can't eat, has breathing problems, and is coughing badly. Her urinary system is giving her trouble. By Wednesday, the doctor is summoned and he comes to the house. This is our National Health Service in operation: no decision has to be made about whether or not we can afford to pay. Our doctor is local and he can walk to his patients in the town.

When we girls come home from school, we learn that the doctor has diagnosed this strange illness which is called bronchitis, and she must stay in bed. She is delighted at the prospect. Nevertheless, we children and a husband are to be looked after, and the rallying-round of the neighbours begins.

First of all Mrs Prosser steps into the breach. She knows how our household works because she has been helping my mother with domestic tasks already, and is kind and reliable. She agrees to take the boys out in the afternoons, with baby Stephen in the pram and Johnnie and Richard alongside. We big girls can play around by ourselves after school. The doctor visits again on Thursday, and then, the same afternoon, is the time when I manage to get the nail into my leg while playing in Christine's garden.

My child's world is within my mother's, but it is far from its entirety. Writing her diary that evening, she records that while lying in bed she wrote a letter or two, glanced at magazines, looked at the pigeons on the roof and dozed. She then tacks on to the day's events one which was central to my own. "Great excitement when the boys came rushing home with garbled tale about Bridget having a nail in her leg and lots of blood, and was at the doctor's. The doctor dressed it and put in two stitches. Luckily, no ill-effects." My accident is only a small part of her day.

More lack of supervision results in Richard getting into mischief. On Friday, he breaks a huge pane of glass in the playroom window, an expensive calamity. She gets up to put the midday dinner on, but goes to bed afterwards. The doctor comes again that day, the third day in a row. He is pleased with her progress, but her temperature is still sub-normal. There is no mention of medication, and no definite diagnosis. Rest and support seem to be the remedy, while he keeps an eye on things.

The neighbours step in with feeding us. On Saturday, we watch my mother in her dressing gown making our midday dinner of omelette and chips. This is food I like. Mrs Jones the Clock Tower brings blackcurrants and white blancmange for our pudding, which my mother eats in bed.

That day, I have been invited to the Barnardo's party. I have a papier-mâché money box that was given out at school, to fill with pennies for the charity. My mother agrees that I may go by myself as I am nearly nine years old. The party is in a marquee in a field in Cusop, which is a village over the Dulas Brook, and hence in England.

"The winner of the children's money box collection is Bridget Ashton," says the announcer. "Please come and receive your prize."

I am so proud. Such a surprise is totally unexpected. I am presented with a box of Maltesers, malty chocolate-covered crunchy balls. A whole boxful, all for me. I've never had anything more than a sixpenny bar of chocolate to myself before.

While I am at the party, Mrs Prosser brings the boys home after their afternoon walk, and they all sit down for tea. Mrs Basil Watkins lives in a house a few yards from us. She brings the children a blancmange and jelly. This is all delightful, and later she even arrives with some ice-cream.

"Mrs Basil Watkins insisted on washing up," my mother writes, "and Helen helped her. Then Richard, Johnnie and Helen sang their songs for our visitor, and she stayed to bath them."

Mrs Biddle, our Catholic family friend, offers relief by taking Rosie home for the rest of the weekend.

142

On Sunday, we are excused from going to church because my mother is not well enough to attend. She is getting out of bed more though, and makes the dinner. Mrs Biddle brings Rosie home and supplements our meal with a blackcurrant tart.

Over the next week or so, her diary records that she improves slowly, with rests in the afternoon, food offerings from kind friends, and the invaluable assistance of Mrs Prosser. The entries do not include one mention of help from my father. It seems that a mother's illness is a woman's affair.

Old-fashioned ways have got us through. Neighbourly support, a little paid help from Mrs Prosser and the new care from the National Health Service doctor have helped the crisis to pass.

As for childbirth, during 1952 I had become used to seeing mothers with big bulging tummies. My mother and her friend Mrs Galsworthy of the clothes shop were both pregnant. The midwife delivered our little brother Stephen at home because home births are normal, and certainly what my mother wanted. After the birth, she and Mrs Galsworthy breastfed their babies, and we observed the course of nature as they sat and chatted in our house, first expressing drops of milk in a fountain across the room.

When Rose Jones, the sixteen-year old sister of my friend Christine, found herself in labour, she had been taken to Hereford to give birth. My mother's diary records: "Heard today that Rosie Jones had twin girls in Hereford hospital. What a situation for the poor girl!" But she wasn't left to struggle at home as might have happened before the National Health Service.

Dr Trumper sometimes gives advice that extends beyond medical matters. My mother's friend Mrs Dilys has a foster son. She records: "Mrs D took Bobby to Dr Trumper for a check-up. He said all he was in need of was a good hiding now and again!"

....

Measles

In 1950s Hay, we have all been vaccinated against smallpox and diphtheria, but everyone knows that children can catch any of a range of illnesses: measles, mumps, chicken pox, German measles, whooping cough and scarlet fever.

In 1953, measles is circulating in Hay, and comes to our family.

I am lying in my darkened bedroom, hot, sleepy, sweaty. I drop in and out of slumber in the silence of the room, the only sounds being the pigeons cooing on the roof outside. Helen is in her room nearby, also ill, and then I hear my mother come in.

"Just get out of the bed for a moment, dear," she says. I tumble dozily onto a chair while my mother takes off the sheets and pillowcase, throws them on the floor and carefully remakes the bed with fresh ones. I flop back into bed, feeling the cool cotton against my hot cheeks. I am comfortable and sleepy. This is not a painful illness. The skylight is covered over because measles is supposed to be bad for my eyes.

One of these days, I hear my mother's footsteps on the first set of stairs. She turns on the landing and then comes up the wooden stairs to our attic bedrooms. She is carrying a tray with a boiled egg and some bread and butter for me.

"Try to eat a little, dear," she says. Normally I love this food, but I can hardly make the effort to open my mouth. She encourages me with a spoonful of egg, and places a square of bread and butter in my mouth. I don't want any more. I want her to sit beside me and talk to me. I feel a little dejected because she doesn't stay more than a few moments. She goes to the next bedroom to attend to Helen, and then I hear her footsteps going back down the stairs.

Helen had the illness first, feeling hot and sticky. Her eyes were sore and her nose was running. Measles will run through all of us, and there is a constant record in my mother's diary:

Saturday 11 April: Helen developed measles this morning and Bridget followed her to bed later on. Went to see doctor who was not anxious to visit her but gave her some medicine.

Sunday 12 April: To Mass and Communion without the children – seemed strange. Helen very poorly indeed, B not so bad. She has no spots, so don't know if it is really measles at all.

Monday 14 April: Helen better, Bridget worse. Read several more chapters of the Fairchild Family to them which they both much enjoy and appreciate.

Wednesday 15 April: Bridget's rash came out today and she was very poorly all day – just lying flat with eyes shut, not even wanting stories. Had to feed her all day – not that she wanted much. I was exhausted after a huge wash including two double sheets off B's bed.

Thursday 16 April: Bridget very ill all day. Did not stir her head off the pillow and I had to feed her. What an exhausting day! I seemed to go up and down the stairs a hundred times! I'm so tired these days I drop asleep every evening in front of the fire, when I sit down.

Friday 17 April: Bridget a little better today much to my relief.

As we begin to feel better, we are sometimes treated with a comic or a glass of Lucozade. I am very happy to be presented with a Beano which has cost tuppence, and a drink of golden, fizzy pop:

Saturday 18 April: Rosie started measles this morning, with Richard an obvious runner-up. Packed Richard and baby up in the pram and went for a nice walk in the afternoon. Helen came, her first day out. Bridget got up for tea.

Sunday 19 April: To Mass and Communion, alone again.

On Wednesday, two-year-old Richard is being querulous. "Don't want it," he says when he is offered his breakfast. He won't play with his toys, and throws himself on the floor.

Next day, it is all too obvious. He won't stay in his bedroom, and threatens tantrums. He wants to be near his mummy. Rosie is in tears. We have a cosy velvet-covered chair, all floppy and misshapen, in our kitchen. "I want to come downstairs too," she says. Our mother gives in:

Thursday 23 April: Richard started measles in good earnest. His spots appeared today. He would not stay in bed so I made him a bed on the sofa in the kitchen and he stayed there all day sleeping and dozing. Rosie also on the armchair with strict orders not to move.

While we patients go through our various stages of the illness, Johnnie and baby Stephen are well. Although my mother has many nursing duties, she still cooks, cleans and entertains visitors around us. Father O'Reilly comes in for a chat on Wednesday and Father Brady, similarly, on Thursday of the second week, staying for an hour. She regularly takes the little ones out on afternoon visits down to the river, and on two occasions manages to go to the cinema in the evenings. Her friend Dilys visits several times, even staying once overnight. While ill, we are part-players in the complex drama of her life:

Friday 24 April: Another day wholly devoted to nursing, and another terrible night, in and out of bed all night. I gave the kitchen a good turnout and did a lot more washing. Richard still flat and no interest in anything much. Seemed to get a second wind by the evening and went to the cinema with Dilys. She stayed the night.

Saturday 25 April: Dilys departed at 6.15 am. Mercifully had a better night. Richard called twice, but John saw to him. Spent the afternoon ironing and baking – four lovely loaves.

"Let's all get up and go to church this morning," my mother says on Sunday 26 April, and Helen, Johnnie and I go with her. When we come home we are able to crunch more of my mother's delicious bread with our breakfast. Being observant Catholics, we have had nothing to eat before Mass.

The following day Helen and I are well enough to go back to school. Rosie is recovering, although Richard is still in bed:

Monday 27 April: Simply poured with rain all day, so didn't wash. Dismantled 'ward' instead. Took camp-bed back upstairs and put away all medicine bottles.

Wednesday 29 April: Richard got up this morning so we're nearly back to normal.

Measles has thus been working its way through Helen, me, Rosie and Richard for eighteen days from 11 to 29 April. We are fortunate that there are no long term ill effects and that our symptoms did not require visits from the doctor. He was there, though, if he had been needed.

Help is available for people with more serious ailments.

Our neighbour Mr Ottowell has an illness which requires him to go to hospital in Birmingham for a specialist operation. My mother has been helping with his meals while Mrs O goes to work. In July, he needed to return to the county hospital in Hereford.

"The ambulance came at 2 pm," my mother writes in her diary. "He didn't want to go, but alas, these things must be."

As the hospitals are in distant towns, we are fortunate that there is a personal ambulance service for people on low incomes, few of whom have private transport. The National Health Service, part of our post-war welfare state, is our background and our strength.

Pauper funeral

Sometimes when we are out on our walks, near the parish church of St Mary, we pass two high iron gates which lead to a building called Cockcroft House. Most people call it 'The Union'. It is an institution which has evolved from the workhouse, and it still houses some elderly people.

In July, my mother attends the funeral of an old Catholic man, Israel Pimrod:

Mrs Biddle and Mrs James were there too, and Clive Grant, assisting Father Brady. It always seems sad when one of those old people die, all alone with none of their own blood about them. Often they have been very self-respecting people in younger, happier days.

The Union is a surviving relic of an older more heartless way of living, pre-dating our welfare state and the National Health Service, which is there for all of us in 1950s Hay.

10 My Father the Beeman

"Special delivery, Mr Ashton," says the postman, knocking on the coloured glass window of our door. He hands us a package with a buzzing sound coming from inside. The postman has delivered these packages before addressed to Mr John Ashton, 3 Market Street, who everyone knows as Mr Ashton the Beeman, and he has learned not to be worried about the buzzing.

"What is it, Daddy?" we all ask, clambering around.

My father carefully unwraps the outer covers. Inside are a dozen small boxes, one inch by four lengthwise. Each box has a round opening in the middle with an air grid, and inside we can see the brown bodies and wings of moving live bees.

"Can you spot the queen?" he asks, as he shows us. "There she is, the big one," one of us has noticed. "That's right," he says. "The others are her worker bees, and their job is to look after her during the journey in the post to Hay."

"But aren't they hungry?" we ask.

"There is a little lump of sugar in each of the boxes," he tells us. "It is enough for them to eat until they get into their new home. Now I must put each of these queens and her helpers into a hive full of bees. The queen will lay lots of eggs, and so by the time the flowers are ready, there will be many workers ready to bring nectar in to the hive, and we will all get lots of honey!"

....

What does my father do?

My father is the most professional of beekeepers. From learning the craft in Norfolk during his wartime work as a conscientious objector, then to employment at Rothamsted Experimental Agricultural Station and moving his growing family to the Welsh borders, he now runs his own business from his workshop in Hay.

While my mother feeds and clothes and washes for the family, every morning after breakfast he goes two houses down the street to 1 Market Street. When we children go there, we immediately breathe the delicious smell of honey and beeswax. The workshop contains piles of wooden boxes and frames in various stages of construction, the metal extracting equipment and all the tools of the trade. The smoker too, a metal contraption with bellows in which rolled up cardboard is burned, adds its smell to the workshop. This is where he starts his day before going out to his hives in the spring and summer seasons, and where he does his bottling and carpentry at other times of the year.

"What does your father do?" We children are always asked this.

"He's a beekeeper," we say.

"A what?" We are used to the raised eyebrows. Our friends know about shopkeepers, teachers, farmers, public house and chip-shop owners, postmen, firemen, factory workers, engine drivers, doctors and nurses. Hardly anyone knows what a beekeeper does. How do we rank in the priority of professions? We are the children of the unknowable hard-to-define Beeman.

When he is out with his hives, the veil covering his head, clouds puffing out of the smoker, and lifting the frames covered with hundreds of moving bees, he is a wizard working his spells. At the end of the procedure, he produces red and gold-labelled jars bearing the dragon emblem of Wales and the product name, Ashton's Welsh Honey.

"Isn't he afraid of the bees? Doesn't he get stung?" people always ask us. He does get stung, but not enough to make a fuss. His bees are wild creatures and must be handled gently. By understanding their behaviour, he works along with them. When the weather is mild, and the bees are outside the hive collecting nectar, they are too busy to sting. This is when he goes into the hives with his smoker. Windy and rainy weather prevents the bees going outside. This is when the guard bees will be much more likely to attack and they are best left to themselves. If it is essential to go into the hive, to inspect them, or to remove the honey, he smokes them carefully, just enough to move them down into the lower brood chamber where the young ones are. If after all the precautions he does get stung, he doesn't panic. He quietly removes the sting from his skin, and gets on with the job.

We children often see a bee crawling out of his clothing. If this happens at mealtimes, we know that it will fly towards the window while heading for the light. We are used to this. We virtually never get stung ourselves.

When he comes home for his meals, he plunges into the domestic round with six active children and a tired woman who is often ready for some help and appreciation.

....

A big row

"How can you say that, John? How can you be so cruel?" An argument is brewing as we all sit round the table eating our dinner. I am struggling with cold mashed potatoes, with my father seated at the head of the table. We children observe the developing situation. My mother is really upset. As the words build up, she is so distraught that she throws a plate onto the floor. It smashes into pieces. Then she dashes, weeping, out of the room and up to her bedroom.

"Eat up your dinner," our father tells us, and we do our best, in silence. We older ones go back to school for the afternoon, and our father has to deal with clearing up the dinner and looking after the little ones until she comes downstairs. That evening, my mother writes in her diary that she flung herself onto her bed and fell asleep. "I suppose it is only this beastly flu," she writes after two more days of dinner time rows, "but John seems very unbearable at times, tho' I am bound to admit he means well."

What sense can children make of all this? We get on with our own activities, cautiously watching the grown-ups, and when the rows erupt, wait until calm is gradually restored.

....

Pussy willow

We are out on a Sunday afternoon walk, near the River Wye at Glasbury. My father is ahead of the rest of us as he usually is, and he is looking intently into a large bush covered with yellow flowery catkins. It is early in March, a couple of weeks before Easter.

"The bees are working the flowers," he says when we catch up. We know them as pussy willows, and we like to stroke their silky buds. He tells us about the pollen that they are collecting for their grubs, the word for the babies in the brood chambers of the hives. To my mother, the willow catkins are the flowers of Palm Sunday and she is not keen on the worm-like creatures in the beehive.

She sometimes says, "How can anyone like those cold-blooded creatures so much?"

But we learn that the pollen from the pussy willow is an important food for the new beekeeping season. The worker bees must bring in enough food so that a new generation of bees is ready for the summer and we will have honey. My father is in tune with the seasonal relationship between the insects and the flowers because it is his great interest and our livelihood. He reads books and has long conversations with other beekeepers on the minutiae of honeybee management. My mother reads poetry about the natural world, and writes some herself. They are both close to nature and yet there is a difference.

....

Politics and actions

My father is an activist. Having been a conscientious objector during the war, which led him to becoming a beekeeper, he keeps himself in touch with current affairs through newspapers, BBC news on the wireless and the publication Peace News. Unlike my mother, he has not left much written information about his opinions. We must look for clues in my mother's 1953 diary.

On 5 September, after a busy morning cleaning the attics, shopping and baking an apple and rhubarb tart, treacle tart and jam tart, my mother leaves my nine-year-old self in charge of baby Stephen while she takes Helen, Rosie, Johnnie and Richard to the cinema to see Jack in the Beanstalk. Those activities are her priorities. At the end of her diary entry, she records: "John went to Brecon to picket the Labour Exchange in company with several others – it was registration day for 16 to 17 year-olds. All went well."

Registration for what? Probably for the army, as national conscription was still in place, the Korean War being officially ended but with no peace treaty signed, and the Mau Mau and Malayan emergencies are ongoing.

Who were the 'several others'? He is a member of the local Labour Party, so perhaps he has colleagues there who share his views.

One other political comment makes sufficient impact to be recorded in my mother's diary: "Mr Tudor Watkins gave a Labour Party talk at 8 (in pouring rain) and I listened to it."

Tudor Watkins is the Labour MP for Brecon and Radnorshire at this time, and it seems likely that my father and mother are listening to the wireless in the sitting room while we children are tucked up in bed.

My father is not the kind of person to discuss his ideas with his children and we are very young. However, he likes to encourage us to be active, and to believe in possibilities.

I am reading a book called *Brownies at Number Seven*, and I am desperately keen to be a Brownie. There are no Girl Guides or Brownies in Hay, and I am not allowed to join the Girls' Friendly Society, the closest equivalent, because of its Protestant connections.

"Ask your teacher if she will start a Brownie group," my father advises. My friend Christine and I pluck up our courage and knock on the door of her house. We have grown beyond Miss Stephens' class a couple of years ago, and remember her as an approachable and friendly person.

"I am sorry, girls, but I really cannot do it. I don't know anything about Girl Guides and Brownies," she says. We are disappointed, but nothing has been lost by trying.

I am obsessed with cardboard cut-out dolls and their clothes. The back cover of one of our breakfast cereal boxes has a series of these dolls dressed in national costumes, and I have the Welsh one, a girl with a tall black hat surrounded by a white frill, red skirt and black cloak. I really want another, a different one.

"Daddy, I wish I could have another doll like this one," I mention one day.

"Then Bridget, why don't you write and tell the company that you would like one," he says. I do, but with no effect. Another time, I see errors in a drawing in Playhour magazine which is being read to my little sister and brothers.

"Write to the editor," he advises. I do this, explaining that the story is wrong, that badgers do not hibernate, and when he 'wakes to find the moon is new', the artist has drawn the new moon as a waning crescent. I am just learning about these things. I get a personal typed letter back from the editor explaining that badgers do sleep for long periods in the winter, and apologising for the mistake in the drawing.

Later, when we are planning to go to London for a holiday, I would like lots of information about things to do.

"Write to London Transport and ask them," he says. These are the days before telephones and tourist information offices.

"But I don't know the address," I say.

"Send a letter addressed to London Transport, London and it will probably get there," he says. I do this, and receive a bumper package full of exciting information.

What I find out is that it is always worth asking even if it doesn't produce the desired result. I can write a letter to some remote organisation and I may be gratified by a result. This is my father's attitude and this is what he teaches me.

....

Springtime

The delivery of the new queens is part of the springtime preparations. My father must ensure that his hives are at their strongest when the flowers come into bloom. Older weaker queen bees must be destroyed, and new ones who promise to be powerful layers put in their place. He must also control the hive from swarming, a May activity, or he will lose his worker bees.

During May and June, inexperienced beekeepers lose many swarms as the bees fly off to look for a new place. This is the normal way for bees to propagate. Often at this time, people come knocking at the door.

"Is Mr Ashton at home? There is a swarm in my garden. Can he come and take it away?" Sometimes he obliges.

"Come and look at this one with me, Bridget," he says. He takes me to a garden where a huge buzzing weight of bees is dangling from a branch. Swarming bees are unlikely to sting anyone. He is calm, and thus so am I. He places a wooden box under the branch and gives it a sharp knock. The swarm, which is surrounding the precious queen, drops into the box, which my father then covers. He has a small but potential new hive of bees.

More often, the swarm is in a roof or in a shed or some difficult place and he can't stop his work to deal with the problem. In any case, most swarms are temporary, and he tells the worried person that the bees will soon move away.

He must find good locations for his hives, places where the flowers are most productive. There is honey to be obtained from hawthorn, mixed hedgerow flowers, fruit trees in orchards and importantly from clover. In these days before widespread use of nitrogenous fertiliser, clover is widespread in pastures and grasslands. My father has a good relationship with local farmers. He is a countryman himself, and they talk weather and crops and animals. The farmers generally welcome his hives. They agree a suitable unused corner of a field, protected from strong winds, and my father will pay the farmers a honey rent in due course.

We are out in our van on a Sunday afternoon going for an excursion along the Brecon road. Five of us are rattling around in the rear, with Stephen on my mother's knee in front.

Suddenly, my father puts on the brakes.

"By Jove, look at that field," he says. It is full of brilliant yellow flowers. In 1950s, there are no fields of stark yellow oil seed rape flowers. Such a field is unusual enough to cause us all to get out and look.

"That is a field of charlock," he tells us. "It is a weed which has taken over the crop." Like all the plants in the cabbage family, it is good for honey bees. The yellow flowers have four petals in a cross-shape, which accounts for its Latin name of *Cruciferae.*

Charlock is one of the most troublesome weeds of cornfields, and its seeds can lie dormant in the soil for twelve years or longer until brought to the surface by ploughing. The farmer here may have got a real surprise when his cereal crop turned yellow like this. Being the children of a beekeeper, and a mother who teaches us about wild flowers, we are well-informed botanically.

....

Strict and sometimes funny

My father is the disciplinarian. When we are naughty, which is often enough, my mother may be so aggravated that we get a slap, usually on the leg, and it doesn't hurt very much. However, when our daddy slaps us, the sting is lasting and often we burst into tears. In our house, the boys sometimes get slippered rather than slapped, but severe punishments using canes or belts are never used.

Poor Johnny, our orphan foster-child, seems to get the worst of it. Certainly, he is often troublesome. In Hay in the 1950s, a good spanking is deemed to teach better ways. Odd how the word 'good' always precedes the action. A 'good hiding' was recommended by Dr Trumper to my mother's friend Mrs Dilys for her foster son.

One April day my mother records: "John vexed about poor Johnnie. I think he'd be glad to have him away from us. It makes my heart bleed to hear him speak so unkindly. I certainly feel these days a great desolation in my inmost heart. Every day, I think of the joy and peace of Heaven and wish I were there."

The spoken word can be as hurtful as the sharp slap. My father has left nothing in writing to explain his actions, and we must bear in mind that my sister Helen has a story where my mother was also unkind. Which parents are perfect?

They certainly do have rows, and they are often at mealtimes. "A row with John at dinner time – on the subject of children fussing over meals. Felt very fed up and slammed out for a walk all afternoon leaving dinner things unwashed. John took Richard to Brecon, so only had Stevie."

Which leaves the unanswered question about who cleaned up the kitchen and washed the dishes afterwards.

Sometimes I want a favour. I really need tuppence for a copy of *Sunny Stories* because the next episode in a serialised adventure in this children's magazine is tantalising me. But I don't have tuppence. I struggle with myself. Children are not allowed to ask for things. My father is in his bee workshop. I pluck up my courage "Daddy, please could you give me tuppence?" I venture.

"What do you need it for, Bridget?" he asks.

I explain as well as I can.

He umms and aahs. This is a serious request. He is not a man to answer quickly.

Eventually, he says, "Well, I suppose I will give it to you this time. But don't think you can come and ask me again!"

I take the two pennies and escape. We children know our place. My father is not to be treated lightly.

And yet, he is sometimes different – funny and friendly. We are all around the piano in our sitting room. My mother has us all singing her favourite songs from the Oxford Song Book, *Early One Morning, Oh No John, Mr John Blunt*, all her classics.

"Daddy, do your song," we all plead. "Do *Richard of Taunton Dean*."

If he is in the right mood, he puts on his best West Country accent, and starts:

One Zunday morn as Oi've heerd zay
Young Herchard he mounted his Dobbin Gray
 And over the hills he rode ameen
A-coortin the passon's daughter Jeeun
With my doombledum dollykin doombledum day

Our tall, handsome father relaxes his usual seriousness, and we all curl up with laughter hearing how Young Herchard tries to woo Miss Jeeun:

Fur Oi've a pig poked up in a stoi
As'll coom to us when Granny do doi
And if you'll consent fur to marry me now,
Whoi feyther he'll give us his voin vat zow
With my doombledum dollykin doombledum day

cannot resist his wonderful enticements and agrees to his proposal, so:

Whoi he gee'd her a kiss and her coom'd away.

From his West Country childhood, our daddy has an even better offering involving snuffles and snorts and whistles:

There was an old farmer who had an old sow –
Snort how, phew how, who piggledy how
Suzanna's a funny old man
Snort how, phew how, who piggledy how
Suzanna's a funny old man.

We can't often persuade him to do this one, which is his best party piece. Sometimes he can drag himself away from his beekeeping, forget his responsibilities to bring us up properly, and have some moments of sheer fun.

....

Summer

My father has an unpleasant shock in May. My mother's diary records:

Mr Ingold came yesterday from Harpenden to see John's bees. He finished his inspection today. Forty percent of the hives are infected. What a lot of terrible anxiety after all these long years of struggle! Heaven only knows what the end of the chapter will be.

Probably it was a bacterial infection of the larvae called foulbrood. Despite this unfortunate news, my father must have sorted out the condition in his hives. There is no further mention of it in my mother's diary for the rest of 1953.

During May and early June, he makes regular inspections of his hives. Wearing ex-army khaki dungarees, face covered by his veiled hat and using his smoker, he chooses sunny, wind-free days when the bees are busy bringing in pollen and nectar. When they are active, they are too absorbed to be upset by the intrusion. He takes the lid off the hive, placing it slowly down on the grass, being careful not to squash any bees. Gentle handling is the art, and will reduce the likelihood of stings. He puffs a little smoke onto the working bees, which causes them to drop lower down into the brood box.

He is looking for eggs and developing brood. If there is plenty of both, he knows the queen is laying well and the hive is in good condition. If the hive is weak, he will combine it with a stronger one. He checks the hives every nine days, and keeps regular records.

By late July, he is ready to remove the crop of clover honey.

This is one of his most important products, a creamy white honey holding the distinctive scent of the flower. He must first put bee escapes on top of the heavily laden frames so that the bees can get out, and then he can take off the honey harvest.

At the beginning of August, the hives are ready for the journey to the hills. He ensures there are plenty of empty frames ready to be filled with heather honey which is the beekeepers' gold.

This time is the annual migration of the beekeepers. The hive entrances must be closed up in the evening when all the bees have gone inside after their day's work, and lifted into the van. This is a hard, heavy job. After arriving on the heather hills, the hives are placed in the new site, the entrances opened ready for the morning when the bees will adjust to their changed location.

For the next two or three weeks, my father anxiously watches the weather. There must be the right balance of rain, sunshine and temperature, with no strong winds, for the heather flowers to secrete their nectar. Our livelihood depends upon these few days. Remarkably, my mother makes no mention about the weather in connection with the heather in her 1953 diary. Her mind is elsewhere. She records the water shortages and on 12 August that the weather was 86 degrees in Hay and 90 degrees in London.

When we have our family days out on Sundays, we children play in the fields while he inspects the hives to see how they are doing. He is focussing on his bees, while my mother has her entirely different thoughts as she watches over the activities of her own brood, her six children.

September harvest

When the heather flowering is finished, it is time to bring home the honey crop before returning the hives to their winter location.

Now the honey must be prepared for sale. Some of it is pressed from the comb, gently warmed and then strained before being bottled. The highest prices are earned from honey produced in sections. These are small wooden frames which the bees have filled with perfect honeycomb, sold complete. Managing the bees to produce honeycomb this way is a highly skilled procedure in which my father is an expert.

Appreciative gourmet customers enjoy the honeycomb, pollen, wax and all, as a delicious natural food. In our household, we get the out-of-shape oddments, which are scrunchy and sweet. The wax is almost as good as chewing gum.

One October Saturday, my father decides to take Johnnie with him to the bees. My mother writes: "John went off about eleven for the day, to collect more honey, and took Johnnie with him – the first time they've spent a day together." Our little foster brother would be safely veiled, watching the smoker and the bees being handled, something he is unlikely to forget.

Bridget goes to South Wales

"Eileen, I think Bridget is old enough to come with me to South Wales," my father says one day, and my mother agrees. This is a privilege indeed for me, the oldest daughter. My mother gives us a picnic tin full of sandwiches and homemade cake. We have a flask of tea for my father and a bottle of water for me.

The van is packed carefully with honey jars and sections with the red and gold labels bearing the red dragon of Wales and the ditty 'Ashton's Welsh Honey, Well Worth your Money'.

I am really excited. I sit in the front seat of our van, and we leave Hay, driving along the main road to Brecon. From there we head for the hills, and I know these are the Brecon Beacons. Up the steep slopes we go, and then, suddenly, my father stops the van.

"By Jove," he says. "I think that is a golden eagle." We gaze across the open landscape. Perhaps he is right, and in the 1950s, it is still possible to see such a rarity. I am proud that I have seen an eagle, and what is more, a golden one, the same colour as a queen's crown.

The drive seems to take a long time in the chuntering van. My father helps me to be good by offering me a barley sugar sweet from a paper bag in the glove compartment. I suck it happily, and when it is finished, I want another one. I can't stop thinking about it. Eventually, I say, "Daddy, please can I have another barley sugar?"

I know I am not allowed to ask for things. There is a long silence. "I suppose so," he says, "but don't ask again."

We pass over the uplands of the Brecon Beacons and then from there downhill to Merthyr Tydfil, the land of coal mines.

My father points out the rows of miners' houses lining the valley sides. This is where children like me live and go to school while their fathers are working underground in the black darkness. It is so different from Hay. I watch in surprise as big hanging baskets carrying slag move slowly along aerial wires. My father points out the huge pyramid-like heaps where the waste from the coal is going. The air and the buildings are a gloomy grey, but my father tells me that the miners earn good money, and they love to buy his honey.

We go from one shop to another. Usually, I am told to wait in the van, but one time I am allowed in. The shop is lined with well-stocked shelves, and the assistants behind the counter are serving the customers. When he has finished dealing with the manager, my father buys a big jar of cream.

"Your mother will like that," he says.

When all the honey is sold, he has a big wad of one pound and ten shilling notes in his wallet. He doesn't tell me how much of course. Now we make the journey back home, another 35 miles in our trundling van, over the uplands and down the other side. It seems to take a long time, but I have learned so much. I've eaten two barley sugars, seen a golden eagle, had a view of dark mining towns and met shopkeepers who love my father's honey. Now we are so rich that my father can afford to buy a big jar of cream.

Honey selling days are always important. In January, my mother had written:

John went out selling to S. Wales. I was glad to see him return safely, and with nearly £50.

In April:

John was off all day selling honey in S. Wales. He came in rolling with cash.

He nearly always brings some presents when he comes home, once some doughnuts, and another time wooden tops that spin by using a whip. These are the rewards of my father's work with the bees, and briefly, we are flush with money.

11 The Town is Our Playground

"Mrs Ashton, I am sorry to have to say this," said our neighbour Mrs Gwilliam. "But really the constant thumping by your children on our wall is intolerable."

Mr and Mrs Gwilliam run the haberdashery called Paris House, just down the steps in the alley from 3 Market Street. The back of the shop has a smooth wall, perfect for Helen and me who play Two-balls against it.

We are skilled jugglers, keeping the balls moving at a grand pace, one always moving through the air and one through the other hand, non-stop.

"One two three four five six seven," we go, to start the game. This is called 'sevensies' and is a straight throw at the wall which we catch on the rebound, one ball after another, at a rhythmic speed. 'Sixies' involves letting the balls bounce once on the ground while keeping up the speed; 'fivesies' lets the balls fall to the ground and be caught on the rebound; 'foursies' means throwing one ball onto the wall and letting the other drop to the ground; 'threesies' has alternate balls thrown straight at the wall and the other overhand, 'twosies' is where one ball goes into the air and one to the wall and One-Two-One is throw-bounce-throw at the very end. If the player gets through all that without dropping a ball, it is a great achievement.

We practice for hours, and there are many variations. But the thump thump thump, even with the small rubber balls is very annoying to the Gwilliams whose living quarters are behind their shop.

"I am very sorry about this," our mother says, "but I really don't think I can forbid the girls playing their game. Perhaps we can say that they should stop after teatime, so that it is quiet for you in the evening."

....

Around our house

The streets around the house are our playground. We are inventive children, and with a few toys such as balls, sticks, planks and a piece of rope, we can always find games to play.

The square, in front of the castle but just outside its ancient boundary walls, is a good open space to play, with few parked cars. Kicking a ball around, and catching it, or batting it with a piece of wood occupies us for hours.

Market Street runs out of the square between the arches of the council building and the former market tavern where our frightening neighbour Mrs Jones lives. She peeps out of her dusty windows as we play in the square.

If we go out of the back door of our house, we come to some garages and a yard. The wall surrounding the castle is right there, just a bit too high for us to climb, which is a shame because my friend Gillian lives somewhere up there. The back entrance to my father's workshop is here, often with bees buzzing around, so we must be careful. There are endless possibilities for play. When our daddy is busy in his workshop, my brothers might get hold of some wood and an old chair and make a seesaw.

Here, Helen and I practise our skipping skills with single pieces of rope, skippety tip, skippety tip, round and round we go. 'Salt mustard vinegar pepper', speeding up faster and faster until we trip and have to start again.

Sometimes we get hold of a piece of chalk, or otherwise we find a stone with which we can draw a mark. This is for hopscotch. We find a smooth piece of tarmac to draw the shape. There are two patterns, one a simple rectangle divided into six numbered squares, and the other is a one-two-one-two-one-two-one pattern of seven squares. We slide a flat stone into the first square to do 'onesie', and hop from one square to another, not standing on any lines, and picking up the stone on the way back. It gets harder and harder to slide the stone into the right square as we progress to 'twosies', 'threesies' and all the way to 'sixies' and 'sevensies'. We girls are the hopscotch experts, but boys sometimes ask if they may join in.

Cardboard masks are a source of excitement, Rosie screams as I chase her along the street. Kellogg's Corn Flakes boxes have big flat sides, and masks of skeletons, monsters and fairies can be cut out and some elastic threaded through so that I can scare my little brothers and sisters.

At one time, Helen and I find some buttons which have the word CD imprinted on them. We decide the letters stand for Club Detectives. Civil Defence is beyond our knowledge.

They make good badges, and we have secret meetings in my attic bedroom. We make rules and write messages. There is a cupboard with a hidden shelf above it upon which we can put our private papers. No grown-ups know about it. But one day, we have a visitor staying with his son and his friend, and I foolishly share the secret. The boys take out our papers and spread them around, laughing at these silly girls. I have been betrayed and I burst into tears.

"What is the matter, Bridget?" says my startled father. I tell him the wrong that has been done to me.

"Never mind, dear," he says. He has a good reason to be sympathetic because one of the boys is the son of my mother's friend James. "Would you feel better if you have an ice cream?"

I am astonished. Such suggestions are rare in my life. Of course I would. So I take my fourpence and go off to buy a Walls ice cream sandwiched between two wafers.

It is always sunny while we play outside in Hay. But one winter morning it had snowed overnight, and I write a story at school about how dark my bedroom is with the snow covering the skylight. While we were at school, our daddy went into his workshop and built a sledge for us. The Tumpy Field is near the church, which is the motte of Hay's earliest timber castle, and it makes a grand sledging site. The big children whizz down and throw themselves off before they fall into the stream at the bottom.

....

A busy girl

My mother has given me her deceased brother Richard's stamp collection. This is much more developed than my own simple paper album to which I am very attached. My version has the name of each country at the top of the page and the population of its capital city. This is one way to learn about the outside world, and I am an avid collector. My mother has a small international correspondence, and I am allowed to remove stamps from her letters. With my pocket money, I sometimes send away to Stanley Gibbons for a small packet of stamps from their catalogue. I have King George VI stamps from the post that came in to our house from the days before his death in 1952. Then in 1953 appear some double-sized coronation stamps, the tuppence-ha'penny red, the threepenny green, the fourpenny blue and the sixpenny grey. The national emblems of the rose, thistle, daffodil and shamrock represent the four nations of our kingdom, and are decoratively arranged around our queen, who is wearing her crown.

The British Empire stamps all have a picture of our pretty queen in the corner. They show engravings of people in those faraway lands, all waiting to be explored by me when I am grown up.

I can spend hours swapping with my sister Helen and my friend Christine, having long debates about the virtues of each stamp.

My uncle, who died in 1944 in Thailand, had a collection arranged in a smart cardboard album which my mother has handed over to me unperturbedly. I unstick his stamps and put them into my album. I am impressed with the penny red stamps of Queen Victoria, and others from the next king, her son King Edward VII. There are the pre-war stamps of King George V showing his lively, up-curling moustache. I have many labelled Deutsches Reich in a range of colours and prices. They bear the face of Adolf Hitler with his tight, short moustache, a slight smile on his face which is engraved to make him look handsome. I know nothing much about him except that he was our enemy.

King George VI appears handsome to me too, with his clean-shaven face, hair parted and upturned. My uncle's collection also included stamps from the brief time of Edward VIII's reign, showing his sleek, sleazy profile. I unstick and re-stick all these rare stamps without a thought in the world, and not a murmur from my mother.

I also collect paper cut-out dolls. The doll itself is made of cardboard, and has to be cut out with scissors from a booklet. Her coloured clothes are made from paper, and they have little paper pegs which must be folded over her shoulders to keep them in place. I choose what outfit she will wear according to the stories I am making up. I arrange all my dolls in rows according to size, as though they are children in school classes. Some are boys, but most are of girls, whose clothes are brightly coloured and more interesting.

At one point, I am being taken shopping by the wife of one of my father's beekeeper friends, and I see a booklet with a paper cutout doll on the front. She is bigger than any of my existing dolls, and I immediately covet her. Dare I ask? I decide to try.

164

"Mrs Sturdy, please would you buy that doll for me?" I ask. Such a request is considered an impertinence, but after a mild reprimand, she buys it for me. I call her Peggy, after Mrs Sturdy's daughter, and she is always at the top end of my lines of dolls.

"Why don't you children go outside to play? It is such a lovely day, and here you are mooching around the house," our mother often says. But I am happy for hours, cutting, sticking, and making up my own stories with my stamps and my paper dolls. Dreams are created inside the house as well as outside.

....

Not fit for adults

Not all our games are fit to be seen by adults. When we wander a little further from home, we can get up to mischief. On a rough green area down by the Dulas Brook there are some very old-fashioned houses, and there is a primitive outdoor lavatory.

A naughty girl of my acquaintance has found some soiled toilet paper. She waves it around, chasing after us, calling out 'cahhy, cahhy', while we run off shrieking. Without realising it, I am learning a Welsh word. Decades later, I check the spelling and realise it is 'cachu, cachu' and what it means. An odd relic of Welsh survives in our childish culture.

Then there is the Cwm Mawr, some fields behind the castle, which everyone knows is called the Coomoors. It doesn't occur to us that this is a Welsh name which means a large valley. It is just a field where we can go and play, and we do.

There are a few bushes clustered around with elderberries to be picked.

"We'll play doctors," says an older more experienced girl. We do naughty things behind the bushes. This is definitely a girls-only game, and without a word being said, we know we will not tell our parents.

....

Are we safe?

We are very free children with little sense of danger. But after the school holidays, we return to find that our playground has been painted out with a set of white roads complete with junctions and safe crossing points. Schools are aware of a new danger.

"We are going to learn about road safety," our teacher informs us. We are trained in how to cross the road:

At the kerb, Halt.
Look Right.
Look Left.
Look Right again.
If all clear, Quick March.

A day is arranged when those of us who have bikes or scooters or prams, or anything on wheels, can bring them to school. I come with my toy pram, inherited from my mother's childhood. It is a deep, brown old-fashioned design, and I have my Victorian china dolly inside. I become aware, as we wheel our vehicles around the new roads, that my friends have new brightly coloured prams with gaudy covers, and their dollies have pink plastic heads and blonde curls. They have clearly been paid for with money and hence are superior to my antique toys.

Another danger is caused by bad weather. After some heavy rain, the river is filled with brown, surging floodwater. Those boys who betrayed my trust are staying with us.

"Let's go to the river and make a raft," they say. We take some rope down to the river where we find some broken pieces of tree branches and tie them together, making something which to us resembles a raft. When we put it on the water, the river begins to pull it away.

"Hang on to the rope," one of the boys says. "I'm trying to get on."

But the raft swings around and is uncontrollable. After a while, the rope escapes our hands and the raft disappears.

"Where have you been?" the grownups ask us when we get home.

"Down at the river. We made a raft, but we couldn't get on it."

They are aghast.

"You mean to say you tried to make a raft on the river when it was flooding!" my mother says, pale with anxiety, but also with relief. These boys and their father are guests in our house. "You could have been swept away and drowned!"

166

Another episode is more sinister. I am playing in our back lane when a red Royal Mail van pulls up.

"Hello. Would you like a ride in my van?" the young postman asks me.

Of course I would, and I get into the front seat. No-one sees. He drives out of town towards Cusop. When we are in a quiet spot, he parks, telling me he has an itch, and asks me to do something improper. I have no reason other than to oblige.

Somehow, he pulls himself together and realises what he's up to. Not having laid a finger on me, he tidies up his clothes and we drive on, parking at every letterbox where he takes out the letters. As we return to town, he tells me to duck down so that no-one can see me. He explains that he will get into trouble if he gives people rides, and so I should not tell my parents. I don't.

The lanes and villages around Hay are there for us to explore in our more adventurous moments.

My mother's friend, Mrs Dilys, lives at Forest Farm, a mile or two away up a beautiful valley towards the Black Mountains.

"Let the girls walk home with me," Mrs Dilys asks my mother one fine May afternoon. She agrees, and Helen and I go to her house where she gives us delicious food. We are enjoying ourselves and eventually she sends us on our way home. We can play along the way, and we take our time.

We find a field where we can have a game of hide and seek. First Helen covers her eyes while I hide myself among the tall grasses, and I call out, "Ready!" When Helen finds me, I cover my eyes while she hides.

We are having a happy game until a loud voice yells, "What are you doing? Stop that this minute!" Fearfully, we look up at the angry farmer whose hay we are spoiling, before escaping away from his wrath. We feel indignant. How are we to know that this is special grass? It is still a little way to walk. Darkness begins to fall.

"Girls, it is nine o'clock. How dare you come home so late!" my mother cries when we enter the house. She sends us straight to bed without our supper of cocoa and biscuits.

....

In later years

A decade later, when I am in Hay staying with my friends, we often see the erring postman whom I easily recognise. He lives a normal life in the community. We compose a ditty which we sing to a calypso rhythm:

Never trust a postman
Never trust a postman
He'll always do whatever he can
So never trust a postman.

On the bus

In spring, the wild daffodils are flowering in the Herefordshire orchards. These are real, big golden flowers. My mother often buys produce from the 'Lady from Dorstone' when she is on her selling rounds in Hay. The lady tells us that we may go to her orchard and pick as many as we want. With Lorraine who lives next door, Helen, Rosie and I are allowed to take the bus to Dorstone which is six or so miles from Hay, in England.

We play around among the apple trees with their pinkish-white blossoms, semi-wild daffodils in profusion under our feet. We pluck and pick and bunch the flowers, and revel so much in the green spring freedom that we miss the bus home. There is no-one at the bus stop. We are abandoned. Our heaps of daffodils begin to wilt in our fingers. The kind woman sees our tearful faces, and takes us into her house. We will have to wait there for the next bus. Our parents will worry and wonder where we are, but there is nothing to be done.

"Would you like me to make you some cocoa?" she asks. We love cocoa, but when she brings it to us, it is dark and watery, not sugary and milky as my mother makes it. Dark cocoa and daffodils and missing the bus at Dorstone – the drama of our day.

This is all put down to experience, and we are allowed to use the buses again. On the last day of the summer holidays, our mother arranges that Helen, Rosie and I will take the 9.25 am bus to Whitney to spend the day with Mrs Biddle, our Catechism teacher. She takes us out to pick blackberries which my mother will bake into a tart for us, a treat for when we come home from our first day back at school.

....

Expedition to Whitney

My mother records nonchalantly in her diary: "Bridget, Helen and Lorraine walked the four miles to Whitney after dinner and came home on the train, which they thought great fun."

This is a serious expedition. Lorraine is considered old enough to supervise us. She is eleven years old, I am nine and Helen is seven.

We set off along the country road to Whitney which runs parallel to the railway line, the River Wye on our left. There is not much traffic and we are able to hear cars coming well ahead of time.

We pass an empty house, the windows bare of curtains, and the garden full of overgrown flowers and weeds. We peep through the spidery dark windows and we are sure we see a creepy old woman disappearing from one room to another. "That's Aunt Aggie," we say to each other, giggling nervously. She is a kind of witch, or perhaps Desperate Dan's auntie from our Dandy comic.

Near here is a sign which says 'Hay on Wye 1 mile'. I look back, picturing how far it is, and how long it has taken us. Three more of this length ahead of us, this becomes my standard mile now and in the future. It is a long way for young children.

We are slowing down, and there is a train to catch. At last, we come to the bridge over the River Wye, just before Whitney. On the other side of the river, the autumn colours of Whitney Wood face us, beyond the station. First, we cross the toll bridge. We can see the river below us through the railings of the bridge.

Mr Stanton, the red-faced toll-keeper, comes out of the tollhouse. A board shows charges for all the animals, vehicles and people who want to cross.[17]

Mr Stanton must open the gate for cars and animals, and hand out the ticket for the return journey. There is no charge for children, and he waves us on our way.

When we reach Whitney Station, Lorraine pays for three half fares to Hay at the ticket office. The train comes steaming in, and we clamber up to our compartment feeling very grown up. We cross the Wye on the railway bridge and soon we are back in Hay.

The quiet on the country roads, the toll bridge and the steam train, the wild daffodils in the apple orchards, the raft on the flooding river, walking in twilight along country lanes, and the dangers closer to home in the streets of the market town.

Were we safe? Probably, our parents were so busy that they were hoping for the best. They had no time to supervise our every move and understood that there is always an element of danger. Thus, we rambled and played in the streets of Hay and in the surrounding countryside, with the freedom of children in the 1950s.

12 Mother Nature

"Come on children. It is such a lovely day we'll go down to the river and commune with Mother Nature," my mother says.

Rosie is very excited. She knows who Mother Nature is.

She has seen pictures in art books of a naked lady, and has no doubts.

Baby Stephen is piled into the pushchair among buckets and spades, with a picnic in the basket behind. Off we go, down The Pavement to Market Square, and past the clock tower. We make our way along Bridge Street, past the Crown Hotel, and turn left down to the iron bridge that crosses the River Wye.

On the other side of the bridge is a gate and a path that leads down through the trees to the riverside.

Rosie is looking out all the time as we go through the trees. Mother Nature is surely hiding behind one of them. She looks this way and that, quietly, and then she glimpses the naked figure silently slipping away from view. Running to catch up the rest of us, who are on our way to the sandy beach, she will always know that this is the place to see Mother Nature, in the trees beside the river.

....

Town walks

The sandy beach is a favourite spot. River sand is like seaside sand, and almost as diggable, allowing us to make sandcastles and channels to fill with water. This is educational, this is the way to bring up children and this is where my mother takes us on many a sunny afternoon. She trained in the Rudolph Steiner School before she was married, and knows that children need to learn among the basic material of the earth.

Her friend from the Netherlands, Mrs Galsworthy, often meets us here, with her two children, Jeannette and a baby of the same age as Stephen. "Mrs

Galsworthy is the only mother in Hay besides me who takes her children out for walks," we hear my mother say sometimes.

Between St Mary's church and the Tumpy Field is a path which leads to the Bailey Walk. Turning right takes us along a path with a steep drop to the river. Down there, some older children have made a house. Helen and I scramble down.

They have made seats and a roof of branches. They also have some pieces of broken china, and wood scraps for seats. We are allowed to look but not to join them as they don't know us. We would really like to have a house like that.

"Come on girls," my mother calls. "Don't drag behind." Don't drag. That is always being said. The path ends near the station.

In the summer, we turn left instead and head for The Warren. Here is shallow water with pebbly beaches. We try to skim stones, making them bounce on the water, and sometimes we are successful. "Did you see that?" I would say with confidence, but the others usually look too late. We have fishing nets and jam jars. It is not easy to catch tiddlers, and my mother sitting on the bank and watching Stephen is too tired to help. Bigger boys and girls from the town are more successful than we are. We paddle, fall in, get wet and cold and have our picnic.

There is bracken on the bank, and we can play Indians, hiding among the fronds. The Warren is a place where Helen and I and our friends can come by ourselves as we grow up: stones, water, fish, undergrowth to hide in and freedom.

Our parents sometimes take us on a walk to the hamlet of Cusop. This means that we cross the Dulas Brook into England. There is a bridge over the brook, with a steep drop down on the left hand side. My mother doesn't look too closely as I walk along the wall of the bridge. She doesn't say, "Don't do that, Bridget, you might fall!" This is a lesson I learn from her, that I should have confidence, and not be negative and fearful.

But sometimes this attitude shocks people. Once along this walk, I am up a tree, as I often am, while my parents walk ahead. Roddy's mother is walking by, and she sees where I am. "Mr Ashton, Mrs Ashton – one of your children is up in that tree!" she exclaims.

Her intention to be helpful is met with indifference by my father. "If she has got up the tree, then she can find her way down," he says, and doesn't bother to go back to help. This is an oft-told story about the Beeman's family in Roddy's household.

There are many places a family can go to freely. One time my mother wrote that she sat in the Coomoors with our baby, resting in the sunshine and enjoying the golden buttercups. We cross the Coomoors when we go to the woods collecting ivy and holly for our Advent ring or moss for the Easter Garden.

One winter the floodwaters collect there and freeze, making an ice rink for all the town's children to slide on.

Often my mother takes us walking part of the way home with Mrs Dilys who lives at Forest Farm, a good mile uphill towards the Black Mountains. Her friend is a business woman who runs a guest house at her farm overlooking a wooded valley, and she has horses. She doesn't have a car or a van, and so whenever she comes into Hay, she rides downhill on her bicycle. It is a long hard push back up with her shopping hanging off the handlebars.

Then there is Mouse Castle, a little way out of town on the country road towards Hereford, in England. The meaning of the name is lost to us. Perhaps it is a deviation from Welsh, and perhaps it is a prehistoric hill fort. Our parents discuss this, but they haven't an obvious answer. Thus, for my sisters and brothers and me, it is a castle for mice. As we walk in that direction one day, baby Stephen in the pram as usual, a woman with long dark hair comes towards us. She is wearing red knee-length socks. My mother exchanges compliments with her, and afterwards we are told that she is Egyptian. Thus, I learn that red socks are a mark of an Egyptian woman.

On the approach to Mouse Castle, we might take a left turn and wind back into town past the timber yard where Italian former prisoners of war are still working. This way brings us out at the station where we cross the brook and turn back into Wales.

Sometimes, our walks are longer, especially on a Sunday. Llanthomas is two miles each way from our house. We learn that 'Llan' is a Welsh word for a holy place, usually a church, so the place is the church of Saint Thomas. We are cautioned that it is not a Catholic church, but it is holy enough for a Sunday outing. On the way there is a smooth bark-free fallen tree which we christen the Llanigon Log, and here we stop for a snack and a game.

Or we may walk to Clifford woods where there is a ruined castle built by a conquering French-speaking lord in ancient days. It is three miles there and back. In her diary, my mother writes: "The girls gathered primroses and violets, and we found wood anemone and butterbur, the first time this year. And lady's smock, almost out."

And yet, my mother is often sad.

One mild day in February, there are outbursts and tears at midday dinner time as often happens. We older children go back to school and my father returns to his workshop:

I went for a walk, just baby and me. It was a glorious sunny day – blue sky, warm sun. Went up the Clyro road, then turned round and looked at little Hay, shut in by its mountains. When one goes outside the house, everything seems to fall into its true proportions.

There are many walks like this with baby Stephen and Richard who in 1953 is three years old, and too young for school. One day in October, she writes: "It was such beautiful day, dropped everything and took the boys for a long walk along the Clifford road. One of those perfect autumn days – everything so beautiful."

On these walks, Stephen is facing my mother in the pram, while Richard is perched in front because the distances are too long for him to walk for much of the time. Although my mother does not often write in her diary about conversations with her children, when she takes the boys on walks she has time to talk to them. They are facing her, and smiling and perhaps singing little ditties together. They will stop somewhere to have a snack. In the lanes and countryside around our town, her little boys have her all to themselves. But the greatest excitement of all is right in the centre of town.

"We'll go down to see the 'choo choo' trains," my mother says on many an afternoon. At about four o'clock every day, the steam trains come in to Hay station. Stephen is put in the pushchair, with Richard alongside. Often Johnnie, Rosie, Helen and I go too. We stand on the road bridge which goes over the railway line and from there, we can see the station.

First, the train from Brecon comes steaming in from our left. Choo – choo – choo – choo. The clouds of steam cover us as it goes under the bridge. Richard shrieks with terror and delight as we run excitedly over the road to see the steaming engine with its three purple carriages come out under the other side of the bridge. It halts at the station, and the girls and boys from the Brecon grammar schools climb down. The train can't leave yet, though, because this is a one-line track. Soon the train from Hereford steams in from the other direction. At the station, the line diverges into two, with a platform on each side and a bridge connecting them. The trains are now side-by-side on the tracks. We watch the Hereford passengers alight.

Then, choo – choo – choo – choo, the engine comes steaming towards us on its way to Brecon. It goes under the bridge and we are briefly lost once again in the steam, rushing madly to see it come out on the other side. This is the best time of the day for Richard and Stephen, and we big ones love it too.

I am looking at the steam and the smoke. I ask, "Mummy, where does the smoke go?"

"Oh, I don't know, dear. It just disappears into the air," she says.

And that is what I think for many a year. It simply disappears. It turns into nothing.

One October Sunday, my father agrees to stay home with Stephen and Richard so that we can go along footpaths without the pushchair. We cross the bridge over the River Wye.

There is a wall with a doorway. "This is the way to Fairy Castle," my mother tells us. Helen is entranced. We discover a beautiful flower, like a pansy, yellow and purple. The sight of it fills Helen with joy, and she learns that it is called heartsease, the name of a plant to repair troubles and pain.

Next, we find a magical tree. It is huge and spreading, near the river edge.

"Look at this, children," says my mother in wonder. "It is a willow tree – it is hollow, and a sycamore tree is growing out of the middle of it." We can see that she is right, and her delight infects us.

We come to Fisherman's Reach. We have often seen men wearing long waterproof leggings with fishing lines wading in the river. Now we are close to two men and their rods, with a large dead salmon lying on the grass. Even though we like to eat fish, this is disturbing.

My mother's diary describes the day: "Heavenly walk with four older children past the Fairy Castle and Fisherman's Reach, along the river bank towards Llowes. Discovered a lovely spot which we christened 'The Glade of King Willow', and farther on a little pebbly beach ideal for bathing in the summer. I climbed two trees, and felt very supple and youthful."

Sometimes we go along Cemetery Lane, which has mossy flowery banks. It leads past the town cemetery, and further on towards the town reservoir. Along the way, we come to a house with what my mother calls an 'overgrown garden'.

Rambling roses struggle up amid big white daisies, marigolds, blue delphiniums and brambles, all winding around each other in a disorderly way. 'Overgrown' has storybook possibilities as in Francis Hodgson Burnet's *The*

Secret Garden, a book which our mother reads to us. It implies an impressionistic whirl of colour, and the word embeds itself in our minds.

On this occasion, my mother is pushing Stephen in the pram, and along with our family are Lorraine and Peter from next door and my friend Gillian Coombes. Our mother often allows our friends and neighbouring children to join her expeditions. She seems to enjoy a sort of Nature School.

Richard who is not yet three is the youngest of those running around. We are playing in a roadside brook when his chunky little legs lose balance. He tumbles in the water 'with an awful crash and got very wet, so wrapped him up in a pram blanket and hurried home'. Thus, he has earned a special mention in my mother's diary.

We are just settling down for a picnic by a stream one day.

Suddenly, a herd of bulls comes charging towards us, heads down, tails up, hooves thundering. "Run children – run!" our mother shouts, grabbing up Stephen, and in terror we flee towards the gate, leaping over at a rate never known before.

"John, we were charged by a herd of bulls," she tells my father when we are safely home.

"Don't be silly, Eileen," he responds. "Bulls don't come in herds. They were just excitable bullocks. They wouldn't hurt you." But of course we know my mother is right. Bulls they definitely were.

As we get older, we will grumble: "Oh no. Not another walk. Do I have to go? Can I stay at home?" But once we get out, we often see wonderful things, and on an August Sunday in 1953, we encounter a relic of disappearing days. Up the Clyro road is a field which has just been harvested. The stalks of wheat have been cut, tied into bundles and made into stooks which stand evenly spaced out in the field. This ancient harvesting system seems specially designed for us to have an exciting game of hide-and-seek. We play for hours. It may be the last time I shall see such a field in my own country.

....

In the countryside

When we were fairly new in Hay, in 1951, and our little brother Richard was the one-year old baby, my mother wrote the short final entry in the nature notebook which she had kept since 1943. We were visiting Ireland, a farm in a remote corner of Radnorshire, near Painscastle. My father was driving, baby Richard was on my mother's knee in front, and Helen, Rosie and I were squeezed together behind on the side-to-side swinging seat that my father has ingeniously constructed in the van.

'Jim the Ireland' is the name of a farmer that my father has come to see while looking for sites for his beehives. This farm is along a distant lane where some of the old people distrust modern ways. Even into the 1960s, the story goes that one old lady would only switch on her electric light so that she could see to light the candles, after which she turned it off.

My mother notes what she sees as we tumble around in the fields at Ireland farm: cross-leaved heath, bog pimpernel, cotton grass and sheep's bit. We will learn these less well-known plants in due course. In the meantime, we are learning everyday flowers: celandines and buttercups, dandelions and daisies, violets and bluebells, herb robert and stitchwort, and that the great big butterbur leaves are so-called because you can wrap up a pound of butter in them.

On Sundays, my father is usually prepared to take us further afield in his van. We have been to Mass, had our Sunday dinner, and the dishes are washed. The discussions start.

Where shall we go? Hay has so many appealing places nearby for adventures.

"Let's go to the Brickyard today," my mother says, and we jump up and down enthusiastically. On Stephen's first birthday in July, the bracken is high and the grass-covered bumps and hillocks from historic workings create good hidey-holes for hide-and-seek. In celebration of Stephen's birthday, my father puts a film in his camera.

And there begins the problem! One of the boys decides he needs to do his 'hardwork' among the bracken, and thinking this will make an amusing photograph, my father picks up the camera.

"John, whatever are you doing that for?" my mother cries, quite horrified. But she is too late. "You must take the film out of the camera and destroy it!"

My father refuses and thinks this is very funny.

"But John, the photographers will see the picture. We can't let them see it," she remonstrates.

We children are watching this scene. Mrs Jones the Photographs is a friend of my mother's and films are processed locally. My father is unrepentant. He takes other photos that day, and even persuades my mother to pose with all of us around her.

The film is processed, and when the pictures come home, we all manage to see the offending one. It doesn't survive into the album, and to my mother's permanent embarrassment, Mrs Jones the Photographs will certainly have seen it.

The Black Mountains are nearby, long green hills, beyond Mrs Dilys' New Forest Farm. When we go there, my father likes to build us a fire. We are lucky because not many of the fathers of our friends would do that sort of thing.

There is a remote school in the Black Mountains where one of my mother's Catholic friends is the headmistress. She and her helper are always called 'Miss Chappell and Katsie' in our household. Her pupils are children of farm families who live in the remote countryside. One day just before the end of the school summer holidays, our parents decide on the spur of the moment to have a long day out. We start by visiting the school at Capel y Ffin.

We are all standing outside the school with Miss Chappell and Katsie, and my father takes a photograph. "What a wonderful view," my parents exclaim as they look over the valley to the hills beyond.

"What is a view?" I ask. I can't see what they are talking about. To me it is the usual sort of thing, lots of fields and stone walls. Now I am presented with a new idea. For the first time, I am considering a landscape.

"We visited the Monastery where we were very kindly welcomed by Mrs Williams and shown around," my mother writes. "Father O'Reilley and some of his boy scouts were camping below so we visited them too. Next, we went to Llanthony and saw the ruins – then to Abergavenny and Crickhowell. We had tea by the river – a perfectly beautiful stone bridge, and so home at 6.30."

For a family of children who live in the little town of Hay, this has been a wondrous excursion. There are others. We go to Llangorse Lake where we watch the sailing boats; to Whitney where we help with a garden fete; and make regular visits to our favourite Brickyard. Harry Avery and Mrs Annison had bought our former home at Top o' Lane, and we visit them, where we are treated to bread spread with butter which is unforgettably white and made from goats' milk.

Mother Nature and my mother are mixed together in my sisters' and my girlhood minds. Wherever we go, she is aware of the flowers and plants and she teaches them to us. She shows us the different trees, and where she knows them the names of birds. Going for walks with my mother is our education. She and Mother Nature are our teachers.

She teaches us that mud is not the same as dirt, and that red berries are not wicked and poisonous but must be treated with caution. Nettle stings are not to be feared but soothed with rubbings from dock leaves which mysteriously are always found nearby. We nibble the three-part leaves of wood sorrel and young hawthorn leaves. Hazel nuts and field mushrooms can be collected and eaten. And if my father is around, we learn which plants provide pollen and nectar for the bees so that they can produce our honey. In this, we are doubly blessed.

13 Hay Before the Bookshops

"Richard, show me the lady in the red dress!" our mother says. Richard points to the illustration on the front page of the magazine.

"Good boy! Now Johnnie, show me the yellow hat!" she continues, and then to Rosie: "Where is the washing machine?" Rosie beams proudly as she finds it in the picture.

Now the harder questions begin.

"Helen, where is the pink petticoat?" and to me: "Bridget, where is the notice with the prices on?"

....

Around the Woolly Chair

It is story time. Most afternoons, after tea and before bedtime, my mother reads stories to the little ones. Even though Helen and I can read for ourselves, we often like to listen.

Our mother has the youngest ones snuggled in beside her on the big, velvet-covered horsehair-filled Woolly Chair near the Rayburn in the kitchen. Richard and Stephen are on her lap, Johnnie and Rosie are on the arms of the chair and Helen and I are leaning over the back.

Our heads are full of stories and songs we have heard since we learned our first words. Rhymes from Willebeek de Mair's *Little People*, dedicated to me at my birth in 1944, with its depictions of well-to-do children's lives, their nurseries and nursery maids, delicate china, and girls in 1930s dresses:

Look at careful little Joan,
Bringing tea in all alone.
See what careful steps she takes
So that nothing spills or breaks.

Through the French window, into the drawing room, Joan is carrying the tray. Helen would like to be that little girl.

The naughty baby, who has thrown the contents of his Nanny's workbasket all around, is strictly reprimanded. When our Granny Izzie visits us, and reads these verses, we share his unhappiness because we have a little baby brother too:

Baby, you naughty boy,
What have you done!

The picture of the sorrowful little boy, finger in his mouth, touches our hearts as our granny, with her gentle, quavery English voice, finishes:

But if you don't want your Nanny to scold,
Darling, you know you must do as you're told!

We are exposed to a different world which my mother and Granny Izzie knew as children, artistic, sophisticated, with servants to help look after the children.

Marigold Garden, illustrated by Kate Greenaway, is my mother's girlhood book. As our Granny Izzie read it to her in the past, on her visits she reads it to us:

When I go out with Grandmamma, Mamma says for a treat
Oh dear, how stiff we have to walk as we go down the street.

It is our grandmother's own childhood world. Tumbling down the decades, it is all a world away from our life in Hay with our often-exhausted mother.

Sometimes she reads her own childhood favourites to us. *The Fairchild Family,* nineteenth century stories about Emily, Lucy and Henry and how they learn to be worthy of heaven, which fits in with my mother's idea of good behaviour.

As we grow older, Helen and I are able to read E Nesbit's *The Bastable Family* books for ourselves. These stories, which my mother read when she was a girl, inspired her ambition to have a large family. The children's adventures, their *would-be-good* ways, were set in a middle class pre-war world, very different from her cooking and washing lifestyle in Hay.

We have nursery rhyme books too, filled with rural imagery from only-just fading times, Little Boy Blue who has fallen asleep while watching the sheep and cows, *Goosey Gander, Higgledy Piggledy My Black Hen, the Old Woman and her Pig, Ride-a-Cock Horse*; we know dozens of these rhymes.

....

Enchanted world for children

The world of brownies, pixies and goblins is also alive for my sisters, brothers and me. Enid Blyton enchants us with her stories, and those about toys which can speak and come alive at night, and about naughty children who learn better ways. I am addicted to them. I gobble up every word I can find, and still want more. Even stories aimed at the younger children, like *Noddy in Toyland* and *Mary Mouse*, draw me in, and Helen and I listen when my mother reads to the little ones.

In the library at school, so minimal that it is all held in a small box, there is one Enid Blyton book about pixies. I take it out over and over again. Sometimes we get one of her storybooks at Christmas or birthdays, but there is never enough. I must wait until I am older, in less impecunious times, to get more. In the meantime, I daydream as I read what I can. I want to become her; to write stories as good as hers; and from time to time I begin some scribbles.

We listen to stories about Rupert Bear who lives in Nutwood with all his animal friends, Bill Badger, Podgy Pig and Edward the elephant. They have adventures with wizards, magic carpets, a Chinese conjuror and an old Professor. They are mainly boy animals, the absence of girls barely noticed.

Racial and gender stereotypes are there, as they are in Enid Blyton, but we are unaware. Wherever Rupert goes, to castles in the sky, over lakes and mountains on the magic carpet, threatened by ogres and villains, he always comes home safely to his mother whose arms are spread out in welcome at the cottage door, his father wearing plus-fours in the background. That is his, and our, security.

But when people ask me, as grown-ups always do: "Bridget, what do you want to be when you grow up?" I have a clear answer. I am going to be a trapeze artist. I know all about that exciting occupation because of stories about Mimi, the French circus performer, which are delivered to my house every Wednesday in the children's comic *School Friend*. Mimi outperforms her rascally competitors by her graceful sweepings from one trapeze to another. Her opponents' antics are clever, such as balancing a chair on a high rope, but far less elegant. I shall sweep through the air as she does.

My mother manages to find sixpence a week for the high point of our week, Helen's *Girls Crystal* on Tuesday and my *School Friend* on Wednesday. We have a strict rule – neither of us is allowed to look at the other's comic first. It is so hard to wait.

As well as becoming a trapeze artist, I want to go to a girls' boarding school. There I can dress up in a cloak and mask with my friends, like The Silent Three, sorting out injustices suffered by other girls and earning their gratitude. I will have midnight feasts, and dodge unkind prefects and bossy teachers. And in between times, I shall be cast away on a tropical island like Jill Blair and her friend M'lani who has an exotic head of black hair such as I have never seen. Jill always needs the help of M'lani, who speaks in an imperfect form of English, but who has instinctive local knowledge. It is a British Empire lifestyle example for children, and although I don't understand that, I am charmed by these interesting people.

Sunny Stories costs tuppence, and my mother sometimes buys it as an extra extravagance. Enid Blyton has been writing this little magazine since 1926. It is 5 x 7 inches (13 x 18 cm) in size, with a cover picture set in a bright red frame. Enid Blyton's last copy was written on 19 February 1953.[18] It shows a picture from the main seven-page story inside. A boy who bullies a group of children is taught better ways by a circus performer on stilts. This is followed by Simple Simon, who starts out with a lovely new tricycle and through a series of badly judged exchanges ends up with nothing more than ice cream, hence earning a spanking from his mother. A two-side crudely drawn comic sequence about a bunny is followed by an episode of a *Secret Seven* adventure which Enid Blyton will later publish as a book. Finally, there is a four page story about fairies, a colouring competition and a letter. The back page carries an advertisement for a sweet malty drink, Ovaltine. All this for tuppence!

Enid Blyton's writing has a magnetic power over a 1950s child. The children are always cleverer than the adults, and there are inevitable rewards of sweet, delicious food. The pet dog understands what the children say, and helps to solve the mysteries. Noddy, the little wooden man in Toyland, is well-meaning but gets things wrong. We children sympathise, but know better, so this makes us feel grown-up. Mr Plod the policeman is a symbol of authority who is always wrong in the end. And as for fairies and goblins, elves and pixies, only children can see them. The baddies get punished and the goodies rewarded. When the author invites the child readers to offer their own opinions, she brings them into the story too. It is a potent mix. I have many years ahead of me to develop a more sophisticated taste.

....

The Hay Washerwoman

Helen and I are readers, and the younger ones have stories read to them. The world opens up to us through the imagination of others. We benefit because we have a mother who reads.

In the front of her 1953 diary, she lists every book she read between 1 January and 31 October, a total of 35, almost one book a week. She put an asterisk next to the books she finds most significant.

Her diary entries occasionally mention what she is reading:

10 February: Finished my book in the evening, 'Matador' by Marguerite Steen. A powerful book, it has made a great impression on me, and given me vivid dreams.

19 May: Relaxed by reading some more of 'Love and Fear' by Elizabeth C which is interesting and rather terrifying in a subjective way.

12 June: Took the opportunity of a day of unlooked-for leisure to start Gandhi's autobiography, 'Story of my Experiments with Truth' which is of fascinating interest.

15 July: Got the children to bed early and enjoyed a quiet evening, reading 'War in Heaven' by Charles Williams.

Her reading range is wide, including H E Bates, Evelyn Waugh, J B Cronin, Agatha Christie and Francis Parkinson Keyes. She reads crime, travel particularly in the Himalayas and the east, detective stories, and novels with a strong social content. The majority of the books are of her time, the 1940s and 1950s.[19]

Some quotations of importance to her are written in the early part of her diary:

O little house,
O dear and sweet my dwelling
O little house, for ever fare thee well!

The trees stand round thee with their singing branches
A little flowering wood forever fair.

She notes this is from an 'Eighth century poem by a monk, on the cell that sheltered Alcuin, then dead'.

There is a quote from Paul Brunton, probably from *A Hermit in the Himalayas*, which is starred on her reading list:

Nature must and does possess an aura, a mental atmosphere no less than man. Whoever is at all sensitive feels it, absorbs it and is consequently influenced by it. I write that statement not as a poet but as a scientist.

"Come on Bridget," she says sometimes. "Let's just slip down to the library before bedtime."

When she has chosen her books, I watch the librarian's skilful fingers flick through the box of cardboard pockets to insert the tickets, before stamping the return date. In post-war Hay, a small town with a population of about 1500, the county council library service in this way brings the wider world into our everyday lives.

I find a children's book, the only one at this time. It is a volume of Grimm's fairy tales with a yellow cover. I am allowed to take it home. The print is small and dense, and it has tiny black and white engravings at the head of each story. Despite being difficult for me to read at my young age, I consider it a treasure.

The weekly magazine, *John Bull*, with its bright covers which lead to our game on the Woolly Chair adds interest to my mother's life. Granny Izzie forwards it by post because the cost of sending printed paper is reasonable. The magazine costs fourpence, but up to four ounces in weight can be forwarded for 1½d, a penny ha'penny. Several can be posted at once costing only a ha'penny for each additional two ounces.

For fourpence, the readers of *John Bull* get 40 lengthy pages to read. There is a letters page, an editorial and many hefty stories. Some are several pages long, in a tiny font, interspersed with advertisements. In one copy, for example, a story is set in South African Boer country intermingling a romance with gold mining. There is a war serial placed in France, and a domestic drama of a grandfather with his ageing white pony. Cartoons and documentaries add variety, with an article on a home for the disabled stretching to two pages. A two-side article is about car racing. Some are illustrated with photos, as with one about BBC presenter Wilfred Thomas and his folk song collection.

The ads reflect the target readership. There are colour spreads on the glamour of smoking strong unfiltered Players' cigarettes; for bright green Batchelors tinned peas; fizzy Lucozade for energy; and washing detergents for lucky housewives. If you boil your whites in Surf, you will have lovely white nappies. There are health aids, and you can buy the best quality Aladdin paraffin for the heating stove in your home. The ads are for householders, both men and women, middle aged and middle income, representing the evolving consumer society. After wartime shortages, an endless supply of new goods is tempting people to spend, spend, spend.

The paper is poor quality, the colour printing basic, and the print miniscule. The tightly crammed text gives an unavoidable feeling that time was slower. The stories need concentration, and they move slowly. There is no sense that the readers must rush through, but are sitting back and relaxing, and taking plenty of time.[20]

Sunny Stories, for little children, is equally dense, and my mother must read the long stories to the younger ones. Helen and I can read it ourselves, and happily tackle the tiny font and compact printing. There are black and white line drawings on each page, but as with John Bull, it is clear that we will not rush through the stories. They require sitting down quietly and having adequate time.

My father takes the *News Chronicle*, big uninviting black and white pages. Helen and I wish he would buy the *Daily Express* because it has a Rupert Bear cartoon. No details of my father's reading appear in my mother's diary. It is her taste which shapes our lives. The thoughts in her mind from her reading are part of the world which, through her, we inhabit. Sometimes they make her restless:

> 26 March 1953: Children to bed early, and I mended and listened to wireless, and spent some time reading St John's Gospel and Commentary and some in Greek. Very unsettling for the Hay Washerwoman, I fear.[21]

… …………………………………………

Music, drama and cinema

I am practising one of my favourite songs:

How much is that doggie in the window,
The one with the wagg-uh-ly tail
How much is that doggie in the window
I do hope that doggie's for sale.

"Oh darling, can you sing something different please?" my mother wails. That song is heard everywhere, on the wireless, whistled by workmen, and now by me because I sing in a children's choir in Hay. Listening to it becomes so tedious that someone has invented an alternative second verse, which I can also sing:

I must take a trip to California
And oh how I wish you would go
Take with you that doggie in the window,
Come back in a century or so.

Christine and I belong to a choir which performs in Hay and surrounding villages. We have a concert in Clyro one evening, and I am driven there with a few other singers in someone's smart car. Usually taken around in my father's bumpetty van, I feel like I am flying. We are lined up in the church hall to do our part in the evening concert before the main choir's performance. Another time, we perform at The Crown Hotel, and Helen is allowed to come to listen. Her time to sing will come when she is a little older. Another song we love is *Teddy Bear's Picnic*:

Beneath the trees, where nobody sees…
They Hide and Seek wherever they please

An animal favourite is *The Owl and the Pussy Cat* who went to sea in a beautiful pea-green boat.

But my mother prefers the true Welsh songs in the choir's repertoire even though we sing them in English. We learn All *Through the Night, Sleep my Baby,* and a beautiful descant for *Down Yonder Green Valley.*

Sometimes my mother takes me to a concert given by male voice or a ladies' choir. Wales has a reputation as a land of song, but in Hay music is not perhaps as appreciated as it should be:

In the evening, I went with Bridget to a concert given by the Llandrindod Ladies Choir. All the old familiar faces, songs, chattering audience which latter always annoys me very much.

When she can fit it in, my mother's afternoon piano playing is a pleasing background to our lives. She teaches Helen and me a duet: *dum de dum, bong bong, dum de dum, bong bong* – we thump out. And she regularly assembles us round the piano for singing sessions. *The Children's Opera*, with its nursery rhymes, is a favourite, where Mrs Bond summons her duck Dilly Dilly to come and be killed. Most significantly, we learn from her *Oxford Song Book*. There are offerings from all the four nations. We absorb Scottish and Irish nationalism,

Welsh melancholy and English maidens abandoned by their seducers, or who die prematurely. British Empire values are represented with Rule Britannia and slaves who mourn the death of their master.

This book would never pass muster in the twenty-first century. Still, we have a long life ahead of us to learn better ways, and we sing heartily.

She plays hymns from a children's book beautifully illustrated by Cecily Barker, but she refuses to let us sing *Fight the Good Fight*, or *Onward Christian Solders* because of their military associations.

She is preparing to play the *Missa de Angelis*, an ancient Gregorian Mass, in our church. On Trinity Sunday, she and her friend Miss Chappell lead the Catholic congregation in song. Helen, Rosie and I have learned the *Kyrie Eleison*, which we know to be Greek words. The Latin Benediction follows the mass, with more hauntingly beautiful music and smoking incense.

Hay has no theatre, but it does have an amateur dramatic society, and my father is a member. I am a proud daughter, sitting in the front row, to see him acting in *The Ghost Train*, a story of passengers stuck overnight in a station in rural Cornwall. Professional theatre is beyond our reach except for the Christmas pantomime in Hereford. There Helen and I learn gems such as 'There's a hole in my bucket, dear Liza, a hole', followed by 'Then mend it dear Henry, dear Henry, mend it.' We sing the song all the way home on the bus until we feel sick from the cigarette smoke.

Closer in, and accessible, is the Hay cinema. We go down a lane behind Like's Garage to a huge wooden World War One hut which serves as a cinema. Films bring in glamour from Hollywood and America, and I watch enthralled as Doris Day seated on the front of her horse-drawn stagecoach sings 'Take me back to the Black Hills, the Black Hills of Dakota…'

At different times, Rosie, perched on our mother's lap on the cheap front bench seats, sobs in terror at the wicked witch in *Snow White*. My mother's diary records that Helen, Rosie and Johnny enjoy *Robin Hood*, and that she herself much appreciated *Cry the Beloved Country*. On other occasions, she enjoys a wonderfully funny skit, *The Crimson Pirate* and a British thriller, *Mr Denning Drives North*. She finds an American version of *Charley's Aunt* so awful that she walks out half way through.

The front row seats are the cheap ones, people sitting side by side on awkward benches. The middle rows comprise chairs which cost 1/9d (one shilling and ninepence), and the top price with more comfortable chairs at the back which cost 2/3d (two shillings and thruppence), a whole sixpence more. Sometimes the film snaps, and people in the audience stamp their feet and yell until the repair is done and the show recommences. The whole atmosphere is reeking unpleasantly with cigarette smoke, but the health aspects are not taken into account.

The wireless brings other influences into our childhood world. My father has obtained a 1935-Murphy 146 radio which fits in the corner of our sitting room. Its high-quality sound fills the room, and my mother often listens to plays and concerts in the evenings as she does the ironing or the mending. She and my father both enjoy classical music, and once she recorded being enthralled by the BBC orchestra playing Beethoven's 7th Symphony.

In the afternoon, if we are lucky, we children may be quietly assembled in the sitting room.

"Are you sitting comfortably?" says the wireless presenter, at a quarter to two. It is time for Listen with Mother. 'Ding Ding, da da da da da, Da da da-aa' goes the tune. Rosie, Helen and I are squashed up together on the stuffed pouffé, and my mother has the boys around her on the sofa. First, we listen to a nursery rhyme, sung by an English soprano, with a high-pitched 'wireless voice'. Then there is a story, which we like best, and another rhyme at the end.

Around teatime, there is Children's Hour. The version we hear always ends with 'Nos da, plant', meaning 'Good night, children', whereby we learn another Welsh phrase.

My mother decides that she would like to learn some Welsh.

On 9 January, she starts a BBC Welsh language programme transmitted on the wireless. She has a handbook that goes with it, and listens every Friday night. By 23 January, she is admitting that it is rather hard, and 6 February is the last entry which mentions it.

The great innovation of TV is yet to make an impact. There are only two television sets in Hay in 1952. Roddy Williams's Uncle Sid, who has a wireless repair shop, the Bon Marché in Castle Square, was the first to have one, and his father the second. The little 12-inch screen was only viewable in a darkened room. It was a Marconi set and cost about £100 retail.

Clearly, a weekly housekeeping allowance of around £5 completely rules out buying a television for our family.

Roddy's father, Hay's postmaster, knows who has bought one because the licence must be purchased at the post office.

By 1953, things are changing, and we are lucky because we have influential friends. Helen, Rosie and I have been invited to sit in the flat above Mrs Jones the Clocktower's shoeshop. Andy Pandy is on her television. This dancing puppet lives in a picnic basket, and he has a friend called Teddy. When they aren't looking, Looby Loo, a rag doll, appears singing *Here we go Looby Loo*. We would like to come back every day but we are only occasionally invited. Sometimes we see Bill and Ben the Flowerpot Men, Sooty and Sweep, or Muffin the Mule.

The cultural offerings available at Hay in the early 1950s thus include concerts, the occasional amateur theatrical show, regular films at the cinema, a library, magazines and newspapers, church music and the wireless programmes of the BBC. Television is just beginning to appear. There are no theatres or concert halls, no art galleries and no bookshops with loaded shelves.

If Hay is a backwater, as a child I don't know it. If my mother thinks it is, she will get the chance to test it in the years to come.

14 Upstanding People

"Can I sell you a bunch of lovely flowers, Mam?" says the gypsy who is knocking at our door. Her sun-darkened wrinkled face is bright and cheerful. I peep shyly at her hair which is plaited in ringlets around her ears. She shows us big, beautiful, coloured blooms made from elder twigs.

"I don't think so, thank you," my mother replies. She is persuaded to buy some pegs for the washing line. They are cut from sticks with a slit down the middle and a metal piece to stop the split from going further. They are not very sturdy, but my mother likes to be helpful.

"Do you have any clothes you don't need, for my little ones?" the gypsy asks. My mother manages to find a few bits and pieces, and with a 'God bless you', off goes our visitor to the next house, in this way earning her living.

....

At our door

The rattling of the milk truck stops outside our door in the mornings. The milk-woman has made her way from the farm into town, and then through the streets to the customers of Hay. The cows have been milked that morning, and the filled churns lifted onto a little motor-driven cart. It isn't long since a pony drew the milk-cart. People don't normally have refrigerators, and we certainly don't in our house, so we need a daily fresh supply of milk.

"Milk, Mrs Ashton!" calls the milk-woman, knocking at the door with its coloured glass panes.

These are the days before glass bottles. She has measuring cups of one quart, one pint, half a pint and the smallest, a quarter of a pint. This last is called a gill and is just enough for a customer who wants milk only for a few cups of tea. At our house, she dips the quart measure into the churn, and carefully fills our jug. As she hands it to me, I tell her: "It's my birthday today."

"How nice," she says. "How old are you?" I tell her I am now nine years old. She reaches into her pocket and hands me a shining, golden, twelve-sided threepenny bit with our new queen's head on. Such riches, such unforgettable kindness.

Once a week, along Market Street, there is the clatter-banging of the dustbin men. Helen and I have christened them Fatty and Skinny. The two men drive the truck with its curved sliding openings on the sides. They pick up our bins, throwing them over their shoulders and emptying the contents in the correct side. One section of the truck is for the ashbins. Most households have coal fires, and Bridget Ashbins is the nickname I endure at school. Leaving behind a trail of smells, Fatty and Skinny with their dust-encrusted grey faces and cloth caps move on to the next house.

Ding ding ding – we run outside whenever we hear the handbell of Bumper Howells, the town crier, right outside our front door. He gives out important announcements such as the cutting off of the water supplies in hot weather, and other local events.

"There will be a jumble sale run by the Women's Institute at the parish hall at 2 pm this afternoon," he calls out. Then with a flourishing ring of his bell, and crying out 'God Save the Queen', he moves off to the next location.

For those people who don't read newspapers, with no access to local radio stations, or who don't read posters, this is the way information is relayed. Bumper Howells has a good loud voice. Wearing his workaday clothing, he fits in this work with the other odd jobs he does in the town. He sweeps up after the cattle market with his broom, shovel and wheelbarrow. And he rewards himself with plentiful draughts of cider.[22]

A raggedy, forlorn woman sometimes comes by with a baby in a pram and a couple of neglected-looking children beside her. The woman's hair is lank and greasy, her stockings are slipping around her ankles and her shoes are sloppy. Her brown blouse hangs over her protruding belly and her dowdy skirt.

"Is Mrs Ashton at home?" she asks me. I run to find my mother.

"Oh, good afternoon, Mrs M," my mother says when she sees her. "Yes, I do have some clothes for your children." She fetches a set of hand-me-downs which she had prepared.

Second hand clothes from our family cannot be anything wonderful but our visitor is in no position to be choosy. After chatting with my mother for a while, she leaves with her cargo. She is heading for her new council house on Gypsy Castle estate where she has recently been rehoused from inadequate premises in Brook Street. We visited the house one day and saw the poverty and disorder which was recorded by my mother. "Mrs M has alas taken Brook Street with her to her new house. But they have all been ill with flu, and the baby looks wan and ill."

Mrs Basil Watkins is a very different kind of person. She lives on one of the short sides of the egg-packing station in front of our house. Unlike my mother, with no children clamouring around, she appears mysteriously glamorous. Her dark black hair is piled up tidily, and she wears red lipstick and smart clothes. Her black cat, Friday, likes to visit us. My mother worries that he might abandon his mistress to move in with us which she doesn't want because Mrs Basil-Watkins lives alone. She is a good neighbour, and helped us when my mother was ill.

....

Dramatic woman

"Look at this card," my mother says as Christmas approaches.

She shows us the card signed *From Mrs Dilys Gwillim and Bill*. We are not sure exactly why she is saying this, but to my mother it shows Mrs Dilys' self-importance, her husband's name appearing almost as an afterthought. Her marriage has brought her a beautiful farmhouse which she runs as a guest house, and fields where she can keep her horses. Bill Gwillim, the farmer, makes this life possible, but is a shadowy figure in the background.

Mrs Dilys is my mother's friend, red-headed and vivacious, and learning to become a Catholic. We children love her because she is voluble, full of fun, and a wonderful cook. She frequently breezes into our kitchen, making us delicious pancakes, laughing as she tosses them onto our plates. She leaves behind her a trail of smiles and scandal, friendship and flattery. We make return visits to New Forest Farm, where she cooks us more pancakes on her Aga, and then lets us have a ride on Beauty, her horse.

At first, my mother is pleased with this friendship and writes in her diary:

I think the Lord has brought us together at this particular time for a special reason, a) that I can maybe help her with her religious problems, and b) in family matters. I had a very particular instance today, how my prayers for her have been answered. Well it is all there in the Gospel, 'Ask and ye shall receive, Seek and ye shall find'. When one has found out how literally true that is, one is getting somewhere in the spiritual life.

But things are not quite so straightforward. Mrs Dilys has dynamic moods. She arranges to come for a meal, but then goes to another household and gossips. The two women make up their differences, but then Mrs D reserves the highest cost cinema tickets for both of them, leaving my mother to pay the excess. There are endless small aggravations, but the worst is that she doesn't conform to conventional family standards.

One August day, my mother writes: "She regaled me with a long account of her flirtations with her guests, or vice-versa, which put me very much on edge."

After being let down on one of many occasions, my mother writes: "I learn more and more as time goes on, the vanity of earthly friendships. I often long for the peace and joy of heaven." We children hear her expressing herself this way, tucking it away in our consciousness without full understanding.

Not all women are married with children like my mother. Most of our women teachers are unmarried, some living alone and others with a friend for company and economy, as these are the days when many men never returned from the war. We regularly visit two women friends of my mother, a widow with her paid female companion who lives near St Mary's Church.

We know them as a couple, 'Mrs James and Greenhead'. In the same way, we know 'Mrs Chappell and Katsie' at Capel y Ffin. In many of these cases, there is a strong woman with a more suppliant partner. If there is anything more intimate than simple friendship involved, we children have no idea of such a thing.

My father sees the distinctive roles of the genders as basic and biological, and he tells me this as I become older. The woman brings the children into the world and looks after them while the man supports the family. Catholic teachings on matrimony reinforce this relationship, and a married couple must be true to each other. That is just how it is, and even though certain aspects may rankle, my mother accepts it too.

Mrs Dilys with her irrepressible spirits defies the norm.

....

194

People from far-away lands

We are all used to people with Welsh surnames. The shopkeepers and our friends have names like Jones, Thomas, Pugh, Price, Morgan, Lloyd, Jenkins, and Williams. In Hay, we also know people whose names show origins from the wider world. Families, particularly in our Catholic community, reveal origins in Ireland, although they have long integrated into local life.

There are people with English names like ours, Ashton, Keylock and Galsworthy. The father of my friends Elspeth and Ian Beattie who runs the Red Lion pub has come from far-away Scotland, and from him we hear the Scottish accent.

Our priests, Father O'Brady and Father O'Reilley, are from Ireland, and they speak in the Irish way during the Mass.

Catholic people from other nations attend our church. Wherever they are from, they hear the familiar Latin mass. By meeting them, my sisters and brothers and I learn a little about other nationalities.

The Pyrzakowski family has come to Hay from Poland.

This name is far too difficult for most of us, and for everyday use, we shorten it to Kosky. The father of the family repairs watches and clocks. He has a little workshop on the other side of the egg-packing station. We can see him through the window, squinting into his special eyeglass and using tiny tools to do his repairs.

"Mr Kosky told me that when he was growing up in Poland, every boy had to learn a trade," our mother tells us. "Then no matter what happens in life, he can always earn a living."

Isolated from his own country, we thus understand why he is a watchmender. Mrs Kosky is a tiny woman with pointed features and dark hair tied back in a bun. She is an artist, a pianist and a music teacher, and gives my mother lessons. We children have no knowledge of how this family has ended up in Hay, but we hear the lisping way the Koskys speak English.

My mother is always hospitable, welcoming them as she does all strangers. Sometimes this seems to be at our expense. The Koskys have two daughters, Anita and Yvonne, and one day Helen discovers that our mother has given them her favourite dress without consulting her. It is disconcerting for my sister to see another child wearing her dress. One day, we realise that our mother has given the Polish children our dolls' house, and this too is baffling and upsetting.

Yet we are learning all the time. We gather that Polish people are talented, musical and artistic, and that the boys must learn a useful trade. We must help them by giving away some of our belongings, which is hard.

Hay also has some former Italian prisoners of war who tend to be shy, diffident, and mostly have minimal English. Felipe is our particular friend. They too all attend our Catholic church.

One photo of some of them survives in my mother's album. Their names are handwritten on the back, difficult to read, perhaps Ricuecio Biagio, Adeldo Raffaele, Ricordo and another Biagio. One of them is holding our little brother, two-year-old Stephen. They appear to be in their thirties, which perhaps reflects their having been conscripted in the 1940s. They are dressed in smart suits, three with white shirts and ties, and one with a stylish polo-necked shirt, and their shoes are well-shone. They obviously take pride in their appearance as they walk from the timber yard where they live through the streets of the town.

They love children, and are surely homesick and missing their own families. I learn that Italians eat macaroni, and macaroni cheese is my favourite food. They invite me to the place where they live to eat this delicacy, and I am allowed to go.

I walk down the streets with them, past the station and into England. We turn right on the lane up to the timber-yard. Their living quarters is a corrugated metal Nissan hut, a long curved structure. They sit me down at a wooden table, on a high stool, and present me with my dinner. The bowl is filled with boiled macaroni and red tomatoes. This is not what I expected because my mother makes it with a cheese sauce.

They make a fuss of me, their behaviour being completely proper. I enjoy the attention, and I want to repeat the visit.

"Mummy, please can I go back and have some more macaroni?" I ask from time to time.

My mother demurs. She won't agree, and I can't understand why. People must have been talking. I will never understand this until I am much older.

Thus along with my mother's friend Mrs Galsworthy from Holland, we know Polish, Italian, Irish and Scottish people. One day the most exciting visitor who has ever entered our house comes in after Mass. Tom is from Africa, and is with Father Brady. We have never seen a black person. We are shy, but he is good-humoured and lets us look at his hands and fingernails. The grown-ups talk and eat as usual, and the accepting friendliness all around is the atmosphere I will take with me to adulthood.

In 1950s Hay, we are nearly all fair-skinned people. There had been, however, a posting of black American soldiers at New Moor House, a mile east of the town, during the war. The men were allowed to mix with local people, and one or two children playing around in Hay are likely to have had such fathers. One of my Hay friends of later years has the distinctive beauty of a Diana Ross or a Shirley Bassey. Although she left school at 15, and works at Henderson's, the small engineering factory in Hay, she reads books, asks questions and has an unusual sparkling elegance.

Between learning Welsh at school, hearing Latin at Mass, Italian in the Nissan hut, Polish at the watchmender's shop and variations of English among our friends and acquaintances, we children are exposed to many languages and cultures. The characters of Hay too, the gypsy woman, the binmen and the town crier, the woman delivering daily milk, the red-head flirting with her guests, and the poor woman who found it all too much to cope with, are all upstanding in my childhood. They add riches to our lives.

The Warners of Hay

The gypsy woman who knocks at our door seems to appear magically from nowhere, and then disappear again. But this is not true of course, and sometimes my mother takes us for a walk beyond the council estate where their encampment may be seen, and where the washed clothes are laid out on thorn bushes to dry.

Here is an extract from my later diary written on 5 March 1966:

"The Warners live in a caravan in the corner of a field near Hay. They have been in Hay at least since 1876 when they are mentioned in Kilvert's Diary. They are really semi-settled gypsies though they still seem to get about a bit.

Cecil's mother, old Mrs Warner, is absolutely ancient. She has a wonderful brown wrinkled face, and pigtail ringlets round her ears. Both her daughters, Dorothy and Mary, have fine dark skins and moulded faces.

"Cecil and Tommy, the sons, have twinkly eyes, outdoor skins and leathery bodies. The two men disappeared into the woods as the women talked.

"I wonder at their ways, these people who think through and not around, crafty people, with the wisdom of those who live outdoors.

"Wales was very beautiful today. It was clear, warm and sunny, breezy too, and the mountains stood sharp grey around every skyline. There was clear birdsong, white sheep in green fields, yellow celandines in thick hedges.

"Betty and I went into Hay for a cup of tea in the café. Later, we went back to the caravan, while the evening cool was quietly taking over. The hills all around, the fields between and the little caravan was at the centre of it all. Odd jobs were being done inside and out, the dogs scratching around. Three-year-old Tony was charging round the field on his bicycle. Somewhere out there his daddy Cecil and his uncle Tommy were on some business of their own, between us and the River Wye. I waved goodbye to Betty, and little Tony ran along the field by the road, waving and telling me to come back again."

15 The Coronation and Other Excitements

My father turns on the wireless in the sitting room. The great day that we have all been anticipating has arrived, 2 June 1953, Coronation Day. We are waiting to hear about the Queen being crowned. As we sit down for our breakfast in the kitchen, we get a surprise.

"By Jove, Everest has been conquered, and guess what! By a beekeeper!" My father comes in excitedly to tell us this as we are sitting at the table. New Zealander Edmund Hilary and Nepali Tenzing Norgay reached the summit at 11.30 am on 29 May 1953, and the news has arrived in London on the morning of the coronation. The beekeeper is Hilary, and he and Tenzing buried a few sweets and a small cross in the snow.

They took a few photographs and then made their way back down to their base camp.

Certainly, our new Queen is going to be crowned today, but equally importantly in our family a beekeeper and his companion have conquered Everest.

....

2 June 1953

In the week before the long-awaited coronation, the excitement has been building up. At school, we have been given coloured paper advertisements and paraphernalia to cut out which we take proudly home. There are pictures of the Queen's golden coach, drawn by white horses with red regalia and coachmen in gold and white uniforms. The wonderful crown is full of jewels set in purple velvet. My mother's diary:

29 May: The children brought Coronation mugs home at dinner time, very proudly. There are to be all kinds of exciting events next week to commemorate it. Every house, shop and street is gaily decorated, and a real holiday feel in the air. Took Richard and Stephen to get their mugs in the evening, then came home and put Steve to bed. Then I took the other children to see a Ladies Football Match at Gypsy Castle.

We children all hope to be invited to see this once-in-a-lifetime event on television. It is to be broadcast to everyone in the country who is lucky enough to own a set, of which there are only three or four families in Hay. We want to be able to see the Queen in real life, sitting in her golden coach, pulled by white horses, and the crown being put on her head. Although we cannot be in London, among the crowds lining the streets, here in Hay we can share some of the excitement. My mother records her day:

2 June: The Great Day dawned at last! I got on with the work – cleaned all the upstairs by eleven. We had a snack, then Helen and I went to see the Grants' television – we saw the Queen being crowned in Westminster Abbey. I was glad to have the chance of seeing it. John had dinner ready for us, and we listened to the wireless all afternoon. The children went to the Coronation party at 4 pm, and John, Stevie and I dashed back to the Grants' to see the end of the Procession on the television. A happy day, marred only by weather which was rainy and cold.

My friend Susan Price, whose parents run the Star grocery, have a television, and I too have been invited. Her family and friends are in a darkened room, and some delicious homemade fudge sweets were brought out of a cupboard. The processions and commentary take such a long time that we become restless and go out to play in the back garden behind the shop. What we really want to see is the moment when the Archbishop of Canterbury places the crown on the Queen's head, but we are so busy playing that we miss the moment, to a lifetime's regret. My mother's diary for the next day:

3 June: We all felt a bit 'hangover-ish' this morning and got up late. Did lots of washing, including three sheets and felt a bit fed up. Bridget worn out with excitement and retired to bed all morning, but came down to dinner feeling better. As soon as dinner was over, I went into the sitting room, Bridget cleared the table and Helen made tea and brought me a cup on a tray. The first time ever! It's nice when they get to that age.

A few days before the coronation, five-and-a-half year old Rosie was licking her lips at the Infants' tea. She walked to the Parish Hall along with all the other children in her school class where they were told to sit down among the rows of tables.

The children were reminded of the great event which would soon be taking place, and then they were all given a paper bag which was folded so that they couldn't see what is inside.

"Now children, you may open your bags," said the teacher.

Inside was a crusty, crispy bun, round and fat, with sugar icing on the top. Rosie has never before seen such a creation, and it is all for her. The bun is sliced through the middle and filled with sweetened artificial cream and a splodge of red jam.

"You may eat your buns," says the teacher. So Rosie stickily, smudgily, bites and chews and eats as never before; thus, the coronation as a festival of buns is embedded in her mind for ever.

....

Market day

"Mummy, can we go to the market to get some animals for our farm set?" we would often ask on a Thursday.

The market stalls are set out down by the clock tower. If my mother has a few spare pennies, we might be lucky. We have model farm animals made of metal, and a new cow or a pig or a hen is a special treat. My mother sometimes buys herself a bargain or two. Once it was pansies, and another time a red pullover for Rosie and two pillowcases. The market is important for the country people like those from Painscastle who come in on the bus to sell their eggs. They also take their homemade butter to the butcher, and we sometimes buy some. This is a most delicious treat for me as I love its salty creamy flavour when spread on my bread.

From near our front door, we sometimes see a drover guiding cattle towards the mart through the streets. They leave a trail of dung trodden into the road to be swept up later by Bumper Howells. On market days, the farmers and butchers assemble at Hay's busy mart to buy and sell their animals.

From there, the butchers will drive some of the animals they have purchased to the premises behind their shops, and one of them is the father of my friend

Gillian Coombes. There is a shed in the little alley that runs behind the shop, where smells and sights and sounds are best not mentioned.

The pubs do good trade on a Thursday. Sometimes I peep in at the farmers at The Bear, near Christine's house. Here they eat their midday dinner of faggots, round balls of chopped liver, served with mashed potatoes and gravy. Country women would sit around a table provided by Pearks, the grocer on Lion Street, where they eat their midday sustenance in comfort.

....

The fair

"Mummy, please, give me sixpence," I plead. The May fair is in town. I pester her for so long that she gives in. The fair is behind the castle walls, and just a few steps from our back door. There are bumper cars and a roundabout for little children, a waltzer, stalls with guns, coconut shies and candy floss sellers. And there is one stall where you roll pennies down a chute into a chequer board of squares. Each square contains the number of pennies which you win if your penny rolls into it without touching the sides. Anyone can see how easy it is to roll your penny so that you win lots more. I have the good idea to spend my sixpence in this way, and then I will have plenty of money to spend on the other excitements.

I roll the first, but it lands on a line. Then the second, the third, and all the way to the last, the sixth, of my little hoard. I am distraught. I have lost everything. Miserable, I go back and tell my mother that all is over. No rides for me, no fun.

"The fair is just a waste of money," she says. Later, we all go together, and are allowed one ride each. My mother lets me have a ride too because she knows I have learned a hard lesson. We extend our pleasure by watching each other. Richard, Johnnie, Rosie and Stephen ride on the brightly painted wooden horses and in the coloured fire engine where they can ring a bell. Six children, six sixpences, totalling three shillings. It is a lot of money out of the weekly housekeeping.

....

Seaside holidays

Money had to be found for a holiday at the seaside, even in the restricted budgets of post-war days. One way or another my mother managed it. Before we moved to Hay, in summer 1947, we had been to Jaywick, in Essex. Our Granny Annie with my father's sister Grace joined us at the beach. There is Granny Annie, well proportioned, wearing a straw hat, sensible shoes and nice warm stockings. She, with her daughter Grace, Helen and me in sunhats and my father, are sitting on the sand.

Tiny as they are, the photos taken that day were a special treat. Film was expensive.

The following year, 1948, we managed a holiday at Littlehampton. This time the baby was Rosie, just a few months old.

In 1949, we made a trip to Tenby while we still lived at Top o' Lane, and our Granny Izzie was with us. She was holding baby Rosie in a photo, with Helen and me dressed warmly in double-breasted woolly jackets.

In 1951, we made a family visit to our Granny Annie and Granfer in Warminster. It takes a couple of hours in our van to reach Wiltshire from Hay. Our granny is a firm Protestant, and my mother is a sensitive Catholic. There is a feeling of unease when they are around each other.[23] We know that her brother, our great uncle Jack, is a racehorse owner in Ireland, and he removed my father from his will because he married a Catholic. My father always tells us this with a laugh.

His sister, Aunty Grace, has married his longstanding boyhood friend, Geoff Butcher, who supported him in his wartime conscientious objector's tribunal. Uncle Geoff had built two houses next to each other for them and our grandparents. They look sparse and bare before the gardens have been planted. Our head-scarved mother appears in a photo looking like a farmwoman, holding Richard who was the baby at that time. Aunty Grace and our cousin Sarah are in the group. Grannie Annie with her upright stance, arms behind her back, grandmother of five, looks proud and efficient, and a little frightening.

In the same year, we also had a few days at Aberystwyth. A photo showing three be-ribboned girls covered with sand on the beach survives, and another at Borth where we stayed in a caravan. There must have been some good honey-years to pay for these holidays, which without the photos would be forgotten.

"Christine went to Porthcawl," I tell my mother. My friend has been telling me about the rides she went on, the chips and the candyfloss. Coney Beach Pleasure Park, in the south Wales holiday town, attracts day-trippers from as far away as Hay. It sounds so exciting. My mother, however, has different ideas.

She has been planning our holiday for weeks. We are going to Tenby, a sedate seaside town with two sandy beaches, a saintly tidal island nearby, rocky cliff walks and very importantly, a Catholic church.

Not for us fripperies like candyfloss, or rides which are over in a few minutes, both of which are a waste of money. We will dig and play on the beach, enjoy healthy walks in lovely scenery, and have calm uplifting visits to the Catholic church where my mother is free from responsibilities.

She has been making contact with Mrs Griffiths who runs a guest house. In January, a letter arrived:

> Heard from Vine Cottage, Tenby. Mrs G is willing to have us for 2 guineas (adults) and 5 guineas for six children. Quite reasonable – 9 guineas for 8 people. I do hope we may be able to go.

Guineas are 21 shillings, or one pound and one shilling. The total is something like twice her weekly housekeeping. Possibly our grandparents are making a financial contribution.

In February, things are firming up, and my mother sends a deposit by post for the week beginning 9 May. However, we all go down with measles at the wrong moment. Helen starts on 11 April, followed by me, then Rosie on the 18th. We may not be able to go on our holiday. But my mother goes on with the plans:

> I've now decided that it would be best to go on the coach, 17/6 return. It leaves Hay at 5.10 pm, arriving 9.35. Quite easy as the children will sleep.

Richard's spots appear on 23 April, which is a good sign as he should be better by 9 May, which in fact happens. There is relief all round. We're going after all.

We are to be staying in a guest house, and this still being post-war days of rations, we must provide some of our food. Three days before we are due to leave, my mother who has been exhausted by her weeks of nursing measles patients, writes: "Went to the Star to get week's rations, which I packed up to send on to Tenby. Then went to the Food Office, where I spent half an hour waiting for Veg ration books."[24]

An excited family of father, mother and six children clamber on to the coach at 5 pm on 9 May. Our journey takes us on a scenic ride through the countryside, passing Brecon, Sennybridge, Llandeilo and Carmarthen, arriving at 8.15. My mother writes in her diary that our 'digs' are bright, clean and cheerful, and that Mrs Griffiths is very nice.

Over the next few days, some of which are lovely and sunny, and one of which is cold and rainy, we enjoy our seaside holiday. We spend wonderful hours splashing in the sea in our woolly swimsuits, and building sandcastles. At the same time, our visits to the beaches are intermingled with regular visits to the Catholic church. On Sunday, we go to mass at 10.30 in the morning, and after a sunny afternoon on the beach, we are back for Benediction at 6.30 pm. There is more.

On Monday, Helen and I go with our mother to the Rosary at 6 pm, where we join in with the Hail Marys and Our Fathers. On Tuesday, not to be missed, it is the Rosary again for Rosie, baby Stephen and me. On Wednesday, a rainy day when my father returns to Hay on the coach, my mother doesn't manage to take us to church. On Thursday, we all attend Mass at 9 am, and she notes that we are all well behaved. In the evening, Mrs Griffiths agrees to supervise our little Stephen who has been put to bed, and the other five of us accompany my mother to Benediction.

As the incense billows, Helen and I join in, singing *O Salutaris Hostia*, and *Adoremus in Aeternum*, because we know the words even if we don't understand them. Little Rosie and Johnnie even manage curious words like *Genitori Genitoque* and *Sit et Benedictio*, the latter obviously meaning 'Sit in Benediction', which is what we are doing.

For my mother, church services in Tenby are a relief. She is not playing the organ, hasn't dusted and polished beforehand, and there is no need to feed and entertain the priest afterwards. All she has to do is keep half a dozen children in order, and we respond by behaving well in the less familiar surroundings.

"We've got quite friendly with all the regulars at church," my mother writes. "A family of six children causes quite a stir, I find," she writes.

On Monday, she had to line up to get more rations for the guest house. "Spent half morning shopping at Food Office."

For a hard-working housewife like my mother, someone else is doing much of the work for her during this week, which is her true holiday. She has a cup of tea in bed on Monday, followed by a leisurely wash and breakfast cooked by someone else. After the visit to the Food Office, she came back for coffee, and then had a quiet hour dozing in Gunfort Gardens with the baby asleep in the pram. My father took the rest of us to the beach, and she met us back at Vine Cottage for midday dinner. On Friday, she particularly mentions an 'extremely nice fish dinner'.

Although Mrs Griffiths provides the main meals, our mother supervises the afternoon tea. One day, she buys two sugarcoated jam doughnuts. Helen and I are at the table, and I can see that one is much bigger than the other. We are taught that we must eat as much bread and butter we want before ending with cake, which rule I know well. However, the temptation to get the big one is great, and so I ask if I can have my doughnut.

"Are you sure you have had enough bread and butter?" my mother asks. I say that I have, take the doughnut and cut it in half. I eat the first half, putting the other on the side of my plate.

"I'm still hungry," I tell my mother. "Please can I have some more bread and butter?"

"Bridget, you naughty girl," she says. "You took that doughnut just because you could see it is bigger." I expect I was prompted to own up to that sin of greed at my next confession.

On Sunday and Monday, at 9 pm, when we children were all in bed, my father had twice taken my mother out for supper which is a rare treat. Eating out is virtually unknown in our family in these days of frugality.

The highlights of the holiday are without doubt hours spent on the beaches. Helen, Rosie and I have new swimsuits, one green, one red and one blue. They are made of wool, hanging heavily on us when they are wet and sandy. A few three-by-two inch photos in my mother's album show us playing in the water, with three year old Richard digging in the sand and St Catherine's island in the background.

No candyfloss or thrilling rides, certainly no chips, but an occasional ice-cream, lots of digging and sandy swims, and five visits to church in six days. That is the 1953 Tenby holiday for the Beeman's family.

....

Festivities

Summer brings us garden parties. As a friend of Gillian Coombes, the daughter of the castle's caretaker, I am often in the castle grounds, but a garden party in August opens it up to everyone. "Everything was very wet but it didn't actually rain. The children had donkey rides and lucky dips. There was a nice display of dancing and singing on the lawn, organised by Mrs Keylock," wrote my mother.

On August Bank Holiday Monday, we go off to a garden party at Whitney to raise funds for our church. This is entertaining for us but, as ever, means more work for my mother:

> Did a very large wash in the morning, hot and exhausting. Cold dinner, rest, then great business of changing clothes and preparing for the garden party at Whitney. A lovely day for it. No hope of a restful afternoon under the trees – had to 'sell' all the time. John sold ice-cream, and the children ran around and enjoyed themselves. I went to bed at 9, quite worn out.

"What can we wear for the carnival fancy dress parade?" I ask my mother as another exciting event approaches. She simply has no time to create costumes for us as mothers do who have smaller families. We rummage around in our dressing up box which has all kinds of odd clothes in, old sparkly items, funny shoes, hats and torn sheets with which to play ghosts. We decide that Helen can be Wee Willie Winkie, the nursery rhyme character who runs through the streets in his nightie-gown. She wears a little red leather beret and a white shirt, and holds a candle. I choose a crumpled American Indian's outfit with stitched-on coloured wooden beads. Hanging on to the ill-fitting skirt, which is slipping down over my shoes, I parade happily down the street with my sister amid the fairies, clowns and cowboys.

I know that I have no chance of winning a prize, but like all the entrants, we are lined up in the marquee and the important person gives us each a shilling.

Autumn brings harvest festival in St Mary's church, and we are allowed to go with our school class. The vegetables, fruit and flowers are arranged along the windows and the altar, and we sing *We Plough the Fields and Scatter* to the Protestant God:

We thank Thee then, O Father,
For all things bright and good
The seedtime and the harvest,
Our life, our health, our food.

We are reminded of the source of the natural wonders around us when we sing *All Things Bright and Beautiful*:

The purple-headed mountain
The river running by,
The sunset and the morning
That brightens up the sky.

This makes sense to us because we have the Black Mountains on our skyline, and Hay is right next to the River Wye.

At other times, and without my mother's knowledge, we approach the church gates when the news gets round the children that there is a wedding. When the bride and groom emerge, the groom scatters handfuls of coins amongst the awaiting mob, and we scramble to gather a coin or two among the roughest and toughest.

....

Christmas

"Happy Christmas, boys and girls," says the white-bearded man with the red coat, and carrying a sack. "Have you all been good this year?"

Awe-struck children gaze at him uncertainly until one or two of the bolder ones call out 'Yes'.

"In that case, I'll see what I have in my bag," says Father Christmas.

We are at the Labour Party's Christmas event in the Bear Inn. I am nine years old now, and I find something odd about the red-coated man. I can hardly believe it, but I suspect that he is my daddy. How can that be? I am too shy to tell anyone, and perhaps I am wrong. But the tone and mannerisms, and the way he speaks, is just like my father.

He calls out names of the children, one after the other, and hands them their wrapped presents. Pat Lewis the Half Moon opens hers, and she has a sewing set with all kinds of brightly coloured spools of thread. It is beautiful. When my turn comes, I find I have a colouring book, and this is not an exciting present. Colouring is boring. This doesn't seem fair. My sisters and brothers too have inexpensive presents. I don't realise at the time that the parents must supply presents for their own children, and having a small budget and six children means there is little money to spare in our family. Pat Lewis is an only child.

Yet despite our low-budget family life, we are nourished with other more natural riches. We have made our Advent ring with ivy and holly, we quietly remove a sprig from a fir tree growing in the woods and bring it home to decorate. My mother brings out her crib set with angels, the ox and the ass, and shepherds, Joseph in his brown robes and Mary colourful in her red dress and blue cloak. The kings must wait until later in the Christmas story. The manger is waiting for baby Jesus.

We won't see him until Christmas morning. He is out of proportion, too big compared to the other figures, and not the original wax model.

"When you were a little girl, baby Jesus had disappeared, and I asked you where he was," my mother likes to tell me. "You said, 'I ate him. I thought he was dripping'!"[25]

At school, we learn to plait paper decorations with red and green crepe paper, and my mother buys sticky slips of paper which we lick and make into paper chains.

On Christmas morning, we wake to find that Father Christmas has filled our stockings with little toys, with a tangerine and a sixpenny piece in the toes. Later in the day, we get our presents from our parents, including a *School Friend* annual for me and a *Girls' Crystal* annual for Helen. We immerse ourselves for the rest of the day in the adventures of girls we would like to be: solving mysteries, being heroines, defeating the wicked Nazis by our loyalty to the French resistance, and helping King Charles 1 hide from the Roundheads.

"Parcel from Germany for you," announces the postman one day. Around Christmas time, this parcel comes every year from Willi Beerhorst, the former German prisoner of war we befriended in Harpenden when Rosie was a baby. There are gingerbread houses and hearts with speckled coloured decorations. All kinds of chocolates, biscuits and sweets are packed in neatly, with unfamiliar cinnamon and gingery flavours. For me, there is a silver-wrapped packet of pumpernickel, a malty-flavoured rye bread which I love. It tastes delicious with butter and Marmite. One year, he sends two tea towels specifically for my mother, the *Hausfrau*.

On New Year's Day, the eighth day after Christmas, we go to church again for the feast of the circumcision. Whatever that word means is not properly explained to us, but it is the day when Jesus was given his name. On Sunday, we go to Mass again, and then once more on 6 January, which is the Feast of the Epiphany when the three kings may go in the crib set. It is the twelfth night, and time to take all the decorations down. Like it or not, we will soon be back at school.

16 The Strangeness of James

Weaving its way through the fabric of our childhood is a strange thread. It emerges from time to time, makes itself felt for a while and then slides into the background. It is the appearance of a man called James, and his presence in our lives goes back to the days before our parents married.

"Our Platonic friendship is not so Platonic anymore," my mother had written in a letter to her mother in 1941. "This is very awkward. He told me, taking about one and a half days in the process, that he loves me and I think he does."

Some more details from those times emerge in my mother's booklet, *About the Houses,* which she wrote in 2000.

"I made friends with a good-looking young man called John Ashton. He was a Conscientious Objector and worked in the garden and with the bees. I also got friendly with James Parkhill Rathbone who had been invalided out of the army. He wrote poems which I thought very beautiful. He worked in the nurseries with the children.

"My friend Jim and I often walked into Stourbridge and bought a bag of cakes which we ate on the way home... Before long I was in love with Jim but he was engaged to a girl called Alys Rita. I was also very interested in John Ashton."

James and Alys Rita are marrying because she is pregnant, and he is the father-to-be.

....

Platonic friendship

While we live in Hay, he and my mother communicate regularly by letter, and she explains this word 'platonic' to me. It means friendship, and it is not the same as love. This man fits into our life in a way which my father seemingly accepts, and on the surface it is harmless. As children must, we observe what happens around us without the skills to understand our feelings. Yet something always feels odd.

This friendship is a penetrating influence in our lives. Letters arrive, and are replied to. He visits us in Hay, with his son John, and stays in our house. Alys Rita also visits us with her daughter Jennifer, but on separate occasions.

My mother's diary often records their correspondence:

30 January: Had a letter from James in the morning asking why I had not written, so wrote to him after dinner. Later, I enjoyed a quiet evening reading Jim's poems, and writing a crit of them.

14 May: Had a letter from Jim.

27 May: Had another letter from Jim today – very sweet and nostalgic. Also containing a lot of interesting matter and food for thought. I always feel I must answer his letters at once.

The interesting matter may relate to a magazine called The Idler which we are told that James is editing. Copies would arrive in the post from time to time, illustrated with small black and white sketches of which he may have been the artist:

14 July: Had a tender letter from Jim in the morning and a poem – apparently our little differences are now forgiven and forgotten.

Whatever the differences were is not recorded. In September, she receives a letter from a new woman friend of James:

I had a long and interesting letter from Lynn Carlton this morning. She reveals herself a person of wide interests, an agnostic (self-confessed) and an ardent reader of Peace News and Wilfred Wellock pamphlets, 'Socialism of the Individual' etc., phrases which sound hollow and unconvincing to me on the lips of a woman. However, it is nice to contact different minds and I hope we may develop a flourishing pen-friendship.

Later the same month, she hears from James' wife:

A long letter from Alys Rita which pleased me very much. She strikes me as being a tender maternal type, rather deeply wounded by the sorrows and disappointments of life, including no doubt James, who however ideal a friend, must be the most unsatisfactory husband possible, though she never mentions him. James hasn't written for ages – possibly trouble? I think it isn't worth bothering about. Although my feelings towards him are quite unaltered, I shan't think about him or write to him unless he writes to me.

In October, Alys Rita comes to our house to stay with her daughter Jennifer. This is the first time my mother has met her. "She is more capable, brisk and efficient than I had imagined. She is a trained nurse."

The next day, Jennifer has a temperature and must stay in bed, with Alys Rita running up and down stairs all day long. In the evening: "We had a long talk after supper – it was interesting to hear about James, though painful."

Next day, "I see no trace of Jennifer's father in her, just as well perhaps."

My mother then arranges to return to Alys Rita's home at Frome in Somerset for a few days. This is a sudden decision, and requires many arrangements to take care of us all in her absence. When they arrive at Alys Rita's house, John, James' son, comes in, and my mother likes him at once, noting his likeness to his father.

Then: "James came in about seven. He isn't much changed to look at, thought possibly a little more stalwart."

This is strange. My mother is with the wife and in the household of her 'platonic' friend. Meanwhile, my father is at home in Hay with us. What is he thinking about? He is a rigid man of conventional beliefs. As for James, he is seeing his poetry-companion with the woman who has borne his children. And my mother, in her deepest self, what is she truly feeling?

Next day, James left for work at 7.30 am, and the children a little later go off to school. The two women soon put the house in order:

What blissful peace and relaxation to be away from the children for a bit. We had a cup of tea at eleven – two women in the house – no men – no children. Rita is very much upset at a woman who is apparently madly in love with James and trying to steal him away. A very difficult situation – and my heart bled for the poor girl. I know…

And there her diary ends. The following page is torn out.

This leaves me with many unanswered questions. What does she know? What does she feel? What was so troublesome that the page is torn out, something now missing that my father should not see? Thus far, the entries about James are not incriminating if one accepts that their friendship is harmless. There are no more entries at all for 1953. Whatever her feelings, she no longer wants them to be on record.

There is no surviving diary from Hay after 1953, but James comes to visit with his son and his friend later. As I am a scribbler, with my own self-conceived Enid Blyton-like future, my mother thinks of me as a potential writer, like herself, and like James. Together, they fuss over me in this way, almost as though they are helping, consciously or unconsciously, to form my future. I receive this attention, but respond neutrally. Over the years, I find myself wriggling at the memory. I am the daughter of a beekeeper, not of a poet.

James' son John and his friend are the unkind boys who gave away Helen's and my secret club papers, and in response, my father uncharacteristically paid for me to have an ice cream. I wonder if I am the personification of the child James and my mother may have had together. And perhaps my father feels this, reacting to the extent that I am allowed to have an ice-cream. Yes, it definitely makes me wriggle.

17 Nineteen Fifty-Four

"That'll be sixpence please," says Mr Grant, the stationer. "Another book for your collection?"

I leave the shop very pleased with my new I-Spy Dogs. Now all through the streets of Hay, I'll be looking out for dogs and earning points. I soon see one, but I'm not sure about it. Dogs are often running around freely, but unfortunately there is no category for mongrels which this one probably is.

Then I spy a cocker spaniel which is easy to identify, and this earns me 10 points. It isn't long before Delta, a golden retriever who is expecting puppies, visits our house. This is lucky and earns me another 15 points. I am looking out for corgis, which are the Queen's dogs, and one day I'll be sure to find one.

....

I-Spy the world

The world of the little girl who was standing at the door five long years ago is expanding. My sister Helen and I are at the age when we have a huge appetite for facts, for sorting out individual items from the confusion of the world so that we may make sense of it. It starts right outside our door, at 3 Market Street. One of the ways we do this is by belonging to the I-Spy club. We are among the half million 'Redskins', of the tribe of Big Chief I-Spy, and we have a collection of sixpenny I-Spy booklets which we fill in with all our discoveries.

We have *I-Spy Wild Flowers, Trees, In the Country, In the Street, On the Road,* and *People and Places.* We could have *Aircraft, Cars* and *The Army*, but these are not of interest to us.

These booklets are our education. Finding a new flower, or a wild creature, or nurse in uniform, we can enter our discovery and earn some points. An easy item for us to fill in from *I-Spy in the Country* is 'a wooden beehive' for which we get ten points. In my case, I can add 'swarm of bees', for which I gain an impressive 25 points. We are aiming to have a total of 1250 points in any one book, which we can then send in to Big Chief I-Spy for a stamp of merit, and earn a feather for a headdress, although earning 1500 points, the full score, is virtually impossible. It takes weeks, months, even years, to fill in a book. We make lists of our books, and totals of our points.

In the school summer holidays, we hardly notice if the weather is drizzly, windy, or of the skies are gloomy. Our father is different. He is watching the weather, and it is often raining. The crucial days are here when it is essential to have sunshine so that the flowers will secrete the nectar, and the bees will collect it to produce the honey. It is the clover season, my father's most important crop. While we fill in our I-Spy books and play with our friends, he is inspecting his hives. He can do nothing but watch the sky.

....

Beyond Hay

"We'll go to visit Granny Annie for a few days," he announces one morning. Helen, Rosie and I are chosen to go. We will stay in our grandparents' house in Wiltshire, which is next door to our Auntie Grace and Uncle Geoff and our cousins Robert, Sarah and Matthew. The houses are on a piece of land next to a hill called Copheap. This round hill is topped with beech trees, and it looks like a place for adventure games. But Helen and I are not allowed to go there to play. Why not? Something vague about soldiers and strange men is muttered.

As we visit places in the countryside, I am busy filling in my *I-Spy in the Country*. We must look out for a thatched cottage, and there is one just down the road from our granny's house with pretty flowers in the garden. That earns me 12 points. We don't have anything like that in Hay, but I know I was born in a thatched cottage, so it feels important. I am looking for drystone walls, for a stile and a kissing gate, and for a scarecrow. Hay is still the centre of our world, but as well as going with my father to South Wales selling honey, to Tenby for holidays, and now to Wiltshire, the world is expanding for the Beeman's children.

July draws towards its end. The weather is changeable and often rainy.

"Only two more weeks," my mother confirms one day, "and we will be on the train to London." She has organised a house exchange in a suburb called Thornton Heath. This is the sort of low-cost holiday our parents can afford. Our ramshackle house in Hay is being swapped for a London suburban semi for two full weeks. With my father's encouragement, I have obtained a pack of information from London Transport, and Helen and I have our copies of *I-Spy the Sights of London.* We'll find lots of these places.

Before we leave, my father moves his hives to the hills where the heather will be starting to flower. The hives are not as strong as he would like because the constant rain has prevented the bees from producing enough honey to feed themselves. We children are far too excited to notice. Our heads are filled with holiday dreams.

....

I-Spy the Sights of London

On 17 August, we wake up at 5 am and my mother directs us as we put clean sheets on all the beds. Someone else will be sleeping in them tonight. We head for Hay station. Helen and I are taking turns pushing Stephen in his pushchair. Our daddy is carrying the bag and seeing us off. He must stay at home to care for the bees. We are six excited country children, going to the city where the Queen lives. We take the train to Hereford where we change for Newport and then wait there until the Red Dragon comes steaming in. This is the non-stop express for London. As we get close to the city, Richard sees a great gasometer and causes a chuckle in our compartment when he exclaims, "Is that the Queen's palace?"

When we arrive at the house in Thornton Heath, our mother is pleased to find a letter from James waiting for her. Always from James! The weather is fine, and I am allowed to go out exploring. Round the corner is a chewing gum machine selling little packets of Beech Nut mint-flavoured gum for a penny. Every so often, two packs come out and I work out that this will happen when the arrow points in a certain direction. This is a very important aspect to the holiday.

There is a suburban park not far from our house, with swings and roundabouts, which we explore on the first day. We have nothing like this in Hay. On the fourth day after our arrival, Johnny traps his foot under the revolving roundabout, and has to be rushed to Croydon General Hospital where they discover he has broken his ankle. He stays in the hospital for the rest of our holiday. The National Health Service of 1954 has come to our rescue. The drama is summarized briefly in my mother's holiday diary. She writes notes every day, and collects postcards of the places we visit. Later she will type it all up into a holiday scrapbook.

We visit all the wonderful historic sights, museums, the zoo, Battersea funfair, often with our Granny Izzie. We take the red double-decker 159 bus into the centre of London, clambering upstairs and ignoring the stinking cigarette smoke. Hooray if we can sit in the very front seats. For two full weeks, we are guided around London by Helen and me and our *I-Spy The Sights of London*. At least that is my interpretation of things, which doesn't get a mention in my mother's scrapbook stories. At Westminster, we see the mounted Horse Guards, 10 Downing Street, the Cenotaph, Big Ben and the statue of my heroine, Boadicea. We are able to fill in the answer to many questions like these. What is missing from the statue of Boadicea? The reins. We gain 25 points. What useful articles stand on each side of the door of 10 Downing Street? Mud scrapers to clean dirty shoes. Twenty points for that answer.

We can pass the door because Downing Street is accessible to pedestrians. From there we walk towards St James' Park where we get lots of points from observing the ducks and other birds on the pond. My mother's holiday scrapbook tells the stories:

Helen was in a sophisticated mood and refused to be impressed by the width of the Thames or the height of Big Ben. She said she thought the Wye just as broad, and our clock tower equally high.

The girls had not seen a large Catholic church before and were very impressed with Westminster Cathedral. We explored the beautiful side chapels and visited the one dedicated to Irish saints. Next came the chapel of the Scottish saints, and we confidently expected the Welsh one next. But alas! In this we were sorely disappointed. What an oversight on somebody's part.

The weather is fine and hot. When we come back at the end of the day on Tuesday 23 August, one week after our arrival, we unexpectedly see our daddy.

He has decided he can leave his bees, now settled at the heather, for a few days. We all go together to Buckingham Palace, where three-year-old Richard makes a career decision. My mother's scrapbook:

> Richard is the only one of the children to have noisy leather soles, and he soon found out he could give a very passable imitation of the sentry turning round, with appropriate stampings of feet. He immediately altered his ambition of being a bus-conductor to that of being a sentry!

The sentries are posted on the pavement outside the palace where pedestrians walk by. We can stand really close to them and look into their eyes. These are the days before the guards are locked away behind the iron railings.

We eat in Lyons teashops where we are allowed to choose anything at all from the menu. Self-service is a completely new idea to us. I choose tomato soup and doughnuts with crispy icing.

As we walk around the streets, I am constantly amazed by the bookshops of London. In the windows are displays of children's books, and inside there are whole shelves for people of my age. I didn't know so many children's books existed.

"Mummy, please can we go inside and look," I plead whenever we pass one. Sometimes we do.

Our *I-Spy The Sights of London* comes in handy again when we visit the City of London. Using its map, we see St Paul's Cathedral, St Bride's church, passing by bombsites where houses are not yet all repaired from the war. Pink flowers, London's Pride, are growing among the ruins, and sometimes we see a bedroom wall with wallpaper exposed. We go to the Monument and climb the 311 steps to the top. We answer the question: Where did the Fire of London start? In Pudding Lane. Twenty points gained. We pass the Bank of England. Whose statue is in front? The Duke of Wellington's. Another 20 points. One of the most exciting places is the home of the I-Spy tribe at the News Chronicle office in Bouverie Street. Here we must check the time on the clock, and then look at the time band to see the equivalent in New Zealand. It is nearly 25 minutes past two in London, and nearly five pm in New Zealand. That earns me 25 points. Big Chief I-Spy may be somewhere around, but we don't see him.

The mummies of people and cats in the British Museum attract our interest on a visit to the British Museum. My mother's scrapbook records:

I last passed through these doors when I was seventeen. Miss Bowden, in my post-school days, conducted me there many times, and we did an exhausting course in Egyptology.

Perhaps it is not surprising, but James, the platonic friend, appears in our holiday. He travels up especially from Somerset, thus making a total of seven people sleeping in our house on Saturday night. We go to Mass on the Sunday as a matter of course:

I then took James out for a little walk, and we explored the beauties of Grangewood Park. After dinner, John nobly offered to take charge of the children, so James and I had a real afternoon off. He wanted to show me some of his favorite things in the Victoria and Albert. We visited the Chinese Rooms, the Laughing Virgin and Toulouse Lautrec's ladies. They looked to me like illustrations out of a Strand Magazine for 1900.

My mother writes about interests she shares with James in a way that she never does with my father.

....

Missing the train 1954 style

"I'll phone the hospital to see if Johnnie is well enough to come home with us," my father says on the day we are due to return to Hay. He goes out to a phone box at ten o'clock to enquire, and this is assured. My mother's scrapbook:

He went to the hospital to escort Johnnie in the ambulance, accompanied by Richard and Rose, while Granny Izzie and the two girls and Stephen and I went to Paddington station independently. We arrived there about eleven, having crossed London in a taxi, and had time for tea and buns in the café before the train came in. We then settled ourselves in the carriage next to the engine as we had arranged, and waited – but no sign of John or ambulance. We were in despair, but eleven-forty-five struck, the whistle blew and the train drew out of the platform. Just at that moment, John rushed on the platform, pushing Johnnie in a wheelchair, about five seconds too late. We felt terrible because we had the tickets, the food for the journey etc., but at length comforted ourselves with the thought that John had enough money to see him through, and Granny was there to help with the children.

We had a comfortable journey, arriving home soon after five. John and his party were not long after us for they caught the next train.

Long stay hospital care for a child with a broken ankle, buns in the café, finding your own seat in the carriage next to the engine, personal ambulance service from the hospital for the patient and three of his family to the station. It all seems so old-fashioned.

....

The bees are starving

Four days after we arrive back in Hay, my father is desperate. While we were in London, with the weather bright and sunny, it has been raining in Hay nearly all the time. We have been visiting places, enjoying culture and history, all recorded by my mother in her holiday scrapbook and Helen and me in our *I Spy* books, while all of this time he has been worrying about the weather. Those three crucial weeks when the heather was in flower have been disastrous. After the rain in July, and constantly in August, there will be almost no honey.

Things must change, even though we children are unaware. On 4 September, my father writes a letter, a rare survival, to his long-term friend and brother-in-law Geoff Butcher, the builder in Warminster:

This year has been a worse failure for honey than last year even, and I just can't stick it financially. Last year I scraped through on about £300 worth of honey. This year I have a good deal less than £100 worth. Fortunately, the Agricultural Committee job has kept the wolf from the door, but this ends at the end of September as it is only a summertime job. I have lost about 30 hives at the heather from starvation. I was tired of buying sugar for them and the weather just wouldn't change.

I feel discouraged, and don't fancy the prospect of another 12 months' work with no knowledge of what reward of honey (if any) it is going to bring. I really did my best for the bees this year, there was every expectation of a decent season this year after the very poor one of last year, and they would have done well if the weather was right, but the control of the weather was not in my hands.

I feel like cutting my losses on the bee business and getting into something before I am too old. The Agriculture Committee is no doubt a job for life, but since it is only a summer job it is not all that attractive. I shall at least have to take a temporary job for this winter, and I feel like considering a permanent change.

This is only a sort of first enquiry, but if you thought anything might crop up, I should be interested to know.

My mother will know that he is making an enquiry of this sort. No letter in response from Geoff Butcher has survived. As children, our lives seemingly go on as normal.

....

The 11-plus exam

Whenever we go down to watch the trains coming in, and I see the girls only a little older than myself from Brecon grammar school walking home with their leather satchels, I know that this is probably my destiny.

Geoffrey & Roger Price, Russell Price, Valerie Tap, Velda Blackmore, Christine Jones. The man's name is not known

"We expect that you will pass your 11-plus examination," my parents often reassure me. This year of 1954 is decisive for me. The children in my class at school are all ten years old and every one of us must move to another school in September 1955. It is assumed that most of the class will go to the secondary modern school a few miles from Hay called Gwernyfed. Only a few will pass 'the scholarship' as the 11-plus exam is locally known, and they will go to the girls' or boys' grammar schools in Brecon.

"I will get a bike if I pass the scholarship," my friend Christine says to me. I have a second-hand black bike, which I have partly repainted silver. I'd love a shiny new red one. But my mother does not agree. "If you pass, that is reward enough," she tells me.

Mr Davies, the head teacher, takes the Standard Four scholarship class. He trains us intensively, building on all that has been going on in previous years, concentrating on the basics. These are the pre-decimal days when nothing is reckoned in tens and hundreds and thousands. Our arithmetic lessons are classified in different ways. There is 'Mechanical', which includes knowing the times-tables as far as twelve times twelve up to the important number of 144. 'Mental' means being able to answer to questions in our head with nothing written down. And there are 'Problems', which involve understanding a written question.

We must be competent in pounds, shillings and pence. Everyday weights are measured by pounds and ounces, and heavy items like coal in hundredweights and tons. Lengths and distances are calculated in inches, feet, yards and miles. Our milk and liquids are measured in gills, pints, quarts and gallons. The daily temperature is recorded in Fahrenheit.

We have to know that there are twelve pence in one shilling, and twenty shillings in a pound. There are half-pence which we call ha'pennies, and even quarter pence which are farthings. Guineas are one pound and one shilling. We need to know the number system based on twelve because we have threepenny pieces and sixpences which are portions of shillings. We have a coin called a florin, which is two shillings, and a half crown which is two shillings and sixpence. Because there are twenty shillings in a pound, the number system based on ten must also be used. We have a ten-shilling note and a one pound note.

Two half-crowns are worth five shillings. We need to know that a half-crown is one eighth of a pound.

Equally complex, we must learn that there are 16 ounces in a pound weight, and 112 pounds in one hundredweight. As for lengths, there are twelve inches in a foot (and the inches themselves are divided into quarter and half inches), three feet in a yard and 1,760 yards in a mile. There are 5,280 feet and 63,360 inches in a mile. As well as remembering these figures, we are expected to do complicated calculations in all of them.

We have to know fractions, which are suitable for our pre-decimal system, and decimals too, with the importance of placing the point correctly, and how to convert one system into another.

Then we must deal with the English spelling system. Mr Pound in Standard Three had divided his class into teams, the Lions, the Leopards and the Tigers. We are very competitive. We work our way through the reading books, and by Standard Four, we are expected to be competent readers. Being a good reader helps spelling come more easily.

We are constantly practicing 'Composition'. That means writing stories, and I like that. I can always knock up a respectable story.

"Bridget, you may choose whatever you like for your dinner today," my mother tells me when the big day arrives. That is an easy choice. "Macaroni cheese," I say, "and bread and butter pudding, please."

My classmates and I are arranged carefully around the room.

Some of us, perhaps six or so from the class of 34, may pass the test, but everyone has to undergo it. Colin, the son of the butcher at the bottom of Bear Street; Robert Pugh the Limited, son of the ironmonger; Kathleen Gibbons, the girl with the lovely singing voice; Christine Jones, daughter of the gas works man; Susan Price, daughter of the grocer; Velda Blackmore, a girl with musical ability; Valerie Tap, an undernourished but spirited girl; Elspeth Beattie, daughter of a publican; Ruth Watkins, daughter of a farmer; Bridget Ashton, daughter of the Beeman; cousins Geoffrey Price and Roger Price; and about twenty others. How many of us are suited for an academic education; to go to a grammar school, and then perhaps to higher education and a professional life? Most of us are daughters and sons of traders or artisans or farmers. But there we must all sit, and while some of us are happy answering the questions, others are chewing the end of their pens and longing for it all to be over.

First, we have our arithmetic test. We are then let loose for a run around the playground before coming back for some of the general English tests.

At midday, I run home cheerfully enough with Christine up Bear Street, and consume my high-calorie tasty dinner. After that, we go back for another two sessions. First is 'Composition', and then we finish with 'Intelligence'.

At the end of the day, Mr Davies asks us a few questions. "Who chose item 1 in the Composition test?" Some hands go up, and the same for items 2 and 3. When it comes to item 4, the only hand going up is mine. He smiles and says he is not surprised. This item encourages the writing of an adventure story which he knows I like to do.

Those of us who pass will go to Brecon Girls' or Brecon Boys' Grammar Schools. The number of places available in the schools determines how many children will pass the test, and there are probably more boys who will succeed than girls. A former headmaster explains, "Marks had to be fiddled in order to give more grammar school places to boys; the girls did too well at the Eleven-Plus, both for the number of places available and for the attitude of the times to women."[26] After the exam, life goes on as before. School. Playing. Church on Sundays. I am unquestioning and accepting. My life in Hay is the same as it always been.

....

Job application

"Eileen, just take a look at this." My father is reading Bee Craft, a beekeeping journal which he receives. My mother looks carefully. She is surprised, wordless.

"This is something that could apply to me. I think I would be able to take on such an appointment." And my mother nods in agreement.

They are looking at an advertisement dated 5 October 1954 for a beekeeping officer in Northumberland, a remote a place in the north of England. Suitable qualifications and experience are required, which of course he has. Instruction in schools and advisory work for beekeepers in the county are needed, and work of this nature holds no fears for him. His experience with the Agricultural Committee will stand him in good stead, as will his earlier employment at Rothamsted Experimental Station. The salary is £695–£760 per annum, which compared with how we have managed in the last couple of years would be riches. Paid jobs for beekeepers are few and far between.

The application must be in by 19 October, and thus there is little time. He puts his mind to it, and applies. Northumberland? It is so far away.

My sisters and brothers and I go on with our daily lives as the time arrives for him to travel away for the interview. Our mother is in a state of tension. The money would be such a relief. But to move so far away? As she has no idea how likely he is to get the job, it is better to try not to think too much about it.

However, he is short-listed, and in mid-November is called for interview and travels north. He phones my mother. He has been successful. The details of how it happened survive in a letter which he wrote to his parents a few days after his return to Hay:

> You will be interested to know that I got the Northumberland job. It was all very tiring, the long journey up, the apprehension beforehand etc. There were six others on the short list. They were all talking happily when I got there. I sat glumly in the corner and pretended to read my newspaper. They took us alphabetically, I was first.
>
> To cut a long story short they called me in after and asked if I would accept. All the aldermen and people were very nice and shook me by the hand. I had a medical exam, and was taken round the Farm Institute where I shall work. Then I saw the Director of Education, very nice man, beekeeper himself, in fact this job (a new one) is so-to-speak his baby.
>
> They haven't a bee on the place, the whole thing has to be started from scratch; this is a chance to cash in reasonably on a lot of my own stuff, including bees. I am to have a more-or-less free hand subject to general policy outline.
>
> Everyone was very friendly, introducing me to one another; several other organisers, drama, music, horticulture, youth, domestic science etc.
>
> What frightens me a bit is that it looks so very rosy. I can't see any snags, and will be into the pension scheme at once.
>
> There are plenty of schools in Newcastle and other towns, plenty of houses on the agents' lists up to what we are likely to be able to run to, (say £2500). There is a university in Newcastle with several faculties, good shops, concerts, theatre, extra-mural evening classes, cheap buses. Probably the whole of one's income free of tax.
>
> It looks like a real break at last. I am worn out with planning and scheming to get it and with being on my best behaviour all the time. Slept very badly, as usual on these occasions, and am now giving myself a course of cod liver oil and malt.

We learn that our world will be changing. No longer must our mother suffer the embarrassment of being unable to afford basic needs in the shops or my father worry endlessly about the weather.

For my sisters and brothers and me, this is an entirely new idea. We are going to move. What does that mean? Go to a new place, new schools, new friends? We only know Hay. Is it something like going to London for a holiday and having an adventure? I am excited, and try to imagine what is there – playgrounds, bookshops, the seaside. My mother's mind is in a turmoil. There is so much to think about. She is glad that finally her children will be able to go to

Catholic schools and she will have the cultural benefits of being in a city. But there is a tremendous upheaval to go through, finding a new place to live and selling our rickety lath and plaster house.

The news soon spreads around Hay that Mr Ashton the Beeman has a job in another place, and that the family will be moving. People start saying to me, "You are going to move away? Won't you miss your friends?" I don't know how to react. As I have never been away from Hay other than for holidays, how do I know what it means to miss my friends?

The friends I left behind: R to L, Lecky Adams who was collected from school by car; Gillian Coombes who lived at the castle; Velda Blackmore the musician, Susan Price of the Star, and two on the right whose names are forgotten

My father is a member of the local amateur dramatic society, and on 6 and 7 December he is taking part in a play. My mother and he must fit in their visit to look at houses in the north of England around these pre-Christmas commitments.

Mrs Prosser, who has always helped with childcare and domestic chores, is summoned. She moves into our house for a few days when they leave, with her own temporary rules.

"No Helen, you don't need sugar on your cornflakes," Mrs Prosser tells her. "They are sweet enough."

There is an atmosphere of uncertainty when our mother comes home. "Daddy and I have looked at houses in Fern Avenue, in Holly Avenue, in Forest Hall," she tells us. She describes the one in Fern Avenue which has a trapeze in the attic. This is definitely the one I choose as it will help my career as a trapeze artist.

My father starts his new job before Christmas, and in a letter, he asks my mother to post up handkerchiefs, underpants, socks, shirts and collars. We spend Christmas without him.

There is a feeling of emptiness in the house. I have been moved to his place at the table, making more room for Helen and Rosie on the bench. Our table manners deteriorate. His presence helped to keep us in order, and we become harder for our mother to manage.

On New Year's Day 1955, my mother wrote to him discussing her visits to the bank manager, and advising him about a visit to the Building Society. Our town house in Hay is worth about £600.

She tells him that on New Year's Eve, we all went to a pantomime in Hereford on the bus, at a total of 35 shillings. She justifies this huge expense "as Christmas has seemed so dull this year. The bus journey was pretty frightful and Stephen a nuisance. He said at intervals of one minute during the pantomime, 'All finished now – let's go home'."

....

Canings and rows

Bickering, it is called. Our squabbles, the seemingly interminable and pointless arguments often cause our mother to exclaim, "You children are driving me to distraction!" Almost exactly two years ago, on 2 January 1953, she had written:

Oh dear, what a terrible day! It started with the children's bickering before 7 am and seemed to go on all day. Spent the morning scrubbing…

Now, in her letter of 1 January 1955:

I shall be more than thankful when the children go back to school. They are simply awful, and I can only keep order with the aid of numerous canings and rows.

Has she resorted to caning? She is clearly exhausted at managing six of us without my father's more dominant presence. She finishes her letter: "Don't forget to write – I feel very low."

It is quite normal at this time for children to be smacked or slapped to be kept in order, and we are used to it. In our Beano comic, Dennis the Menace is always

229

being slippered by his father, which seems like justice to us. In fact, we enjoy seeing him get into the kind of trouble we are always trying to avoid.

We are far from angels, and there is always background naughtiness. But canings? This is a puzzle and perhaps an exaggeration. She is a kindly person by nature, but it may be that we really are driving her to distraction with our bad behaviour.

....

Johnnie slips away

Our house in Hay is to be sold, 3 Market Street, the centre of our lives, from which we run out to play and to school, and from where we cross the road to our church. We are to be pulled from our roots. Various arrangements about the new house in Newcastle are being made. It is costing about £2000, and our grandfather in Wiltshire helps organise the deposit.

The finances are gradually put in place. The house we are buying is unfortunately not the one with the trapeze.

The move is dominating our parents' every thought. My father's new job has started, and is going well. My mother has to keep house and home together in Hay, by herself, which includes ordering fuel for the Rayburn and planning the packing. I am getting a sense of uncertainty, missing my father's presence. It is the absence of that large person with his honey-smell, encouraging me to clean up every last drop of gravy on my plate with a piece of bread because that is the best bit.

It is cold and snowy in these winter months, and something important must be decided.

Will Johnnie move up north with us, or not? This is a serious question. He is our foster brother, but he has not been adopted. The orphanage in Hereford is still the legal guardian, and Miss Bolan is ultimately responsible for him:

20 February: Miss Bolan came down the other day to discuss pros and cons re Johnnie. It turns out there is a Catholic lady and her daughter in Hereford who want to adopt a boy.

2 March: Miss Bolan came this afternoon, and he has departed in the highest of spirits. The Youngs live in Victoria Street in Hereford in an old house that is part of the city walls. It adjoins the Convent where his sister Eileen lives, and she will be able to collect him from the Catholic school which adjoins. The Youngs are really keen to have a Catholic lad and I feel sure he will be happy. They have 14 rooms and a garden so he will have plenty of room to run about.

I really don't feel confident I could manage him in Newcastle, and I couldn't bear it if he started kicking the place around, and if he had to go back it would be such a very long and expensive journey.

Johnnie thus leaves us a few weeks before our move. Is he a difficult child who would be likely to 'kick the place around'? Is he misbehaving so badly, or is it that my mother is completely exhausted with all that she has to do? In the hurly burly of the last days, and after being with us for two years, he quietly slips out of our childhood lives.

....

Removal

On 20 February, my mother had written in a letter: "Now when do we move?" and discussed the removal van and packing our belongings. On 1 March, my father's reply arrived with a month's cheque, meaning we will not be moving for another four weeks. But it has been snowing, and so she had to order another five hundredweight of fuel for the Rayburn.

My father is all alone in the north, and he plans to come for a short visit. This will help to fill the gap in our lives. My mother's letter tells how my two-year-old brother Stephen is looking forward to seeing him:

> He sometimes says, 'Daddy loves me.' Today he had a biscuit with the maker's name in large letters. He spelled it out, as if reading, 'Daddy is coming on the bus from Hereford in a minute'.

And then, amid all the plans, on 20 February Rosie had developed the mumps. A swelling appears on one side of her throat, and she has a feverish headache. My mother goes to Dr Trumper who she writes 'did not seem very interested'.

Mumps is common among children in the 1950s and not usually serious. However, it is very infectious, and one by one, the illness works its way through all five of us. We must avoid school for at least five days, and all through March, my mother is caring for one sick child after another. Thus, as well as packing a household of goods for seven people, helping with my father's arrangements for the beehives and equipment to be transported north, and all the normal household duties of feeding, washing and keeping us clean, it is no wonder that she is almost at her wits' end.

At the end of March, Hoults' big maroon and yellow removal van is outside our door, so wide that it is filling the narrow street. The two removal men speak to us in a way which we have not heard before. When we don't understand, we ask them questions. "You're proper little Welsh lasses," one of them tells Helen and me. Are we? It is odd to be told that.

The removal van drives away when the house is emptied. This place, where we have always been, is no longer ours. We are uprooted. Our beds have gone. For the last night in Hay, we will be staying in a guest house.

My mother locks the door of 3 Market Street and drops the heavy iron key into her handbag for the last time. We cross Castle Square, holding hands, a strange little group, and make our way to the guesthouse in Castle Street. It is bleak, cold, black and white.

....

On the train

The train is steaming northwards. It is the first day of April 1955. We are in an enclosed compartment by ourselves. My mother is sitting near the window, completely exhausted, her face red and strained because she feels unwell. We are all in different stages of recovery from mumps. Two-year-old Stephen is snuggling on her lap, relaxed by the rhythm of the train, bumpety bump, bumpety bump.

I want to open the window. To do that, I work out that the thick leather strap must be pulled up and held tightly because if I carelessly let it go, the window will crash down. Then I must pull the strap up to the point where a button goes through a hole, which holds the window in place.

"Don't do that, darling," says my mother. The smell of coal smoke is coming into the compartment. "Close it Bridget. You'll get smuts in your eyes."

"I'm hungry," wails Rosie, after half an hour. My mother produces some slices of bread and butter, and gives Rosie a piece of cheese. She cuts up some apples. We share cups of water when we are thirsty, and our mother pours herself some tea from a flask.

Helen and I ask if we can walk along the corridor, and our mother gives permission. We daringly step on the shaking metal plates and pass through the zig-zag wobbly partitions which join the carriages over the bumpers.

When Richard needs the toilet, my mother leaves Stephen with me, taking Rosie along too. In the toilet cubicle is a sign which says: "Gentlemen, please lift the seat." Helen and I have seen this, and we ask our mother why this must be so. Her explanation is confusing. Train hygienic arrangements are minimal, and we independent older girls know that we must not flush the toilet when the train is at a station because the contents would drop on the ground beside the platform.

The train stops at several stations and this means we are getting further north. The hours tick away slowly, so slowly. When the guard comes in to punch our tickets, the boys watch in awed silence. We girls read our comics, draw pictures, pick things up and put them down again.

"I do wish you children would be still," my mother says, as we fidget constantly.

After York station, it is not long until we will be in Newcastle.

"Daddy will be on his way to meet us now," my mother reassures us. He will be driving along the country roads from the agricultural institute to the Central Station.

I am impatient to see him. Behind us is all that we know, Hay, the little town by the River Wye where our friends will still be playing in the familiar streets.

We are looking ahead to a place about which we know nothing. But our daddy, with his familiar honey-smelling embrace, will be on the platform waiting for us, and one by one we will leap into his arms. I am secure. He will still be taking care of us. We are still the children of the Beeman.

Bibliography

As this book was written from the point of view of a child of ten years of age, reference documents other than those directly referred to in the text have been kept to a minimum. Wikipedia was very useful for small items of information.

Blyton, Enid, *Sunny Stories: You're a Bully, and other tales*; Georges Newnes Ltd, 19 February 1953. This was the last copy written by Enid Blyton. After this date, other authors contributed, including 'Crawfie', the former governess of the Princesses Elizabeth and Margaret

Catholic Truth Society, *A Catechism of Christian Doctrine*, Archbishops and Bishops of England and Wales, 1921 edition. This is the version used in 1950s Hay, first published in 1889, and later revised in 1985

Fairs, Geoffrey L, *Annals of a Parish: A Short History of Hay-on-Wye*. Also see his *A History of Hay*, 1974

I-SPY the Sights of London, News Chronicle, undated, *I-SPY Dogs, In the Country, On a Train Journey, The Sky, At the Seaside*, and others, all available in 1954

John Bull, 13 February 1954, Vol 95, Number 2485. Publisher unclear. 189, High Holborn, London WC1

Stedman, Rt Rev Msgr Joseph F, *My Sunday Missal*, Confraternity of the Precious Blood, 1938–1942

Stephen, Dr Martin, *The Eleven Plus Book: Genuine Exam Questions from Yesteryear,* Michael O'Mara Books, 2008

Collected writings of the author's mother, Eileen Ashton, unpublished

Nature Note Books, 1943-1945, 1949-1951
Boots Scribbling Diary, over 200 entries during 1953
The Story of our Holiday in London 17 August–30 August 1954
My Name is not Ivy, typed collection of her poetry with autobiographical details, 1976
About the Houses, 2000. One A4 handwritten sheet for each of the houses in which she lived from 1921-2000, the year of her death, and containing some details of all the houses in which the author lived

Other publications of associated interest
Basic cookery skills:

Ashton, Helen, *All About Food*, OUP, 1982–1988. My sister's book which was used widely in schools in the UK and overseas contains basic cookery principles
Corbishley, Gill, *Ration Book Recipes: Some Food Facts 1939–1954*,
English Heritage, 1990
Home Recipes with Bero. For recipes typical of the 1950s, look for an early version

Song books:
Buck, Percy C, *The Oxford Song Book*, Oxford University Press, 1916
The Baby's Opera, illustrated by Walter Crane, Frederick Warne, 19th century date uncertain
The Children's Book of Hymns, illustrated by Cicely M Barker, Blackie, 1929

Appendix 1 Three Other Meal Plans

Mon	Chicken soup. Treacle Tart
Tues	Pea omelette & Chips. Apple Pie
Weds	Haddock. Apple Pie
Thurs	Spaghetti Cheese. Apple Crumble
Fri	French Egg. Plum & Custard
Sat	Stew. Rice Pudding
Sun	Stew. Jam Tart
Mon	Rabbit stew. Suet Pud & Treacle
Tues	Rabbit stew. Apple & Custard
Weds	Egg & Chips. Jam Tart.
Thurs	Sweet corn souffle. Bread & Butter pud
Fri	Smoked Haddock, Peas, Potatoes. Plums & Custard
Sat	Hot-Pot. Apple & Custard
Sun	Rabbit. Baked Apples
Mon	Cold Chicken. Rice Pudding
Tues	Chicken soup. Rice Pudding
Weds	Eggs, Apple Tart.
Thurs	Cheese Rice. Semolina
Fri	Eggs. Apple Crumble
Sat	Irish Stew. Rice Pudding
Sun	Roast Chicken. Plums & Custard

Appendix 2 Eileen Ashton Reading List, January to October 1953

* indicates books she particularly liked

Marjorie Williams	Hannaboys Farm	1943
Howard Spring	The Houses in Between*	1954
Ethel Mannin	The Wild Swans	1952
Belton Cobb	Early Morning Poison	1947
Marguerite Steen	The Matador*	1934
John Buchan	Mr Standfast	1919
Francis P Keyes	Once on Esplanade	1947
Allan Michie	The Crown and the People*	1952
Martha Bacan	A Star called Wormwood	1948
Agatha Christie	The Labours of Hercules	1947
Ethel Mannin	Comrade oh Comrade	1947
H E Bates	House of Women	1936
Stuart Cloethe	Watch for the Dawn*	1940
E C Allingham	Gold and Gaiters	
J B Cronin	The Spanish Gardener	1950
Paul Brunton	A Hermit in the Himalayas*	1936
Elizabeth…	Love and Fear*	
Maud Oakes	Beyond the Windy Place	1951
Audrey Lindop	The Singer not the Song*	1953
Clarence Day	Life with Father	1935
M. Ghandi	Experiments with Truth	
G Battiscombe	English Picnics	1948
Bhagwain Patanjali	Aphorisms of Yoga	
Evelyn Waugh	The Loved One	1951
Lowell Thomas	Out of this World	1951
Victor Gallancz	My Dear Timothy	1952

Charles Williams	*War in Heaven*	1949
Francis Beeding	*The Norwich Victims*	1935
G Bernard Shaw	*Cashel Byron's Profession*	1908
L P Hartley	*The Boat*	1949
Edith Pargeter	*Fallen into the Pit*	1951
T H White	*Mistress Masham's Repose**	1946
A G Street	*The Gentlemen of the Party*	1946
Dornford Yates	*Storm Music*	1942
Francis C Shellman	*The Foundling*	1952

Endnotes

[1] Catechism 1921, Q + A 309, 310 and 311

[2] The information in this account, and the full story, was thoroughly researched by Helen many decades later

[3] Eileen Ashton, *About the Houses*, 2000

[4] Many years later, I told my mother this story. Her reaction was: "No Bridget, I am sure I would never have done such a thing."

[5] There is of course much more to Painscastle and its history, as a quick internet search will show. My story here is limited by my own experience as a four-year-old

[6] See Appendix 1 for the other three

[7] To learn more about traditional baking skills, see the bibliography

[8] *Ration Book Recipes*, English Heritage, 1990

[9] This story and the one about Meg Walbee are the versions which lodged themselves in my infant mind. The Moll Walbee story includes input from Roddy Williams. Also see Llowes, Wikipedia

[10] Catechism 1921

[11] Catechism 1921, Q + A 187 and 186

[12] Catechism 1921, Q + A 200

[13] Catechism 1921, Q + A 241 and 242

[14] Wikipedia

[15] My Sunday Missal, p 44

[16] *Central Office of Information, for the Ministry of Health*, Wikipedia

[17] Originally the charges in 1796 showed that animals pulling carts were to be charged fourpence ha'penny with the exception of dogs for which the charge was tuppence, and that foot passengers should pay a penny

[18] Enid Blyton, *Sunny Stories: You're a Bully, and other tales*

[19] See Appendix 2 for the full list

[20] John Bull, 13 February 1954 Vol 95, Number 2485

[21] My brother Richard suggests she may have used an 'interlinear' Greek New Testament, with the Greek original, a word for word translation between the lines, and the proper translation alongside

[22] Roddy Williams provided some of these details, and also told how a friend once recorded Bumper Howells and played it ahead of his patch, to Bumper's annoyance

[23] Granny Annie in later life gave Helen a little dish inscribed with the words 'Buckfast Abbey'. She didn't want anything so Catholic in her house

[24] My mother's cousin Pauline, age 91 at the time of writing, describes that in those days, when her family went on holiday, they posted their ration books to the owners of the guest house who used them to buy the food

[25] Dripping is beef fat which we eat spread on bread

[26] Dr Martin Stephen, *The Eleven Plus Book, Genuine Exam Questions from Yesteryear*